THE SHAPE OF CRAFT

THE SHAPE OF CRAFT

EZRA SHALES

REAKTION BOOKS

To my mother, Rachel M. Brownstein, my first storyteller, and editor, too

Published by
REAKTION BOOKS LTD
Unit 32, Waterside
44–48 Wharf Road
London N1 7UX, UK
www.reaktionbooks.co.uk

First published 2017

Printed and bound in Great Britain
by TJ International, Padstow, Cornwall

A catalogue record for this book is available from the British Library

ISBN 978 1 78023 822 7

CONTENTS

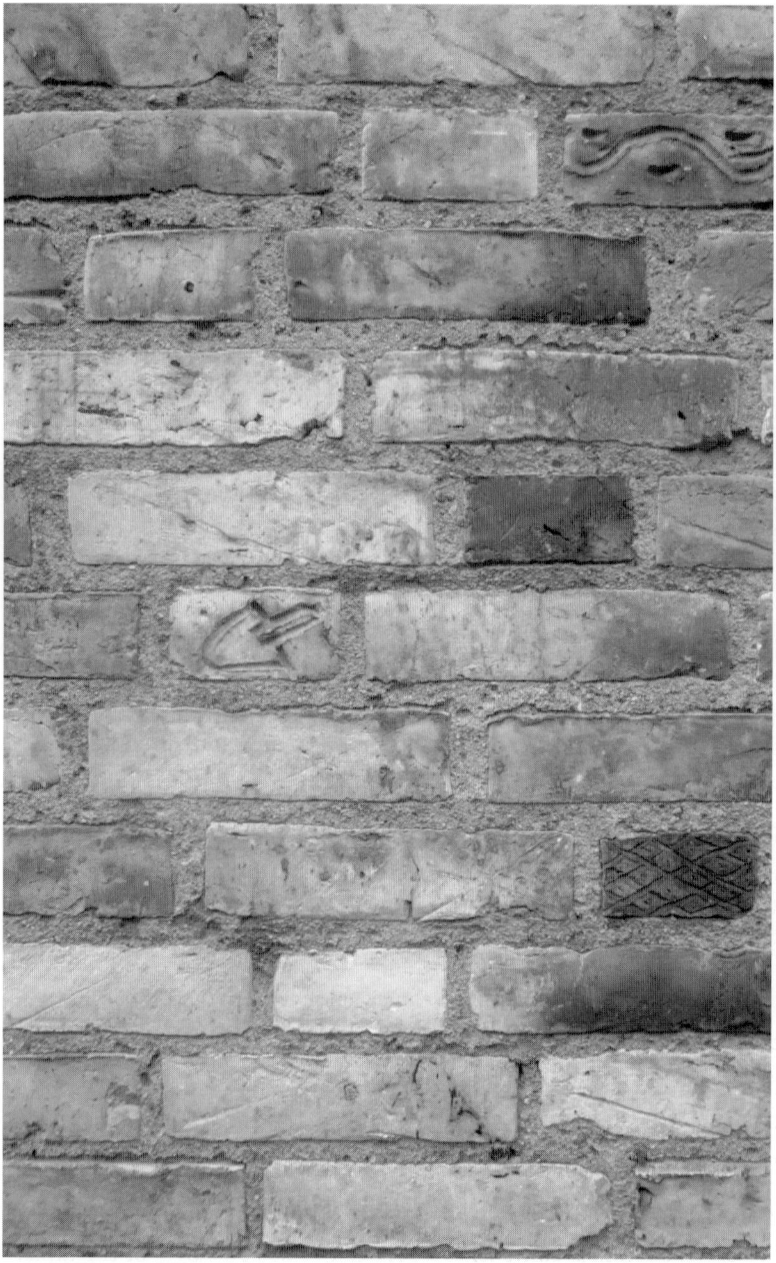

Röhsska Museet, Gothenburg, Sweden, *c.* 1916. Workers at the manufactory in Börringe decorated several moulded bricks with a variety of whimsical sgraffito images, so that self-referential ornaments such as a trowel and drawing of a brick wall are on the facade of this museum alongside Sweden's heraldic three crowns, ships, snakes and the odd drawing of a bottle of wine. The architect Carl Westman and museum curator Axel Nilsson presumably fostered this collaboration.

INTRODUCTION

Children who run alongside a sturdy brick wall and touch the narrow joints of mortar sense the wonder of craft. Their hands imaginatively deduce the rhythmic courses of brick as they meander: – __ – __ – . We adults might apprehend craft more rationally, by knowing the weight of a brick or empathizing with the mason's strained back, but not by following the intervals of mortar with our finger. The pleasures and mysteries accessed by touch create a path to value craft expansively, inclusive of mud, brick, mason and wall.

Can we respect the craft that lies unsigned and underfoot and which oxygenates our lives, giving us tactile joy? To do so can restore our optimism that human manufacturing is healthier for our minds than it is harmful to our environment. The shift in perspective also requires that we begin to value craft as a human instinct, taking a step away from thinking it through metaphorically or reducing it to an exemplary exhibitionist object. The very word 'craft' can confuse: it seemingly stands in opposition to the construction methods and materials of the industrial era, yet it denotes manufacture. Regardless, it feels like the right word to use when I watch someone skilled, whether they work alone in their workshop (or, for the more rarified, their 'studio') or in a large factory making hospital-grade toilets, urinals and sinks. Moreover, because many of us cannot discern the physical composition of much of what we own or the utility of old tools, it can be confounding to attempt to judge which crafts are a dynamic vocation and which an avocation, a hobby. The philosopher and educator John Dewey believed that active hands and agile fingers made us more essentially human. Following that logic, we might say that we grow less human when we fail to see craft as a necessity.

The most resilient craft – in a behavioural sense, not an aesthetic one – is born of necessity, such as a raft, a hut, a hat made of bark or refuse reborn as a child's kite. These begin with environmental constraints as well as empathy. The great majority of craft exposes group identity, not an individual's. Workmanship and tooling are at the centre of craft. If art is a powerful, transcendent allegory, and design is an elegant solution to a real problem, then craft should be thought of as plying usable material metaphors, placing them within reach and asking: what is a tool that nourishes? What is a woven pattern that gathers bodies into dialogue or designates regal authority? The beauty of commonplace necessity can be savoured in many ways.

Craft made a lot more sense when we threw away fewer things and mended more often, when there was a specialized army of artisans for each specific material. Breakage demands an imaginary reconstruction and reckoning: who made it, and when? And is there anyone alive who can fix it? The best definition of craft might be that it is easily understood but not easy to do – and best understood through doing or watching work that needs to be done.

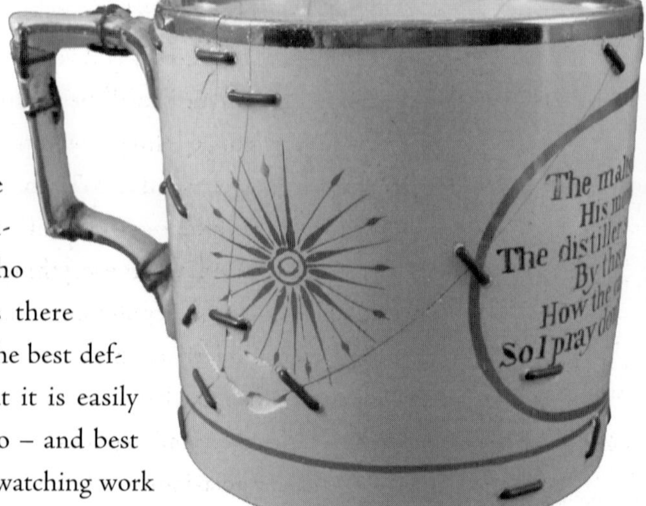

CRAFT WORK

'What real difference is there between a head stuffed with facts without order, without utility, and without connection, and the instinct of an artisan reduced to mechanical operation?' asked Denis Diderot, the Enlightenment author of the *Encyclopédie* (1751–72), who was unafraid to praise the mechanical arts as equal to the liberal arts, the watchmaker as the equal of the mathematician and other 'alleged scholars'. Diderot saw the assignation of respectful and disrespectful terms to labour as a form of class warfare. He asked his readers to value quotidian craft – wondrous stuff in arm's reach, not merely treasures stashed in museum vaults – and to value the unknown watchmakers who over generations perfected the escapement. Do we know craft in relation to everyday life or only as an exotic or aristocratic trinket? Is craft an achievement sustained only by an elite, after years of focused training, or also by the weekend hobbyist? While many have presumed that craft describes primarily rustic or even obsolete ways of working, or unique, one-of-a-kind products, Diderot found it on the streets of eighteenth-century Paris as well as in the regal factories making new luxury goods such as porcelain and silk.

Unattributed English manufacturer, 'Make-do' mug, *c.* 19th century, earthenware repaired with staples. The 46 rivets holding this mug together are so numerous that one wonders if frugality or sentiment motivated the repair. Often, mending is a handicraft requiring skills and tools distinct from manufacture, as is the case in joining broken ceramics with metal staples (a craft now obsolete due to advances in glues).

Identifying craft has mostly been a highly personal affair – an 'I know it when I see it' sort of thing, sometimes validated by training and at other times by monetary value. What benchmark might help people agree when ordinary work becomes craft? Even once upon a time, before the Industrial Revolution, when everything was supposedly craft, some of that skilled work was surely also 'mindlessly mechanical' – and more toxic than the worst modern assembly line, too. An eight-hundred-year-old bowl depicting a woman bent over her work of spinning wool into yarn is suggestive of drudgery and dignity simultaneously. Her sloping shoulders do not evoke our post-industrial 'creative economy' of hobbyists inclined to spin, dye and craft wool: she is at a chore, probably an assigned task.

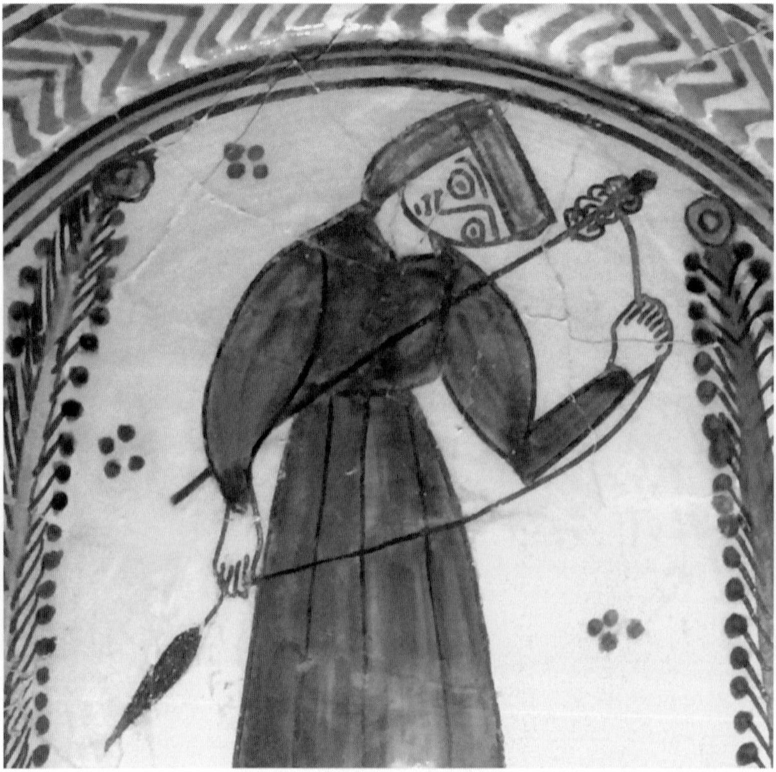

Bowl, *c.* 13th century, tin-glazed earthenware manufacture attributed to Brindisi, Italy. Today this image of a woman spinning wool might appear nostalgic but historically the devotional motif was deployed to transmit religious ideals.

Her taskmaster might have looked at her image on his bowl as a sign of virtue, but an actual spinner might have looked askance, already convinced of the gap between the rhetoric surrounding craft and its actual undertaking.

Use of the spindle and distaff remains a demonstrable skill and involves tedious preparatory labour: we have faster ways of producing a skein of yarn and refining it as desired – either rough and nubby or sleek and fine – through automation. Is spinning a craft that symbolizes old technology or the universality of human ingenuity? In 1916, in the Newark Museum's sweeping survey show 'Textile Industries of New Jersey', Athena Vornazos spun wool before visitors as a demonstration of living history. The exhibition showcased domestically-made silk tapestry, praising America for starting to weave its own Renaissance-grade finery. Specimens included wool hats, silk cultivation and ready wear. A citizen of Newark, Vornazos was described as 'an old Greek woman' in the museum's brochure, a slightly celebratory and also condescending appreciation of her status as an immigrant and local curiosity. Hand-spun wool still provides a sense of continuity and individuality, but not necessarily gender equality: the image of the spinner sends contradictory messages today, too. Was Vornazos 'backward' and from the 'Old World' or a reminder of a thrifty colonial American past? Live potters, weavers and basket-makers undertaking historical re-enactment in exhibitions transmit complex messages

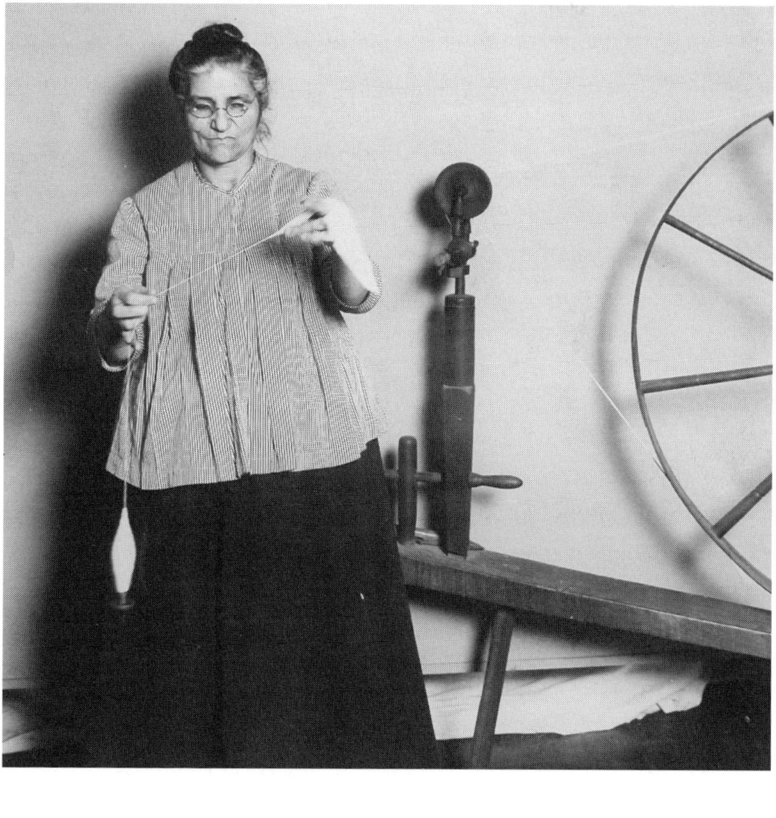

Athena Vornazos demonstrating spinning in the 'Textile Industries of New Jersey' exhibition, Newark Museum, 1916. Demonstrations of handicraft in cultural institutions have served a variety of ideological purposes, and in 1916 Newark attempted to blend 'A Commercial, Industrial, Historical and Art Exhibition' – with priorities in that order.

about progress, power and technological prowess. Audiences usually know craft when they see it. As they stand transfixed by the vitality of pure process, they interpret it in varied and subjective ways, incorporating it into their own personal experiences and values.

The Internet has motivated a groundswell of action to forge a digital commons – free resources of data and techniques. This idea of increasing access to tools is markedly similar to Diderot's *Encyclopédie*, which was the first of its kind to make the trades visible – his graphic inventory of each workshop's instruments and hands might well have originated in his admiration for his own father, a cutler. Such a democratization of education remains relevant to craft today, too. In Diderot's time, most people who accessed his *Encyclopédie* understood by touch the distinctions between wool and linen, brass and copper, earthenware and porcelain, mahogany and oak. Today, less experientially mature Internet surfers are seduced by videos of brickyards in Bangladesh, hat weaving in Korea and the hammering of bronze cymbals in Massachusetts. There, I join tens of thousands to watch meaningful labour; it is a peek into manufacturing that traverses cultural boundaries.

BEYOND 'HANDICRAFT'

To begin with vigorous statements as to what is not craft is to fall into seeing it in opposition to industrial mass production, as a rejection of standardization and anonymous commodities. If we really value craft then we should be able to define it by what it is, not by stating what it is not. The expectation over the past century has been that craft denotes something of virtuosic quality, of limited quantity and an endangered skill, restoring to our homes and clothing a vague sense of something 'soulful'. Arguing that it is better if things are 'made by hand', 'unique', 'useful', 'personal', 'organic' or 'tactile' – usually the pseudo-critical terms used when dealing with the 'C-word' – lays the foundation for romantic absurdities, such as celebrating ancient flint-knapping as the best way yet to make a knife. We don't want to go back to carding and spinning our own wool, and we don't want our whole world to be individualistic. We like conformity and anonymity in craft, too – especially in our toilets, right?

Although this book might well be better described as one about 'handicraft', the prefix of that word is misleading. Most crafts were never solo tasks but required recombining many sets of hands – what I call 'collated craft' or 'multihanded-crafts'. Numerous interdependent craftspeople produce museum-quality wavings, not solo artists. Fibres dyed in clay vats required dyer and ceramicist to work together, and since an understanding of metals was intimately connected to the development of dyeing, diverse bodies of material knowledge relied on one other, too. 'Manufacture' can mean using the hand (*manus*) as well as mechanized tools. The most artistic ancient weaving was at times as 'mindlessly mechanical' as automobile production today. All glorious textiles required looms and organized, divided labour and yet are surely still craft – try to do any one of these steps solo. When labour and materials add up, craft flashes in our hands and minds as 'potent manufacture'; the energy of human intention in the material world feels resonant with meanings and metaphors, and a prosaic artefact or a luxury good seems like a psychic necessity.

In the nineteenth century, handicraft became a pseudo-technical and also a romantic word, and in the twentieth century it ossified into simultaneously both utopian dogma and hollow advertising. Tourist craft items and pseudo-indigenous knick-knacks are still purchased because they look 'handmade', even if they might actually be produced on an assembly line. These versions still get handed from parent to child, teacher to student, salesman to consumer. Most dictionary definitions amplify confusion, because they suggest that craft is both strength and deceit, both a viable skill and an obsolete manual trade. An advertisement from 1964 selling 'the handcrafted television' is a good reminder that manual assembly has never stopped entirely and that a human using pliers is not inherently superior to automation. Perhaps we must first retrieve the adjective mechanical as a middle ground and hold it close to our hearts, as Diderot did the watch. Misplaced enthusiasm has damaged the reputation of and respect for genuine skilled workmanship, as much if not more than the assembly line has.

Reader beware: this book will not begin by ruling out the computer or mindlessly celebrating 'the hand', or claim that 'natural materials' are innately superior or more soulful than engineered ones like plastic and

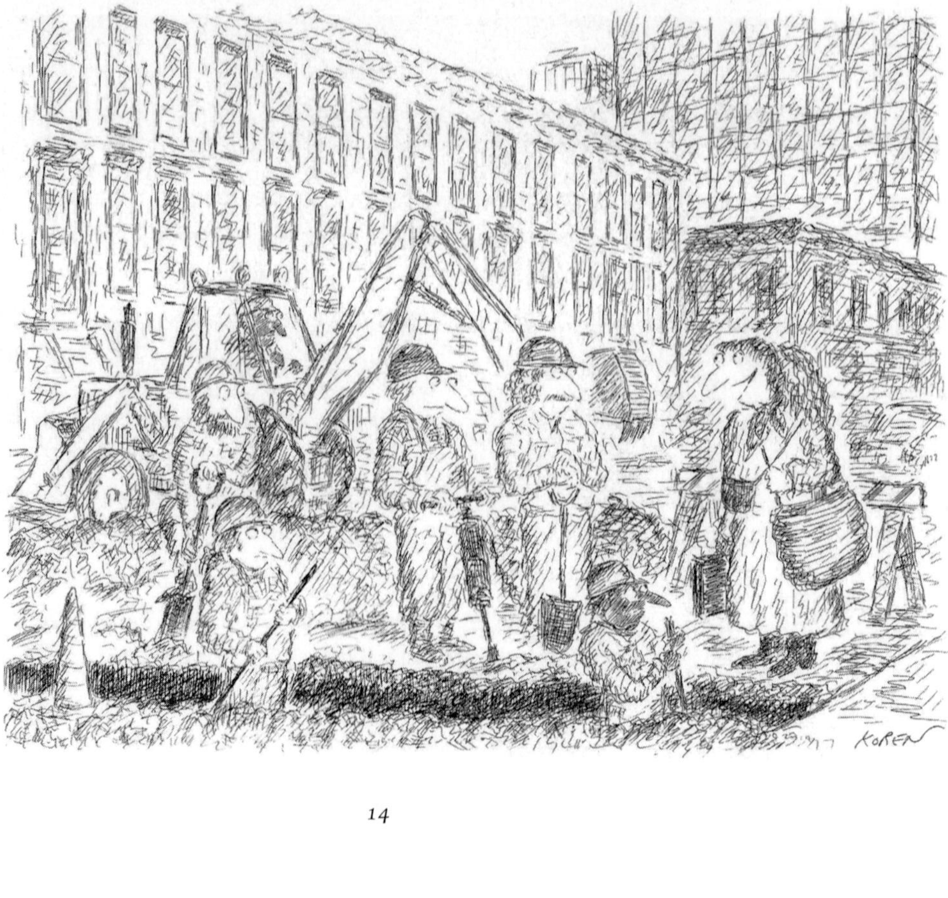

Zenith Corporation advertisement, *Saturday Evening Post*, 1964. Would the promise of a 'handcrafted television' be desirable to anyone today? Advertisements that promise the superior quality of manual production are not new and will not fade despite the tendency to increase robotic automation – but which objects become more desirable with this distinction certainly does change.

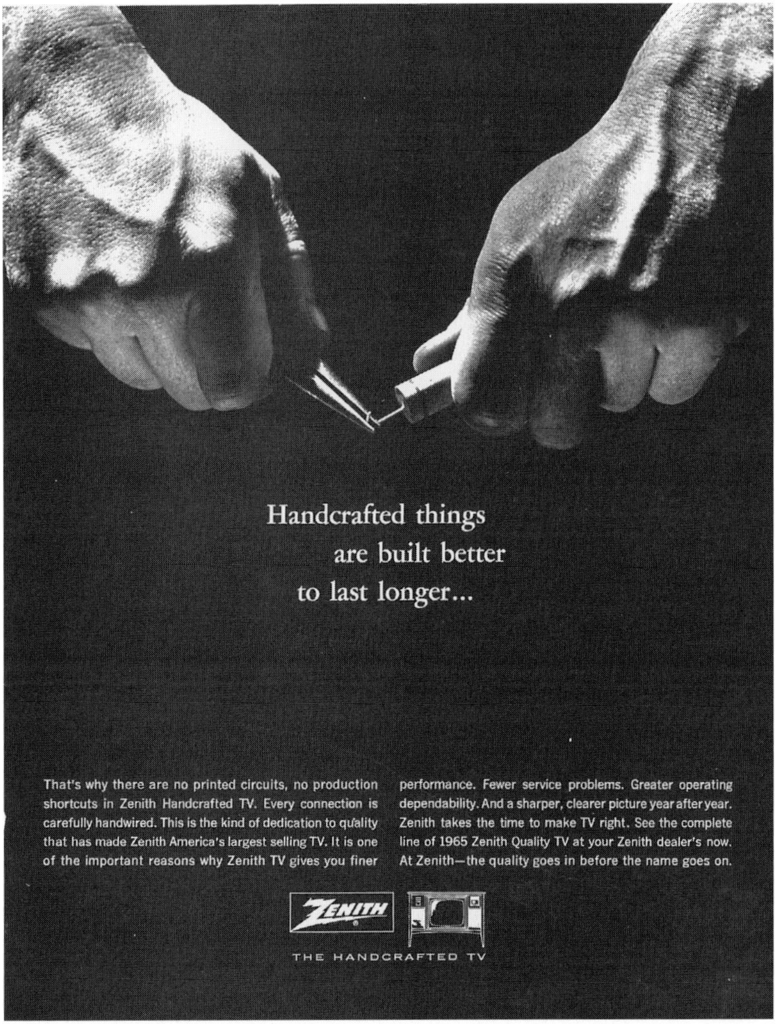

Edward Koren, 'What's it Like, Working With Your Hands?', *New Yorker*, 17 December 1990. Skewering gendered archetypes and the romanticization and abstraction of labour, Koren's satire also evokes David Pye's admonition that little work is really done without a variety of tools.

rubber. The British wood turner and educator David Pye (1914–1993), a professor of furniture who published two books arguing on behalf of thoughtful labour, argued that glamorizing 'handicraft' has not improved the quality of everyday life or of our possessions. If you have not yet read Pye's rebuttal to over-romanticizing craft, 'Is Anything Done by Hand?', then put down this book. No one should have used this nostalgic term since 1968, when Pye pointed out that even letter writing does not happen independently of materiality – we are addicted to standardized paper and other flat surfaces that are rarely products of the hand. Pye preferred to identify types of workmanship and to move away from the hand as a defining and constant value. In his eyes, craft was too often applied selectively to confer praise and status. Pye had a noble goal: to increase respect for more types of work and workmanship, not to circumscribe craft's existence.

Craft might be made by hand, but more often it is cultivated by money or physical constraint. Material reinvention and elaboration always take place in relation to a marketplace, caught at a crossroads where money and patronage intersect with labour. Commercial production – ephemeral roadside whirligigs, touristic jewellery and carnival masks – might be worthy of attention and more than 'mere trade'. Why is the proximity of craft to commerce always a tortured topic, whereas we pretend that art has a lofty remove from capitalism? The craft shop is inevitably closer to street traffic, depending on it for vitality, even existence – and yet as such is more susceptible to being considered ruined by commercialization. Consider this paradox: craft is a term that has lost credibility in direct proportion to its use in advertisements and in our commercial culture, and yet to prove that handicraft survives we identify elite, bespoke fashion accessories for the extremely wealthy, such as a Lamborghini roadster or the Alexander McQueen boots worn by Lady Gaga or the Duchess of Cambridge. To lament the encoding of social status and hierarchies in material possessions is tantamount to calling for sumptuary laws. Hedonism and exclusivity always result in patronage of handicraft, so we should applaud the long lines that queue up to see McQueen's couture or the crown jewels.

IS CRAFT ART?

Just as speech preceded writing, craft came before art and architecture. It seems unnecessarily basic to say, but yes: craft and art are often one and the same, and at other moments become specialized, discrete. Since 1900, increasing numbers of people have looked to art (in addition to real estate and religion) to serve as the defining objects in their lives. Since 1950, art appreciation has increased, largely fuelled by photographic images and video, but two-dimensional familiarity far outstrips tactile understanding. Basketry holds dirty laundry, not the zeitgeist – or so it seems.

But no – to take craft seriously is to note that baskets can articulate the springy tension in human musculoskeletal systems and the push and pull of our desire for earthly connectivity in everyday life more humbly and acutely than any work of art in bronze, marble, oil paint or pixels. Even though consensus dictates that a book about craft must begin by enumerating its distinction from art, to do so is akin to claiming that the separation between materialism and spirituality is clearly discernible. Contemporary humans do not have habits or needs that are radically different from those of a thousand years ago; we only express ourselves differently. Art and craft have similar aims: to render material, psychological and spiritual markers concrete. Craft gives us crowns and thrones to distinguish pretend princesses from bona fide queens; these artefacts defy easy categorization in regard to their functions.

Craft's relationship to contemporary artistic production is often summarized by three points of contact: by seeing it in relationship to the computer and the genres of painting and photography. If the computer is the latest tool in our bucket of instruments, to its detriment, craft is conceived in comparison as filling the role of an obsolete technique, as if obsolescence were a natural tendency and did not emerge from commercial pressures. In fact, the computerized car still needs trued wheels, and the modern type designer still needs to understand how much ink will bleed within and from letterforms: these are skills of craft. Painting remains the yardstick with which to measure national and individual artistic genius in both the marketplace and cultural institutions, even though many paintings were made in workshops. In contrast, craft is regarded as of a lower status because it is handled and not treated worshipfully with eyes alone. Moreover, painting is born of the icon and remains iconic as it translates better into our two-dimensional world than three-dimensional craft, as does photography. Photography freeze-dries labour, tricking us into thinking we know what it is like to set an axe into a log or raise an ingot of silver with a hammer – but labour needs to be engaged in order for us to truly commune with a handicraft. This maps a critical Bermuda Triangle in which craft gets categorically and ontologically misunderstood amid oceans of digital images.

In the past five decades, exhibitions have installed optically pulsating quilts vertically on the wall, moving them away from beds and from arm's reach. This orientation celebrates the visual but not the tactile and physical qualities of the textiles. Does it validate them to liken them to abstract paintings or weaken them? Such retrospective cannibalization of craft seems to intentionally obviate the social lives of things. 'All degradation of art veils itself in the semblance of an intellectual advance,' stated William Morris, a leader of the British Arts and Crafts revival, in his 'Lecture on Textile Fabrics' (1884). Morris was right, as these days we can easily find a choir of twenty-first-century craft enthusiasts typing out verbal arguments to invent a new conceptual craft, instead of arguing about the ways weaving and other ancient complex manipulations of material have always prompted theoretical reflection. Recovering ancient techniques in dyes and weaving, Morris argued for simplicity while he manufactured and sold luxuries.

Ironically, exhibitions of quilts often purge the context of production from view, so that conditions of isolation or poverty become invisible.

Cotton appliqué quilt, unattributed, mid-Atlantic United States, *c.* 1850. We fail quilts if we admire them as mere pictures and not complex material expressions of social identity and physical relationships. Quilt sizes convey meaning the same way automobiles preserve the memory of horse-drawn carriages.

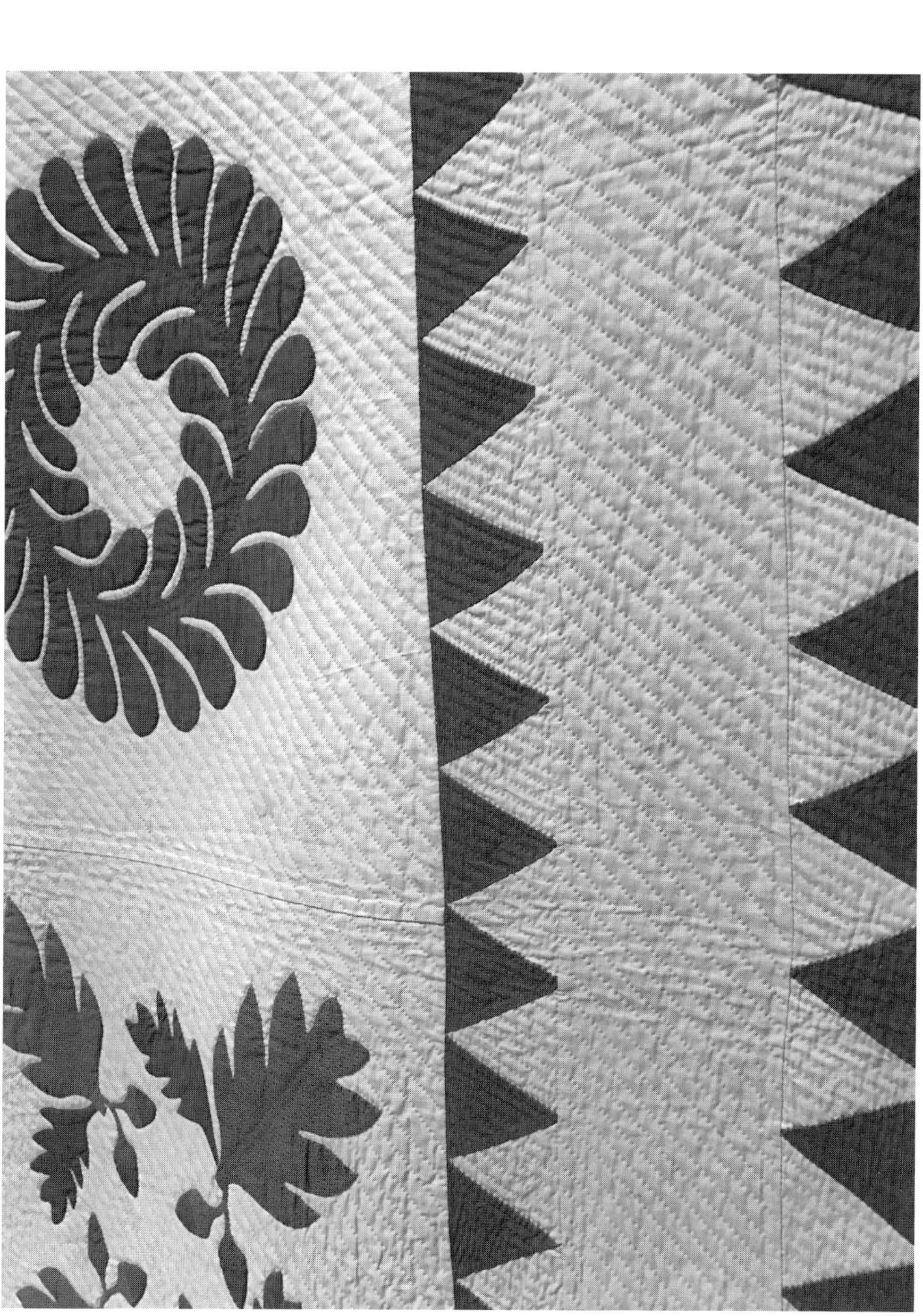

Praise for quilts should map them as social and cosmic geometries. Bedspreads should not be regarded as equivalent to altarpiece canvases but as human-sized, to facilitate our coupling. There is additional political potency in many an African American quilt that reclaims cotton, appropriates the colours of flags and emphatically declares the rightful breathing room of people as a human right. Quilts were used lightly and kept tightly thereafter, usually in chests. Such textiles are a template of humanity's bonds for remembrance and ritual re-enactment. We fail these artefacts if we look at them as merely pictures and not as expressions of self-determination, as agents of social bonding.

CRAFT COMMONS

The least interesting craft objects might be ladders and chairs that are uniquely carved of wood in a hyper-individualistic way, while the most compelling might be worth little money and reveal deep cultural habits. The great majority of craftspeople have repaired things rather than just made them from scratch. Virtuous reclamation is a timely redefinition of craft in our era crying for sustainability. The twentieth-century creed 'Make It New!' rings hollow these days when we look at toxic waste sites, polluted beaches, abandoned strip malls or fraying cities like Detroit. Craft is not filling empty space with more things but a responsive articulation to a need. Fixing an old glass requires a great leap of intuition, empathy for inert matter, and often includes reverence for a dead artisan's labour. Craft will remain a necessary compulsion to get our world out of its current mess.

Commonplace craft is where human necessity and empathy for materials flow together. Sometimes a bent twig or stapled pot can help us cope with fear or anxiety. Designers Charles and Ray Eames's wonderfully impish rhetorical question 'Who would say that pleasure is not useful?' leaves the binary opposition of uselessness and the useful in proper disarray; life is not so clearly either/or, it is often both/and.

Bending bamboo or pulling on a skein of wool requires – and teaches – communion with materials. Craft demands that humans meet material at some middle ground that is not entirely anthropocentric. 'Empathy for material' is a much better rule than 'truth to material'. Humans respond to woods and clays in a variety of ways: some delectate over plasticity and others seemingly extrapolate cellular structure or alchemical properties. Craft has too long been hung up on the principle of 'truth to materials', which sounds wonderfully ethical but has mostly been an excuse to condemn plastic, machine-made goods or ornament as well as people, on aesthetic grounds via moral pretexts. There is no one truthful way to use any of the more than six hundred species of rattan and bamboo in this world. Some of it is brittle, some pliant. Surely most fish traps evolved after centuries of knowing a river's seasonal shifts in current, temperature and fauna. The context of each purpose changes, as seemingly every three or four generations humans use up one set of resources or another or develop new tastes via trade. For thousands of years, before any moralistic anthropomorphic assignations were made to trees or metals, empathetic communion guided fabrication.

Ed Rossbach (1914–2002), when working with rolled-up newspapers and plastic drinking straws as well as raffia and linen when he taught the craft of basketry in the Department of Decorative Arts at the University of California, a vast range of media, reasoned that 'Basketmaking might be a sort of clock, not a measuring device, but something devised by man to enforce an awareness, a savouring, of time through its arbitrary division into rhythmic units.' When Rossbach was stationed in the Aleutian Islands with the U.S. Armed Forces he began to interlace tundra grass into three-dimensional forms, a reality he found preferable to the world's chaos. His first baskets were not aiming to be art, nor were they ever based on a notion of skill; rather, they were ways out of an existential predicament. Rossbach was one of only a handful of craftspeople – alongside David Pye – who articulated a theoretical perspective on their practice, and their thoughts will be touchstones in the arguments that follow. Their openness to their own time and willingness to look forward helps me believe that a ten-year-old building castles in cyberspace might stake the same claim on craft. As soon as towers of pixels are designed they become as embedded in our desires as do memories of French medieval abbeys or the stepped masonry of Mexico's Monte Albán.

When Louis Kahn suggested that his fellow architects ask bricks what they want to become, he was arguing for more listening and less doctrine: 'You say to a *brick*, "What do you want, *brick*?" And *brick* says to you, "I like an *arch*."' Craft has value in that it sorts and seeks out the diversity and plurality of the world's human ingenuity and distinct geographies. Humans have availed themselves of the world's rich stew of materials, from beeswax to baleen to vellum to hemp to lapis lazuli, and the integration of these minerals and vegetables and animal by-products into a toolkit requires sensitive empiricism. Determining the right temperature, pressure, tension and force involves observation but also a sublimation of the self, so that a material conditioning and environmental context are paramount. We must resituate craft as a social instinct and an extension of environmental bonds. The rural basket-maker in Japan knows when to return to a good hillside where the bamboo grows straight and was harvested three years ago; the upstate New Yorker to the wet dell to check on the ash slowly gaining girth: this is attunement to materials.

Empathy and affection: both of these oppose the strategies championed by the so-called avant-garde. The notion of a 'leading cultural edge' has been accepted as a modernist inheritance – and is a military term suggesting continual antagonism as a cultural metaphor – but ought to be seen as an intellectual yoke unsuited to craft. War, aggression and

Weaver, Vietnam, 2012. Basketry has been global for centuries and outsmarts simple frameworks of national identity and concepts of 'folk' production. This photograph could be regarded as a contemporary version of the 18th-century Massachusetts farmer who was a part-time skilled artisan, or of the 19th-century manufactory where hands still outnumbered machinery and automation.

generational upheaval and innovation have been sustained as pedagogical models for cultural production for most of the twentieth century with a net loss of affection and an ever-increasing amnesia and myopia. Most schools and museums give the doctrine footing by celebrating individualism. We need to disabuse ourselves of the notion of avant-garde in order to cultivate craft.

A theory of craft driven by affection might begin with bamboo chairs and rattan wastepaper baskets and the Indonesian and Vietnamese labourers who weave them in sub-par conditions for you to buy on the cheap from IKEA. Basketry still lies outside the academy, just out of institutional control, as a self-taught skill and unclaimed art that is the most global and universal. Baskets prove that craft can still be found in the bargain basements of department stores, charity fairs and tourist highways and byways, almost in spite of the efforts of schools or museums. They show that cultural pluralism is a tangible fact. Valuing both the basket and basket-maker combines appreciation for both human frailty and genius. Baskets can fool national identity and concepts of 'folk' production. They defy frameworks of nationality. Let us delve into them as mysterious spaces where cultural identities are muddied and rewoven into new hybrid forms.

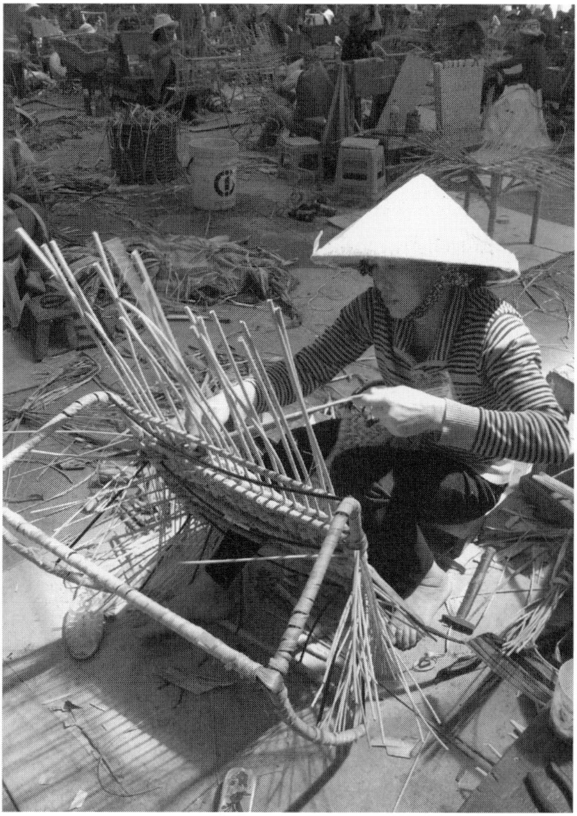

MODERN CRAFTSMANSHIP

Champions of craft who aim to bypass nostalgia often express passion for theory and contemporary art, a tendency that usually ends in elitism of a different type to connoisseurship of the antique or rustic. Instead, can we talk about craft in a way that engages issues of class or historical memory? In most libraries, there are three types of polemical books that meditate on craft (and these are outnumbered by thousands of specific treatises on highly specialized production methods such as lacquering, marbling and lace and a good many thousand scholarly books written out of passion for the so-called minor arts). The noblest advocates, often also the most self-righteous, call urgently for the recuperation of manual skill as a virtuous civic practice and for the reinstatement of the ideal of quality. A more widespread group applauds the production and preservation of individualized and unique 'handicraft' objects that humanize our increasingly mechanistic world (even if these are generally commodities reserved to brighten the private spheres of the affluent or the privatized museums that pretend to be part of a cultural commons). Lastly, many artists, teachers and students see craft as a democratic eruption of creativity that productively threatens elitist cultural canons and institutions. The sentiment of this activist group is as moralistic as the first, but it usually degenerates to a narrow horizon line, a polemic over aesthetic wars or authenticity. I see some value in all three approaches but will try to avoid moral brinkmanship and the myopia of contemporary art discourse by emphatically returning to the context of money and trade and to issues of class and consumption – and the banality of direct encounters with textures and the social space of the workshop.

I will avoid many of the accepted definitions of craft that look to the past instead of defining it as a living contemporary force. Too often, craft is described as embattled, desperate or on its deathbed. Bookshelves are filled with hundred-year-old plaintive cries that one craft or another is an endangered species, such as the cooper's or wheelwright's. Thousands of crafts have been lost in the course of industrialization, imperial domination and colonial suppression – but the human baseline instinct for tooling remains a necessity. Historically, champions of craft encumbered by nostalgia and temporal self-loathing have rejected the icons constructed in their own day. For instance, the railway bridge, Eiffel Tower and Empire State Building were each reviled when they were built as ungainly and inhumane. Today, the distinction between artisanal and industrial craftsmanship in these engineered marvels and factories seems less easy to categorize. Each of these seemingly disruptive technologies actually generated new types of craftspeople.

George Kubler provocatively begins *The Shape of Time* (1962) by asking that all tools be valued as art, especially anonymous things that challenge our customary praise for individual artistic genius. To extend the canon of art, he situates craft as an ongoing force in our world, an instinct to animate matter, and hopes that we will in time slowly become 'aware of the excellence of many craftsmen whose work has only lately come to be accepted as art'. By ceasing to focus on known constellations of stars, he asks us to see positive and negative space anew so that intervals might recombine into alternative imaginary lines and lineages. In Kubler's expansive vision, obsolescence and reinvention are cyclical and often perceptual phenomena, with discarded and adrift tools rising up to shape history unexpectedly. Craft asks art historians and art lovers to willingly forgo the idea of originality and masterpieces and embrace mere tools. Like Kubler's *Shape of Time*, *The Shape of Craft* aims to pursue interpretation that moves away from privileging Western culture and pre-established hierarchies of cultural value.

The roots of this book can be traced back to my stumbling upon a plaque in the lobby of the Empire State Building dedicated to 'Modern

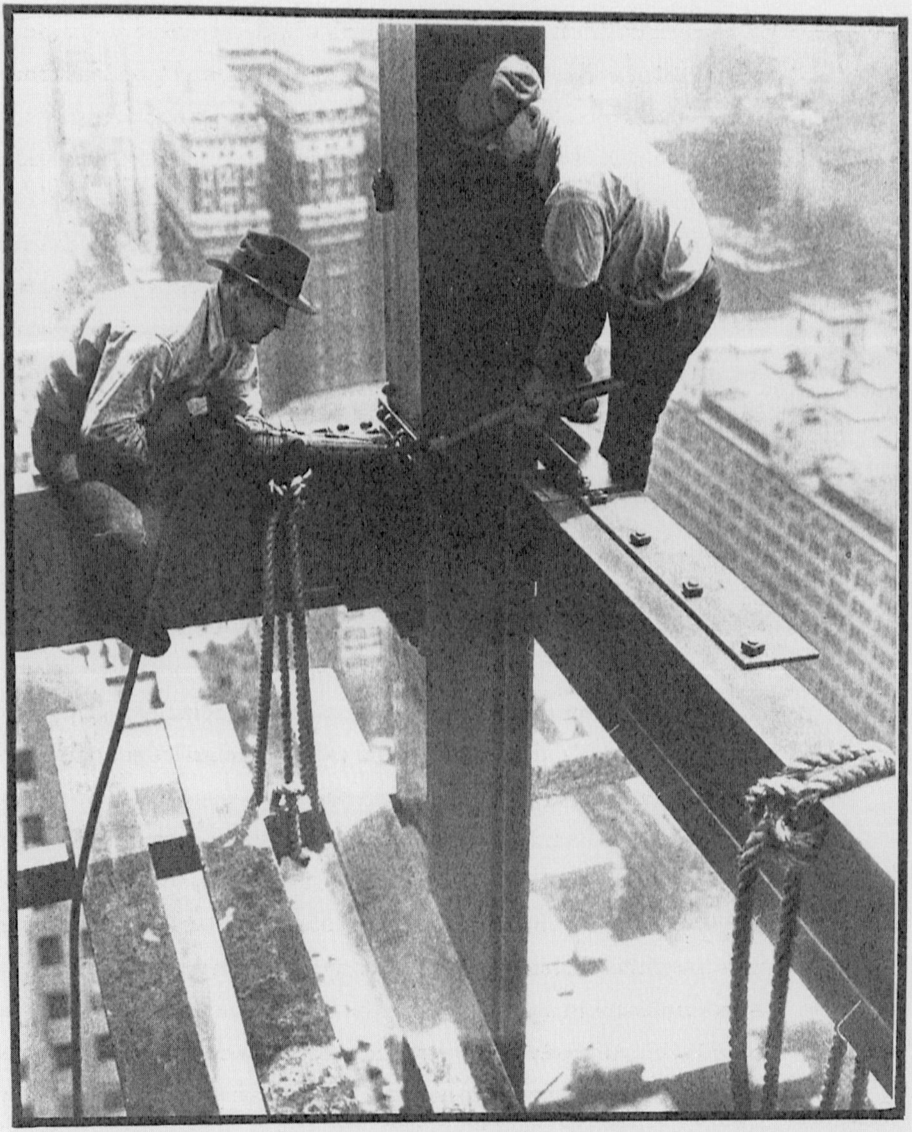

THE ARTISANS ARE DEAD

And these are the new artisans. The master-workmen of our time drive steel to steel with hammer strokes of air. But they still depend upon the judgment of hand and eye. And their necks are still breakable.

Craftsmanship'. Born in Manhattan, I had taken the building for granted as an emblem of capitalism, not handicraft, and had looked at it without really seeing it. The skyscraper stood in opposition to skilled labour, I assumed – a record of standardization, scientific management and business-directed efficiency. But in the case of the Empire State Building there was craft in customization and collaboration. Teams of riveters – the 'master workmen of our times' – were newly invented artisans. By looking closely, I saw that the decoration was a programme celebrating labour – and also that the promotion of its craftsmanship was a scheme to advertise the real estate development. The Empire State Building has become a shared piece of modern-day patrimony – it pops up in films and countless ads across the world. As a photographic icon it symbolizes power, but by looking closely at its construction one can see the fragile contributions of human labour. Five-person riveting teams acting in aerial concert: one worker heated a rivet, then another threw it to a catcher, who passed it on to be held in a massive wrench, where it was driven into place by a worker with a pneumatic drill. These crews, balancing on a steel skeleton without helmets or ropes, expand most existing definitions of craft: their workmanship still did depend on hand and eye, and yet collaboration and communication were intrinsic to their skill.

The plaque in the lobby doesn't list all the skilled workers; it does what we usually do: cut life down to a manageable list, one that serves the purposes of a social or political agenda. Most lists of 'great craftspeople' have a strangely Western cultural bias and boil down objects like bones – storytelling and storytellers get the upper hand. In the case of the New York skyscraper, the construction workers were turned into pawns in the narrative of civic incorporation. The acrobatic riveter was a new trade deserving of recognition, but giving select workers gold pins and limited recognition was propaganda – and cloaked the vain ambitions of the building the same way its grandiose name distracts our attention

Arthur Gerlach, photograph for *Fortune*, 1930. The caption describing the construction of skyscrapers in New York City, in this case 40 Wall Street, speaks for itself.

from the dark money and corporations, DuPont and General Motors, that built it.

Versions of this 1930 plaque honouring 'modern craftsmanship' in the lobby of the Empire State Building exist elsewhere. When Adobe software opens there is a similar list of names that momentarily reveals collaborative authorship and collated multihanded-craft. We need to permit more people and things with an unknown pedigree to enter the canon of great craft – like code written in software and satellite lenses and mirrors. But we also need to analyse the anonymous craft out there. If prominent buildings such as the Empire State Building have been overlooked and under-researched, taken for granted as 'machined', then our analysis of common craft has yet to begin.

CONTOURS

This book is organized into answering basic questions about craft – the who, what, where and when. The first section concedes that the initial way that we conceive of craft is through biography, but after three portraits of establishment figures I move to anonymous crafts to show how much distance exists between archetypes and everyday life. Comparing individuals' lives and *oeuvres*, we see the variety of applications of clay and wood reveal that no material has any singular essence – and is often a process of self-invention and contextual opportunities. This personal essay illuminates the immensity and beauty of anonymous craft in manufacturing. After these sections on 'who', I turn to 'what', querying materiality and our hang-ups about raw ingredients being gendered or caught on some gradient between the natural and the artificial. I seek to salvage the nobility of basketry from the basement of Western civilization where it has been unceremoniously tossed. Turning to the issue of 'where', I speculate on whether there is logic in the way we enter craft as a process of wayfinding and identity generation in twined fibre. In the country or the city, in isolation or as a social act, weaving is a plane – generally a landscape, a mode of place-making as well as an act of self-invention. The final section is an effort to situate craft now, in the present instead of the past. Delineating who, what, where and when sketches out some of the ways that humans use craft to sink roots into their world. Each chapter springs from material-specificity into conversations between crafts, to move from specialization to a search for commonalities and to highlight assumptions. For example, might welders have much to learn from weaving? Can we move away from gendering materials and tools to see them as having fluid, shape-changing values?

We are at a tipping point, when the risk of abstracting craftsmanship into a fetish results in the loss of an ability to empathize with its social and material dimensions. This book will not hide in the rarefied atmosphere of galleries to identify craft-like art, nor praise traditions to run away from the messy contemporary moment. Recently, the declaration that craft is a humanitarian concern has become a commonplace truism (notably often in affluent arenas of privilege, such as the art museum and the academy) – and sadly too often a repudiation of computers and digital technologies. I argue that no forms of craft are stable or pure. Can global craft be valued in a way that does not strive to set back the clock of industrialization or ask an emerging economy to stop developing? A pre-industrial reversion in the so-called developed world is neither possible nor desirable (discussed further in chapters Three and Four). We can chastise each other for our ethical shortcomings, or learn to tango more nimbly with the world's contradictions.

My goal is to delineate a few contours where the reader can touch *The Shape of Craft* in their own lives. Raising craft consciousness can solve only a few of the world's problems. Recovering first-hand touch in our educational pathways is a necessity to compensate for the degree to which navigating glass screens is counted as experience. Communicating through things in lieu of language was once more common, and this is why craft was once more formidable. The shock of novel woods and feathers are potent encounters that resonate years later. Caressing a fabric or handling a basket – sensual knowledge – tells us where we are from, where we want to go and who we feel the need to become. As for a coherent theory of craft, this book holds no such promise; you don't need a theory to recognize what makes pleasure distinctive or life worthwhile. Although I am sure of it when I am in its presence, I will not say where craft ends: new modes of manufacture will continue to be invented and new understandings of old tools will continue to challenge our grasp of the past. The most I can hope is that I whet your desire to touch craft and cultivate increased respect for the myriad anonymous craftspeople at work in the world.

ONE

ARCHETYPES: WHO IS A CRAFTSMAN?

Does the word 'craftsman' bring to mind a barefoot indigenous potter or a boutique chocolatier? All too often, when it comes to crafty hands, the choice seems to be either obsolete rustic or irrelevant luxury production. But the larger field of 'mending' – such as the deft hands of a locksmith, whose calm is contagious as he restores your home ownership – is psychologically potent as a restoration of identity. Such reparative skill is a largely overlooked aspect of craftsmanship but it is essential to our well-being. Critics and artisans have argued that the term 'craft' has become disturbingly flabby in its use in advertisements for motorcycles, jeans and single-batch whisky; what if we begin by recognizing more everyday skills and repairs, like the locksmith's, as craftwork? What else should we call the hands that reweave cane into an old chair seat or turn a dull knife back into a honed blade? Or the mending of larger things: bridges, ships or satellites?

Most construction was craft before machines were invented and glues and epoxies and silicon substituted for joinery, but that shifts the focus to technology, as does the logic of prefabrication. In our Anthropocene era, it is more important to rekindle the fact that craft was once a process of making do, not making anew. As flawed creatures who routinely build monumental piles of trash, we have a stake in recognizing that the most compelling crafts are fixes. 'Willow-work' could entail identifying

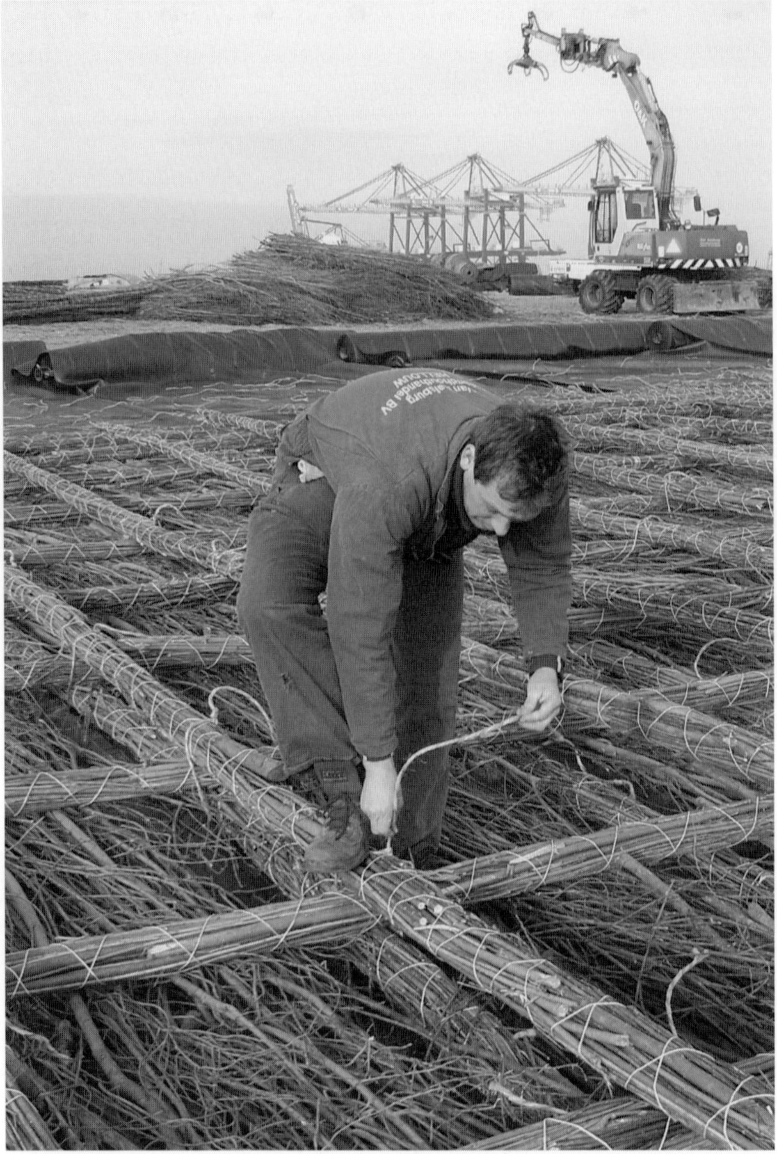

Willow fascine bundles (*zinkstukken*) made and installed by Van Aalsburg Griendhouthandel in Rotterdam. Many skilled jobs defy our established categories, and here the creation and maintenance of sea barriers and dykes could be described as environmental basketry and a craft as well as a technology.

a decorative handmade object, but willow could also be used to address broader collective human needs. Look at the hands of a construction worker tying together a fascine willow mattress to maintain the harbour and dyke of Rotterdam. This knotting and binding of twigs remains integral in a modern industrialized landscape. And the craft of building storm-surge barriers is only likely to grow in the age of climate change. It is worth seeing the willow bundles as pre-fabricated but customized, too.

In museums and galleries, we are told that the modern craftsman makes irreplaceable and unique *objets d'art*, but this contemporary emphasis is problematic. It prevents an understanding of what is common to the crafts and fails to acknowledge that craft is a verb integral to our cultural ecology. Craft is as fundamental as colour and cannot be eliminated in reality; this is a make-believe threat. A gallery of so-called 'modern craft' usually emphasizes eccentricity and hyper-individualization, which might prove more damaging to craft's reputation than the moving assembly line of the Industrial Revolution. To urge each human to be magically distinct is to encourage a re-enactment of the building of the Tower of Babel. The burden of originality weighs on today's young students of art, craft and design. Better for them to seek where 'craft' might meet human need, in the handiwork of a talented floor sander or a useful basket from Indonesia; better to value known and anonymous craft alike. To admire only new, expensive, well-made objects is to dream in the language of airport advertisements.

I begin to answer the question 'who is a craftsman?' by analysing three well-known photographs of heroic archetypes: Nampeyo (*c.* 1860–1942), the Native American potter who was born and worked in a New Mexico pueblo; Constantin Brancusi (1876–1957), the Romanian sculptor who came to prominence in Paris; and Karen Karnes (1925–2016), a recently deceased studio potter born in New York City who worked independently in rustic retreats. Citing genius but intentionally not idealizing it, this selection of snapshots emphasizes a hundred years of discontinuity in criteria for assessing the craftsman and intentionally undermines this gendered term. These examples cycle from a central and representative cultural figure to a peripheral one and, I hope, back again. Instead of portraying Nampeyo as an example of pseudo-pre-contact, pre-Columbian tradition, I want to emphasize the ways she was characteristic of an era when transcontinental travel, Sears, Roebuck & Co. catalogues, photography and rural mail delivery knit consumers across the United States of America into our seamless modern network. If Brancusi is known as a pioneering abstract sculptor, I ask what it means that he portrayed himself as a peasant woodworker, posing with an axe in hand, and his sculpture as a hewn timber. Karen Karnes is less of a household name and yet she was part of a groundswell in mid-twentieth-century counter-culture, and she, like Nampeyo and Brancusi, can be considered an example of the way that histories of craft struggle to illuminate both individualistic achievement and the zeitgeist, as if the uniqueness of the craftsperson were antithetical to the overview. These three figures do not form a sequence of avant-garde tendencies or a conclusive heritage – my selection intentionally breaks against such a master narrative. By alternating between clay and wood, woman and man, I want to highlight the tensions generated when mapping tradition, innovation and gender in terms of workmanship and materiality. Their handicraft lashed together their respective identities. Their portraiture still informs – and misinforms – our understanding of the craftsperson, which is why we must struggle to touch the sandy grit in the ceramic and grain of the wood – and add more portraits to the canon.

These three remarkable figures in craft history mark out the contradictory ways we map Western urbanity and the pastoral. They also reveal the ways we presume tooling to be a gendered activity. Chapter Two develops definitions through first-hand encounters with working individuals. Although heroic craftspeople are good starting points, 'classics' keep us looking backwards into the pre-approved past, whereas many craftspeople work on in the field and factory – much quiet skilled labour continues anonymously, unsigned and underfoot. If we can see Nampeyo, Brancusi and Karnes as lives pushed and pulled by their respective environments then we can begin to understand craft as a process through which we build on the challenges of environmental circumstances as much as individual ability.

Moreover, individuals in the world of craft are rarely discussed comparatively – so biographies are rarely windows into larger issues such as the history of technology or gender. It is useful to jostle images of materials and makers into comparisons. To intertwine the stories of Nampeyo, Brancusi and Karnes, forms – a tin pot, a screw, seating – become protagonists alongside their hands. I aim to make sure that textures, materials and tools outweigh photographs, words and inherited categories. Increasing our appreciation for their tools does not diminish their genius and creativity. Once we synthesize these three characters we can step back to see what pattern emerges – and gauge whether there is room for the unknown factory artisan or handyman repairing a house to enter the pantheon of craft.

NAMPEYO'S INDIGENOUS INNOVATION

The many photographs of Nampeyo atop a rocky Arizona mesa home are evidence that the 'native craftsman' was a modern archetype even at the beginning of the twentieth century. Photo-postcards presented Nampeyo as 'natural history'. Perversely, she was a modern conversation piece and yet also proof of the apparent simplicity of ancient societies. Such images of handicraft implicitly asserted Western industrial progress. Here, the famous Hopi-Tewa potter is photographed with two pieces of work to reveal her process, one a fired pot, highly finished, and another mere raw clay. The incomplete pot emphasizes that her manual labour transforms the clay – her hands alone. Once the wet clay dries she will burnish the surface to a polished lustre, then paint the design freehand with a chewed yucca leaf brush. The laborious nature of these steps was antithetical to modern manufacturing.

For most visitors to the Southwest in Nampeyo's lifetime, the Hopi were picturesque, quaint remains of an ancient epoch, and J. R. Willis photographed Nampeyo in precisely this light. Manual construction of pottery was a telling sign that 'the Indian' was technologically inferior – even at a time when North American factory-made ceramics were in a fairly rudimentary state. Tourists looked at Nampeyo as if she were an earlier stage of civilization preserved in amber. Rolling the clay into rope-like coils, the Pueblo potters placed them atop one another, around and upward, all the while smudging them together so that the layers, initially corrugated, blended, progressing from crude to finished. The absence of the potter's wheel among Hopi reinforced a narrative pitting modern technology against 'the primitive'. But condescension towards the Pueblo potter accompanied acquisitive appreciation of her work. Many realized that her methods resulted in graceful pottery, thinner-walled than that which American factories made. The fine quality of much Pueblo work, the pots burnished with a river stone or deer antler in circular orbit, is miraculous. Potters like Nampeyo dug up and mixed their own clays, fired pots in open pits with no consistent fuels and had no thermometers as aids.

Despite the photographer's construction of an image of primitive, prelapsarian pottery, Nampeyo exudes a contradictory strength-in-weakness. She embodies self-determination and the survival of indigenous traditions: her labour resists Western acculturation even if her product becomes a commodity. Today, we can recognize Nampeyo as among the first self-consciously modern Native American artists. She was aware of

J. R. Willis, photograph of Nampeyo, *c.* 1918, glass negative. The plentiful photographs of Nampeyo suggest she was regarded as representative of a culture and an exemplary artisan, but to emphasize such interpretations is to overlook her own agency.

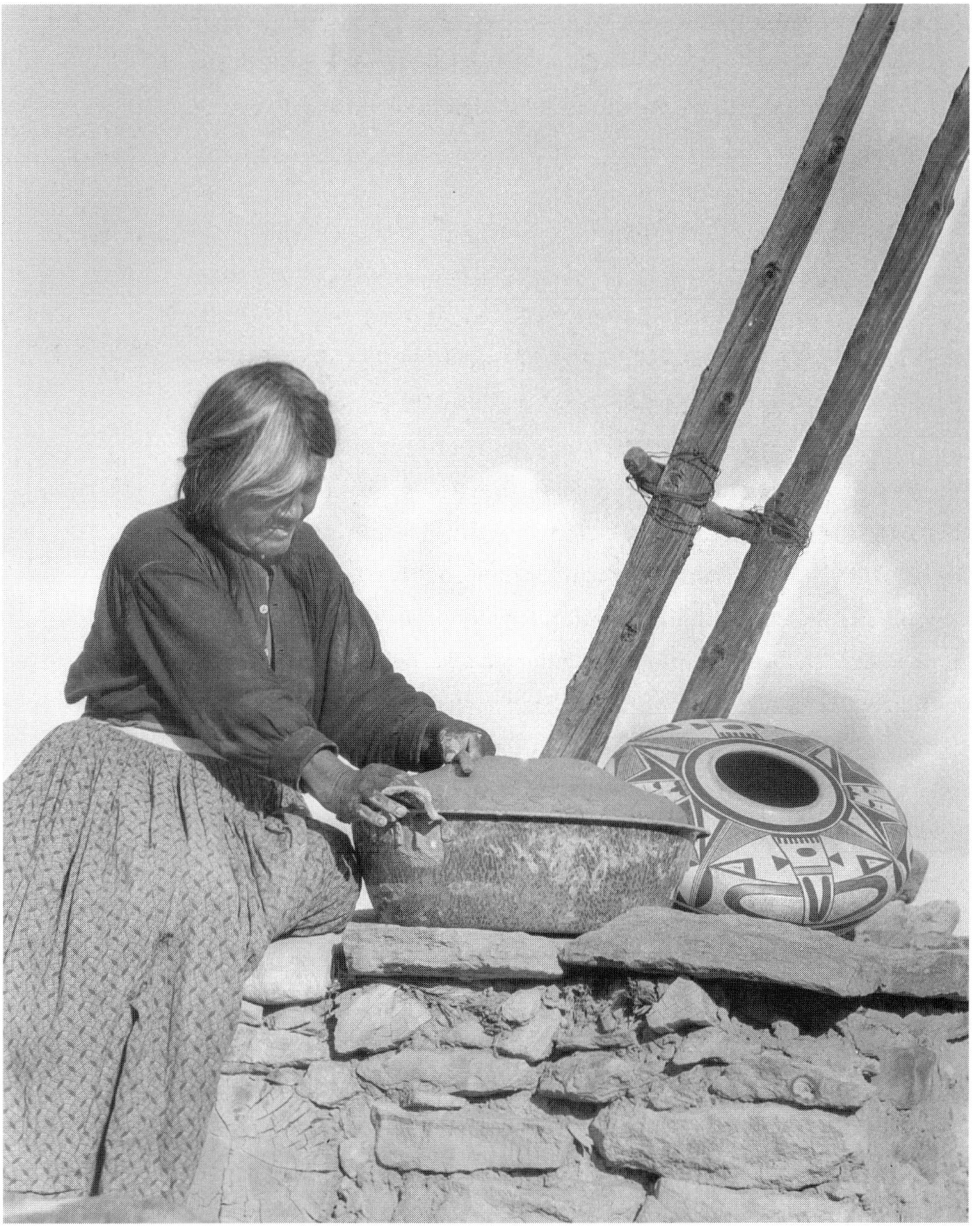

these postcards bearing her image – she herself fed the fascination that veered towards objectification in her portraits and willingly endured hundreds of photographic exposures. She used her craft to leverage a distinct identity.

Nampeyo seems to stand for Native American Indian culture that has not been ground into touristic knick-knacks and yet is complicit in that process. After centuries of imperialism and racism and the incursion of the railroad and mining companies that were chopping apart the land and people, she personified the artisan whose work withstands the vicissitudes of time. On the other hand, the photograph misrepresents her and her working methods: a Hopi potter would not in fact have worked exposed to the sun: her clay would dry too fast. And a seasoned potter would have sought a better work surface than an uneven rock wall. Nampeyo would not have used a worktable, but most likely level ground. Ancient pots have round bottoms, as their makers had no expectations of a perfectly level surface. The oldest pots are propped up in our museums on doughnut-like discs. But Nampeyo knew her customer and understood the tourist trade – and that her pots would sit on level shelves in modern houses.

Her downcast face does not look into the lens but to the dark opening of her finished pot, a black ovoid. Pots have long been anthropomorphic substitutes, with feet to stand on, swelling bellies and a lip at their opening, and this one seems to look at us. Around the rim is a chain of geometric faces – guardians, perhaps, adaptations of spirits, the kachina? The radial pattern is confident and bold, and skill is manifest in the linear decoration painted on a curved surface. Behind Nampeyo in the photograph are two protruding rails, the top of a ladder made of saplings – the access to an underground kiva, most likely. The environmental clues heighten her romanticism and allure as a 'primitive'. The dark mouth of her pot becomes a suggestive prelude to the mysterious subterranean kiva. She sits on a remote mesa, to which the Hopi retreated in order to escape Spaniards. Through touristic time travel, the Indian pot was – and remains – a metaphorical talisman to access a supposedly simpler era and a culture almost lost to modern life.

If you believe that Pueblo ceramics became endangered and impure with the advent of the twentieth century, with its atomic bombs and televisions, celebrity art and computer design, Wonder Bread and Twinkies, then think again: Nampeyo was not in an Edenic state. To her neighbours on the mesa, she was unusual because she was of mixed tribal identity, part Hopi and part Tewa. As a national curiosity, she logged thousands of miles on trains to appear before audiences of millions. She became a live exhibit in temporary expositions as far away as Chicago, where she was seen by the likes of Theodore Roosevelt, Jane Addams and W.E.B. Du Bois – fellow curiosities who attained celebrity status. While these contemporaries had access to podiums, she was displayed sitting on the ground and seen as a 'primitive'.

However, Nampeyo deserves to be regarded as an inventor. When she was a child the railroad penetrated her desert home and brought a trading post within walking distance as well as rapacious archaeologists. She developed her style only after gaining access to archaeological digs run by Jesse Walter Fewkes in the Pueblo environs. Although she is often described as a reviver of traditional pottery, her so-called Sikyatki style referred to an excavated Hopi ruin – literally, 'yellow house' – of which she was unaware before the Smithsonian's excavations. Seeing shards with asymmetrical linear decoration, she transposed them into her own production. 'Finding a better market for ancient than for modern ware, she cleverly copies old decorations, and imitates the Sikyatki ware almost perfectly,' wrote the archaeologist Fewkes, unfairly demoting the artist to the status of his student. In a way, he was right: she saw new possibilities in craft as he dug up the past in the name of 'science'.

Look again at Willis's photograph and note a compelling detail: a ten-gallon metal basin. As mail-order catalogues of Sears, Roebuck & Co. and Montgomery Ward began to disseminate goods via railroad and through the United States Post Office's rural delivery, such mass-produced containers became widely accessible and affordable to the 'cliff dwellers'. Nampeyo's parents had probably not owned this sort of tin tub. Photographs of Appalachia from the 1930s show similar metal basins hanging outside dingy cabins for all-purpose use in agriculture, hygiene and fire fighting. Carried up to the mesa, the pail was a multifunctional and prized possession. Nampeyo is constructing her pots in the conventional Hopi manner, using another bowl as a support. But a ceramic shard, called a *puki*, had historically cradled the bottom of the wet clay, and Nampeyo replaced it with the metal tub. In a role reversal, the standardized factory product literally supports the work of handicraft. Nampeyo inverted acculturation. Human lives are a collage of technologies – a phenomenon sometimes called uneven modernization. The industrial and archaic sit uneasily together, flummoxing 'progress'.

Nampeyo foreshadows the contemporary paradox of craftspeople aiming with equal vigour to reconcile modernization and conservation of tradition. She is the forerunner of twenty-first-century tinkerers who try to integrate the newest gadget into an old-fashioned task, using computer numerical controls (CNC) to mill a wooden bowl or weave on a Jacquard loom. She personifies the soloist who vies with the factory's robotic and human assembly line. Gestural and allusive in transferring centuries-old archaeological imagery onto her pots, Nampeyo riffs on the past, absorbing icons from other tribes that were not part of her Tewa heritage. The modern basin permitted another of her signature formal innovations: it allowed her pots to have unprecedented broad, sloping shoulders, resulting in horizontal top surfaces. There are no extant ancient Sikyatki pots with such steeply raked shoulders, and Nampeyo became known for her spare decoration on these oblong pots. Her white slip surfaces breathe, her painting enjoying ample negative space. Many of her larger pots measure between 18 and 20 inches (45 and 50 cm) wide, and the consistency of their dimensions suggest that this modern metallic *puki*, layered with rags, sand and ash, increased her efficiency and standardized her preferred form, a super-sized seed jar.

To suggest that Nampeyo perpetuated static traditions would be misleading. Indigenous conventions change demonstrably with shifts in identities and technologies, commerce and culture – and have in each century. The tin bucket is a brutal fact, not as violent as the introduction of the horse by the Spaniard conquistadors, but an intrusion nonetheless. The photograph shows Nampeyo using clay as well as the distribution network of railroads. Her image undermines simple generalizations about indigenous art. The metal basin leaves a tangible trail of intention and ambition, if we are respectful enough to recognize Nampeyo's self-determination.

At the age of fifteen, Nampeyo began selling pots at the Keams trading post a few miles away from her mesa home. There she saw other Hopi potters mixing Zuni and Spanish motifs. When Jesse Fewkes and other archaeologists noticed Nampeyo's historicism, her pots came to be valued more than those of her peers. She worked in connection with the market and not in isolation. Her brother, Tom Polacca, left the settlement

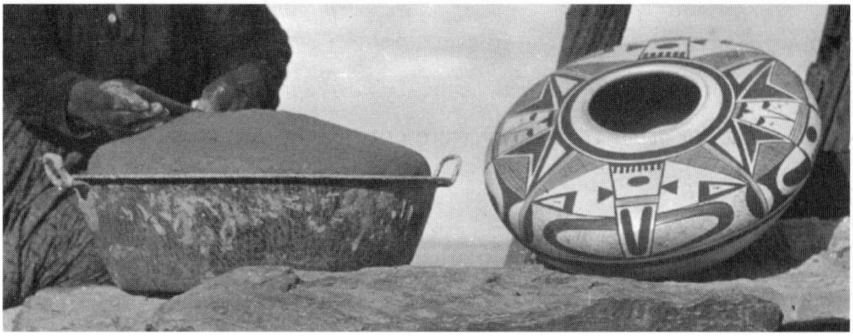

Detail of photographic postcard inscribed 'Nampuya' by J. R. Willis, *c.* 1918. The metal pot that Nampeyo uses is evidence of her historical context, but is often overlooked.

of Walpi to work at a trading post and converted to Christianity, and Nampeyo likely found it easier to transform her ethnic identity because of his self-fashioning. She was caught in a network of consumption and commodities. Even if she made the metal basin her own and was the first to affix her name to her pots on printed labels, she was never dealt with fairly in economic exchanges.

Nampeyo remains a paragon, but as an indigenous modernist, not 'primitive'. Her metal *puki* challenges the view of craft as a static practice. Art historians have rarely classified indigenous potters as inventors, but in fact Nampeyo is disruptive. She scaled up the seed jar form. Clay is heavy stuff that is hard to cantilever without support. Her pots look boldly aerodynamic to the modern eye accustomed to streamlining and presentation. Nampeyo the entrepreneur selected from cultural traditions and craftsmanship what she wanted – the metal bowl, for example – while working within the capitalist retail and tourist market. She was the first indigenous potter to declare herself an artistic entity and to brand her pots. The photographer J. R. Willis might have choreographed the pose, but he also capitulated to the identity she wanted to project: 'Nampuyo, the Hopi Potter', reads the caption. This particular craft practitioner was not engaging in repetitious action; rather, she was knowingly breaking with cultural precedent even as she invoked authenticity.

Today, in the image saturation of the Internet, Nampeyo is everyone's aboriginal potter; she embodies craft broadly because photography permits such kinaesthetic empathy. We feel we know her virtuosity. Disagreement over the constitution of craft comes when general rules are sought, such as the idea that craft must express individuality. Anonymous Native American pottery is susceptible to being undervalued, and the fallacy of such a view is exacerbated when museums consider some handicraft 'ethnographic duplicates': no two are the same, no matter how similar they appear. Note our inconsistencies in declaring signed 'handmade' objects unique and consigning unsigned craft to some shelf lower than 'art'. When presented with her photograph, we declare Nampeyo a craftswoman; every question about taxonomy is swept away.

A photograph of Nampeyo operates as an emotional and psychological fulcrum. She becomes objectified as a type, the 'aboriginal Indian potter', and yet our bonds of empathy also bridge the chasm of time and difference. Contemporary potters' sense of commonality with Nampeyo has continuously grown over the decades alongside distance from her historical context. We believe we can identify with her, that when we handle clay we must be approximating what she felt in making a coil pot. The slippery material is prone to slithery partiality, a spiritual inclination which nineteenth-century German aestheticians came to call *Einfühlung*, a 'feeling into' (although they did not foresee such empathy extending to non-Western art). Despite all the ways that we might regard Nampeyo as an innovator, through photographic consumption her image has succumbed to a false sense of cultural and temporal continuity. Our identification with this craftswoman is altogether misleading but potent, a drug-like hallucination that is too accessible to forgo entirely. Our neo-tribal identification sustains a romantic dream that is broken only by a rational acknowledgement of the metal basin.

There is at least a third temporal possible narrative at play, too, in Nampeyo's photograph, about the threat of craftsmanship disappearing and the arc of its uncertain survival. Edward Curtis included Nampeyo in his photographic documentation of what he called 'the vanishing race'. Scholars such as Ruth Phillips see this 'myth of imminent demise' as a lens to understanding the United States; it is equally influential in the way we think about craft. Is the Indian potter an endangered species? In embodying the threat of extinction, Nampeyo's image suggests that craft is something lost. If we see Nampeyo as a custodian of ancient manual traditions and disentangle her from the messiness of self-fashioning, cultural hybridity, and the damned metal basin, we can insulate ourselves in simplistic myth. Fantasies of aboriginal women potters have had remarkable endurance but are obviously more constructed or imagined than they are real. As an actor acutely self-aware of her cultural predicament, Nampeyo remains incredibly powerful the more we recognize that her pottery is full of paradoxes. Her tin pot rattles aloud with her agency, marking a player, not a pawn, in a turbulent economy and disrupted ecology. Although she does not proclaim, 'I am Nampeyo, the Innovator', her work and metal tub demonstrates this craftswoman's modernity.

BRANCUSI, THE AUTHENTIC WOODSMAN IN PARIS

For photographers taking his portrait, Constantin Brancusi often held tools more commonly seen in Paris's ethnographic museums than in its École des Beaux-Arts, which he had attended. For Edward Steichen, the American shooting for *Vanity Fair*, Brancusi posed holding an axe in two distinct ways in his Paris studio: he stood like a heroic medieval warrior, glaring directly at the lens, and also at rest, perching on his stepped sculpture *Endless Column*, his downcast eyes more introspective. He is flanked by two other versions of the serrated columns, enduring icons across the fields of architecture, art, craft and design. The angular, rough-sawn wood and the axe explicitly exhibit manual labour, flaunting Brancusi's repudiation of his own skill in figurative modelling and of the conventional studio system in which assistants translated models into monuments for maestros like Rodin and Bourdelle. Brancusi intentionally asserted a manly folk identity as a form of artistic rebellion. His direct carving – *la taille directe* – produced 'fundamental, primitive, and honest' forms like *Endless Column* and the chunky off-balance teacup over his left shoulder. His modular forms were an antidote to over-cultivation, yet there is a contradictory tension between affectation and authenticity in his holding the axe.

Edward Steichen, *Brancusi in His Studio*, c. 1927. Photographs of Brancusi in his Paris studio were published in several American magazines, including *Vanity Fair*, where he was featured a number of times in the 1920s and cited regularly as an example of abstraction taken to a theatrical extreme.

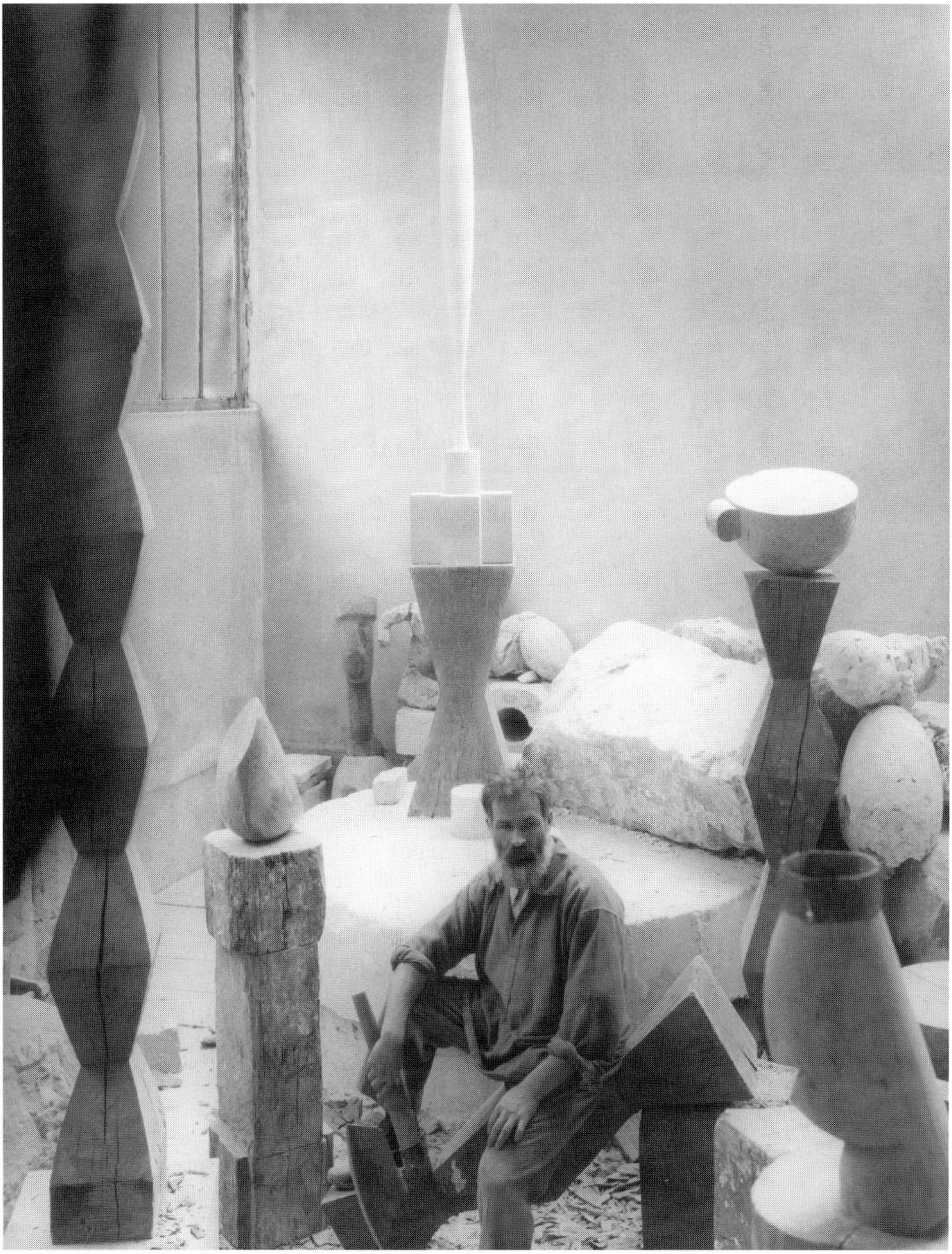

A celebration of manual labour is intrinsic to Brancusi's stature in the story of modern art. When United States customs officials refused to recognize his *Bird in Space* as a work of art, declaring that the sleek bronze was taxable machinery, Brancusi testified in its defence: 'All the finishing from casting was done by me, personally by hand, as also the polishing by hand. No polishing machine or other machine was used.' Several versions of *Bird in Space* exist, in bronze as well as marble, and the thin, slender white form directly above his head in Steichen's portrait is the latter. They were surely made in clay and plaster, too, but these intermediaries were rarely declared photogenic. And even if the 'bird' stands prominently in the Steichen portrait, Brancusi demonstrates that he is a woodsman, not a marble carver in the Renaissance tradition.

Brancusi carefully selected tools and implied action in his self-portraits as well, cultivating a shamanic relationship to wood – always pitting himself against a massive timber. So it is an overstatement to claim that craftsmanship is lesser (or supplemental) to his art: his self-portraiture as a peasant woodworker make his persona and work inseparable. At his death, when he bequeathed his studio to France, the body of sculpture came with over 1,600 photographic prints, many of these self-portraits he had developed in his own darkroom. Brancusi depicted himself as Paul Bunyan in Paris, giving the material a mystical quality. The artifice of his image management has not stained his authenticity or the legitimacy of his identity. Brancusi remains appealing because his work still challenges refinement, and because the idea that there is truth in wood is as appealing as Nampeyo's primal clay – her tin pail excepted.

Regarded as an artist who made sculpture in wood, not as a woodworker, Brancusi remains a crossover in appealing to a vast range of craft and design enthusiasts. An architect in Cologne and a chainsaw carver at a county fair in Colorado might be equally as likely to cite Brancusi as a heroic influence. He resembles a diviner of form. Yet his virility is medium-specific.

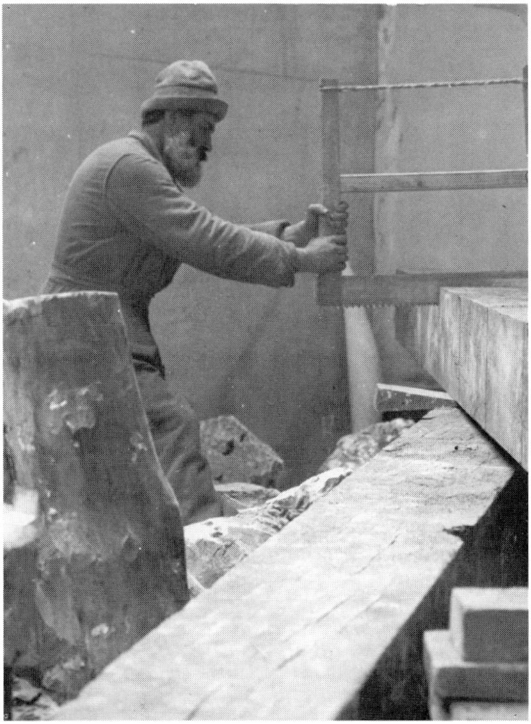

Constantin Brancusi, self-portrait sawing the modules of the future *Endless Column*, c. 1924. Brancusi's use of his own camera and darkroom to create self-portraits demonstrate a self-awareness that specific tools and technologies were ways to fashion his identity as a peasant-craftsman.

Photographing himself thrusting a large frame saw or heaving an axe, Brancusi seems to divine 'the soul of the tree', as furniture maker George Nakashima would later put it, or perhaps to make tooling seem a form of religious devotion. He did not snap pictures of himself pouring plaster moulds or filing bronze. He made woodwork into an animistic process, a vital impregnation of meaning into matter. Trying to separate the identity of the artist from the woodsman is impossible. His Montparnasse studio – plumbed with gas and water, tied to a modern municipal infrastructure and outfitted with a phonograph, radio and 16mm film camera – looks like an austere quarry in photographs. As a photographer and sculptor, Brancusi fashioned a public identity as a fabricator of geometric forms that were strangely both crude materials and weightless abstractions.

Rows of carving and cutting tools hang on the walls of Brancusi's recreated studio in the Centre Pompidou. Many of the sculptures in the room are wood and marble, but some are plaster, a less than revered substance, usually considered an intermediary material, a transitional step on the route to bronze casting. Plaster calls for rasps and lots of buckets: it is dismissed in most art histories as a material lacking vitality or true formal properties. According to both Arts and Crafts reformers and modernists, plaster casts of antique sculpture stood for everything wrong with Victorian museums and the degradation of artisans' autonomy. Plaster is still seen as a pseudo-material and is not what artists or historians point at when they revere Brancusi as a 'visionary peasant-sage'. The material ruptures our association of the sculptor with pastoral or folk art. His serial forms and multiple casts of his *Bird in Space* have long tripped up scholarly explanations of abstraction. Although Alfred Barr, founding director of the Museum of Modern Art in New York (MOMA), drew a diagram showing Brancusi emerging from 'machine esthetics', most scholars since have focused on the wood as self-consciously primitive abstractions (yet have hesitated to acknowledge his sham self-representations). The categorization of his artistic identity diverges with materiality.

Casting bronze is inherently a collaborative process, but Steichen photographed Brancusi as if he were a hermit; studio documentation might have included assistants such as Julio González or Isamu Noguchi, both later famous in their own right. Sidney Geist worried whether Brancusi used power tools to polish his brass and marble forms – as if it were important that he did, as he claimed, grind and polish 'by hand'. One extremely reductive question about craft remains pervasive: 'did you make it yourself with your own hands?' This self-righteous perspective is posed to most guest lecturers showing their work to an art school audience. If his self-portraiture suggests Brancusi was 'hands-on', remember that Noguchi's recollection of his apprenticeship was of time spent polishing the shimmering bronze *Leda* (1920–26) and its nickel-plated steel base every afternoon while it was on exhibition. Brancusi was fastidious in his attention to lustrous metal and marble surfaces, contrasting these with chipped wood. In his self-portraiture, rough tooling is a communion with material and a performance.

Brancusi is often identified with 'primitive art': his chisel chips and striated saw-marks are seen as related to African carving and art from his childhood in Hobitza, Romania. Can they be both at once? To lump these diverse influences together as 'craft' is to dump together everything

Constantin Brancusi, view of atelier (with *Endless Column*, *Leda* and *Plato*), c. 1922. The zigzag edge of the wood screw echoes in the telescoping neck of the figurative sculpture *Plato*, on the right, with its back to the camera, the *Endless Column*, which it faces, and the motif of a crenellated silhouette is in many of Brancusi's bases.

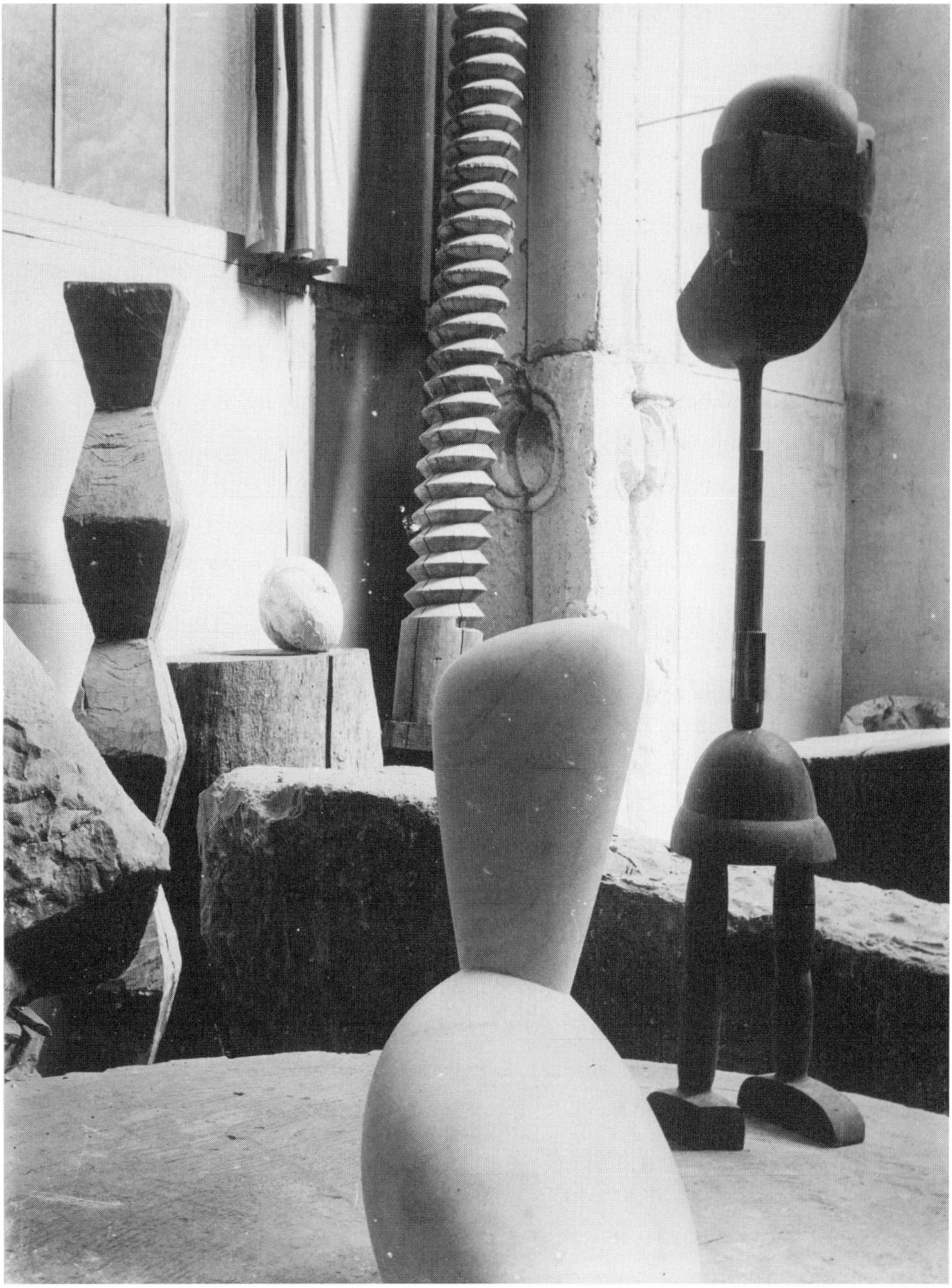

outside the academic traditions of Western art. The elongated necks of *Plato* (1919–20) and *Little French Girl* (1914–18) have prompted comparisons to Gambian and Nigerian fetish carvings of the sort that Picasso was snatching up in flea markets. Horizontal grooves on the telescopic necks of his figurines suggest a substructure and decorative pattern, tracheal rings as well as ritual adornment. The stepped chokers defy the anatomical art in which Brancusi was trained.

While some art historians take Brancusi to task for his 'affected naivety'; we would do well to look at the staying power of his axe and saw marks across our culture today. His version of rough-hewn wood has suffused contemporary decor; from bars and picnic tables to dining rooms, libraries and bedrooms, the splintery texture of exposed joists represents artisanal labour to the general population. Since about 1970, shabby chic 'farmhouse furniture' has brought rough wood slabs straight from the sawmill, into the living room. Brancusi decor is in Los Angeles, London and Milan – anywhere that heavy timbers outweigh the logic of construction.

That rough-hewn wood is perceived as expressive – either of an artist or of 'nature' itself – is confusing. Is it the tooling or the raw material that nurtures this aesthetic? Emphatically coarse surfaces – adze marks – are the visual signals that make Brancusi's sculpture seem so deeply human, and yet those chipped surfaces are both exaggerations and artifice. Such cuts have become indicative of the 'handmade' today, even though Brancusi's chopping applied a patina to a saw-cut plane. Anathema to the notion of 'finish' and refinement in earlier times, saw marks on wood should not be equated with personal drawn marks: it is an intentional texture, but ambiguous as an articulated surface.

And yet to realize that Brancusi made no fewer than six carved variations on a wooden teacup – and more of the *Endless Column* – is to recognize that his indirect carving was a sort of repetition that was hell-bent on appearing anti-mechanical. His workmanship was not intuitive; sawn and planed surfaces were deliberately chipped. His super-sized teacups especially depart from mystical abstraction or notions of freehand tooling: they resemble cartoons of commodities and absurd advertising signs of old, not abstract form. When we see the cups as theatrical props and intentionally rough-hewn versions of social etiquette, Brancusi's friendship with Duchamp becomes more palpable and his relationship to Paris café culture more present.

On seeing the skyline of New York City in 1926, Brancusi said, 'Why, it is my studio. Nothing fixed, nothing rigid. All these blocks, all these shapes to be shifted and juggled with, as the experiment grows and changes.' His photographs of his studio should be read carefully as a stage of intentionally juxtaposed characters. In several, behind the *Little French Girl* and tucked in the shadows of two variants of the *Endless Column*, one can find a long, threaded timber, the only enchanted object in the room not made by the artist himself. Made for a cider, wine or oil press, the wooden screw is formally similar to the *Endless Column* but is much more finely notched into a spiral thread. Anna Chave categorizes this wood screw in Brancusi's studio as 'an antique', underestimating its power. Her taxonomy is decidedly less troublesome than calling it a readymade or a fetishized tool. This helically grooved timber is a peculiar presence that roamed around the studio, a serrated profile that resonates with the angular *Endless Column* and the telescopic neck of the *Little French Girl*. In Man Ray's 1922 portrait of Sinclair Lewis, the photographer transformed the writer's blank expression by using his own winepress as a prop, having acquired one in an antique store most likely after seeing Brancusi's. The screw literally became a modern-day *deus ex machina*.

The 'antique' woodscrew has an obvious relationship to the artist's incised timbers but has a helical thread, an invention that dates back to ancient agriculture, when olives and grapes were first crushed using mechanical pressure. A basic carpenter's clamp is also a threaded wooden screw; linen presses applied pressure the same way. The mechanism was shaped with chisels, with callipers constantly keeping measure. When Brancusi acquired his tool it could have been twenty or two hundred years old. Rural carpenters were still making them in the 1850s (and in Romania and elsewhere well into the twentieth century). Brancusi transformed it into a column by setting the screw upright. This readymade tool either inspired *Endless Column* or it confirmed the idea. Alfred Barr's judgement seems right: when Brancusi photographed his *Column* and the screw together, he made machine art. Or, he handcrafted machines into abstractions. His friend Duchamp saw power in repositioning tools as art, turning a urinal into *Fountain* (1917), a snow shovel into *In Advance of the Broken Arm* (1915). Similarly, Brancusi perceived the wooden screw as an inspired form, not a nostalgic token: the grape press was a tool to think with. Claiming that Brancusi cut his teeth on this bit of Sumerian farming technology might sound like heresy, but it also poses a middle ground that connects abstraction to materiality, the hand to the machine, agriculture to abstract culture.

Is the wood screw mechanical or not? Probably it was partially made on a spindle lathe, but it is purely subjective to identify one object as machine-like in an inhuman manner and another as mechanical and more authentically human, isn't it? Such cultural biases for and against tools and patterning strangely inform many categories of craft, such as disdain for moulds and jigs. Apropos of Nampeyo's pottery, we assume rounded bowls to have flat bottoms and tabletops to be level – or those with dining room tables expect as much. In 1968, David Pye ridiculed the term 'handmade' amid the hippie and yippie search for authenticity; his audience was too engaged in the idea of handicraft as an individualistic ritual of soul-centring to think of tooling in more empirical terms. Can we do that now? As Pye pointed out, nothing is truly made by hand in the studio, and not even in our kitchens, except perhaps for kneaded dough. Pye pleaded for education in tooling – in both the 'workmanship of certainty', using precision, as well as the free 'workmanship of risk', relying on dexterity. While commercial advertisements might be expected to sell the 'handmade' as long as people unwittingly drink snake oil, a higher obligation belongs to artists, artisans and designers, who misinform the public when they resort to categorizing anything in such a vague and romantic manner. Pye was urging the preservation of variety in a built environment that was suffering from increasing industrial standardization, not advocating for an expansion of manual-based production. Scissors, rakes and combs are examples that Pye noted of instruments that regulate texture, and Brancusi's screw was a similar tool. Such implements defy our subjective aesthetic values as they remake organic nature into hard-edged shapes.

To situate Brancusi's 'antique' timber on the antipodes of tooled consistency, we must decide if it is standardized to the point of being dehumanizing or whether the marked surface conveys sentience. Run your fingers up around the taut ridges, lift the timber; then the scale becomes human. The size and weight were appropriate for a small farm operation; one person might have made or used it. I admired an old cider press bought in a Gloucester antique shop long before I secretly caressed a Brancusi sculpture, and I understood it to be virtuosic and utilitarian. Precise without being machined on a lathe, the visible chisel marks are what Pye would have called 'regulated free workmanship'. It was made the same way as olive presses in ancient Athens. It was laboriously filed in the same manner as the first thousand steam engines. The helix is consistent, refined and reliable – no one could use an artistically expressive screw. The gouge marks are signs of yesteryear's efficiency, not like Brancusi's hack marks. To admire the 10-foot-long screw that is 10 inches in diameter one must imagine the conditions of the carpenter who worked on it.

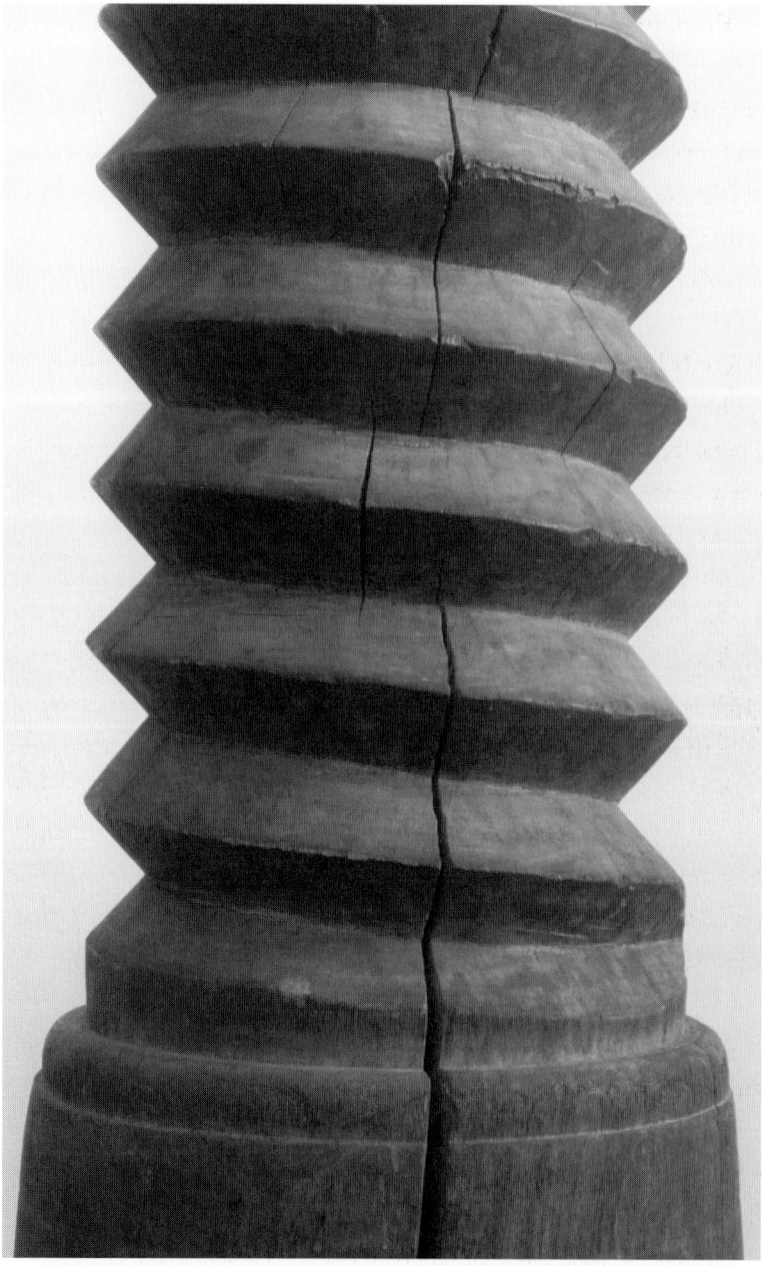

Threaded wood timber (likely part of a cider press), *c.* 19th–20th century, wood, 63 in. (160 cm) tall, 9½ in. (24 cm) width base tapering to 5⅛ in. (13 cm) width at top. Purchased in the 1960s in New England long after it was removed from its original context, this type of tool for pressing apples into cider (or grapes into wine) was still being made in the 20th century in many rural parts of the world. Where Brancusi obtained his we do not know, but it seems to have preceded or coincided with the variations on the *Endless Column*.

The deterioration of and radial splits in wood help us mislabel such a screw as 'handicraft' when in fact it is engineering, technology. Modern routinized screws in plastic or metal maintain their form. When new, such wood screws were smooth and well-oiled machinery and shipped over distances as prefabricated units. For example, a family farm's cider press in Ontario, Canada, made in about 1830, was shipped north from a workshop that was previously a neighbour in Pennsylvania and delivered by cart and canal. Presumably, the carpenter worked according to an agreed-upon verbal plan but without a blueprint dictating the precise dimensions of either the screw or the threading. Refined over the course of the winter months, the form was found and emerged. It sprang from a predetermined design in the mind but came alive through material negotiations and shared expectations.

We could learn from Brancusi and view the screw as a tool for thinking. It is the product of rational handicraft, full of banal labour that adds up incrementally to become awesome. To dismiss it as an antique is to be miserly with our affection. To deem the farmer's woodscrew not contiguous with craft and to allow it to disappear under some other category, like the industrial sublime, is folly. The screw for Brancusi, like the tin pot for Nampeyo, was a simple piece of engineering that edged his hands closer towards imaginative and inventive mimesis. But despite Pye's written arguments in praise of precise tooling, it is rougher work that symbolizes the definition of authentic craft to many who use the term in the affirmative. Can we build emotional empathy for standardized craft like the screw, which is not moulded but neatly cut, groove by groove? Can we respect such an anonymous craft?

Tools are human strategies to modify the built environment, devices aimed to increase control or entropy. Pye himself was a craftsman who relished making small, finely fitted wood canisters. He used a fluting machine to carve structured, elegant patterns of ornament that transformed surfaces of wood grain into rippling algorithms. In contrast, the agricultural-industrial screw does not comfortably enter domestic sentiment even when it enters a dwelling: its scale is imposing. Brancusi's antique tool and his *Endless Column* outline the problem of expecting David Pye's oppositional forces – 'workmanship of risk' and 'workmanship of certainty' – to be equally proportioned in our world. We have always needed the craftsman to be precise more than self-expressive, as Brancusi's work suggests. This might have been the ultimate lesson that Brancusi internalized through the screw and bequeathed to us: mechanical tooling can be suggestive and emotive of humanity.

A few years after the summer of 1954, when MOMA opened what was then the largest American exhibition of Brancusi's sculpture to date, Charles and Ray Eames began to design a series of walnut stools that echoed Brancusi's work. Cultivating a sense of primitive carving, their lathe-turned seats appear estranged from machinery yet are the product of mechanization. Stools accompany – and almost contradict

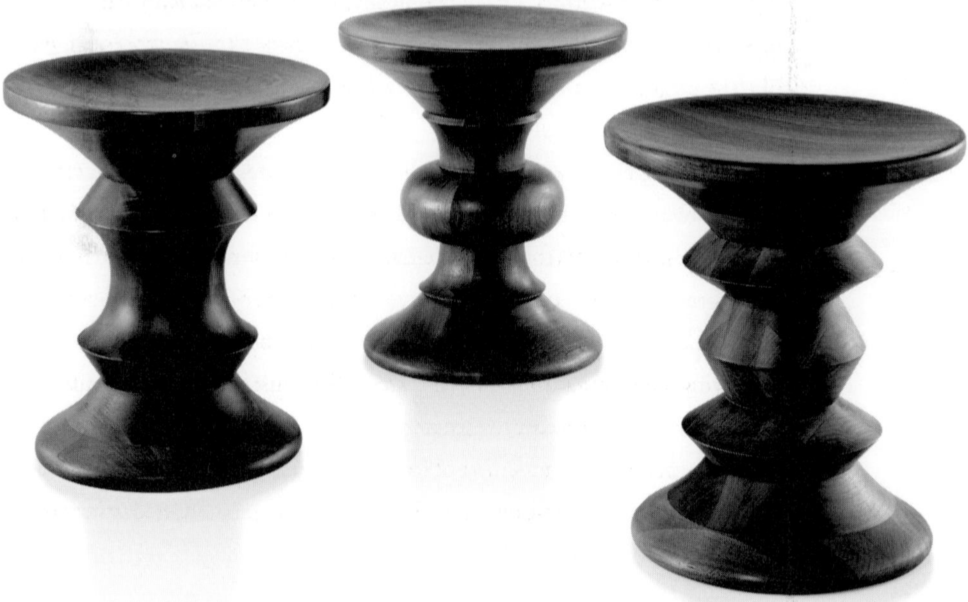

Charles and Ray Eames, walnut stools, manufactured by Herman Miller, 1960–present. Adding variety to corporate uniformity, these accessories were of indeterminate function – a perch for a cup or book? Human feet or bottoms? The zigzag form made on a lathe somehow ends up being associated with pseudo-ethnic forms.

– standardized chrome and leather upholstered office furniture for the nearby Time-Life Building. The Eameses exploited walnut and tool to produce stark rhythmic silhouettes. One dark walnut stool is concave, another convex, and the third has three sharply angled ridges that most closely evoke Brancusi's *Endless Column* – or his cider press. They added dynamic form to the rectilinear white offices, the impersonal corporate headquarters of the Luce publishing empire. Still manufactured by the Herman Miller Company today, the walnut Time-Life stool is a modern factory product that alludes to craft and intends to cultivate sensory relationships. The stools supply tactile and visual variety. The multipurpose object is equally suited to serve as a human seat or perch for feet or side table. When analysed beside the Eameses' plush leather seats that both pivot and swivel, the wood seems rustic, almost clumsy. In their own furniture advertisements and Merchandise Mart installations, the Eameses assiduously cultivated allusions to tribal art, and they were attuned to the ways in which Native American baskets, African and Oceanic woodcarvings and Japanese kites – all often lumped together as 'primitive' – made modern design more appealing and less mechanical. The stools are part of their larger strategy of 'extra-cultural surprise', in the eyes of the scholar Pat Kirkham – folkloric swag.

The long shadow of Brancusi is worth contemplating as a factor in the complex romance of the primitive and the modern. Usually credited to Ray Eames, the stools for the Time-Life offices are shrewd accessories; their intelligence is to be modular but interrupt uniformity. The dark, low sculptural silhouettes acknowledge human diversity: the 'primitive' palliates the alienating skyscraper. In the Eames stool, Brancusi's productive confusion of regulated labour and unregulated material became a theatrical stage – and probably a management tool for men in grey flannel suits. The knee-high stools assert personality differences, perhaps gender distinctions, and other tribal aspects of modern office life.

No degree of commoditization or mechanization can kill the mystery or charm of exposed wood grain – or does that antique cider press seem decorative because it is anonymous and outside our usual mode of brand recognition? To Brancusi, and probably also for the Eameses, the tooling of wood was a part of the craft commons to be reinvented theatrically, when and where the semblance of authenticity was required. Sometimes we need to touch a serrated edge to comfort our minds, sometimes the arc of a smooth-curved body or pot.

KAREN KARNES'S ENIGMATIC SOCIAL OBJECTS

Karen Karnes sips from a teacup she threw on her potter's wheel, looking ambivalently at the photographer, Ross Lowell. Her table is laid with two settings and would be welcoming if her body wasn't recoiling. An educated middle-class woman, Karnes made pots one at a time on the wheel and sometimes refused orders if uniform serial production was demanded. Her aesthetic ideal was to work alone, starting out from ground zero, but her finished work spoke to the traditions of collective feasting. At the time of the photograph, in 1958, she was living in a co-operative community on the Hudson 35 miles north of New York City, selling casseroles to the urban cognoscenti downstream. In this portrait of counter-cultural domesticity, she opts out of the role of suburban hostess, smirks at middle-class ideals or conventional roles for women. Seeking recognition through publicity, Karnes is visibly ambivalent, unsure who or what she will represent to her future audience – independence and self-reliance, or a fantasy of escaping from the modern world of conformity? She was 32 years old, struggling to make her living as a potter and to raise a child alone in an era when most Americans considered both of these ambitions irrational. If her pottery was a tool for people to connect with each other, her craft was a devotion to solitary labour.

Her work exemplifies the residual power of craft, even as a metaphor in the age of mass production.

Karnes mostly made functional pottery over sixty productive years. Living through the apex of Abstract Expressionism, when ceramics were stabbed and torn into ponderous existentialist hieroglyphics, she kept on making casseroles and jars. Six years after this photograph was taken, her ceramic seating, fireplace and bird feeders were awarded a Palma d'Oro at the 1964 Milan Triennale; twelve years later, she was described as 'one of the most successful production potters' in the country. Did success mean competing with factories or adding beauty to everyday life? When she did veer into sculpture, she was quietly demonstrative: her seats are large, but not monuments. If the thought of a pottery in a beatnik cooperative prompts you to visualize a cliché of rustic brown pots, look again at Karnes, ensconced within white walls, tile and cork underfoot

Karen Karnes at home in the Gate Hill Cooperative, Stony Point, New York, 1958. Karnes and her husband David Weinrib bartered Ross Lowell for his photographs documenting their art and lifestyle.

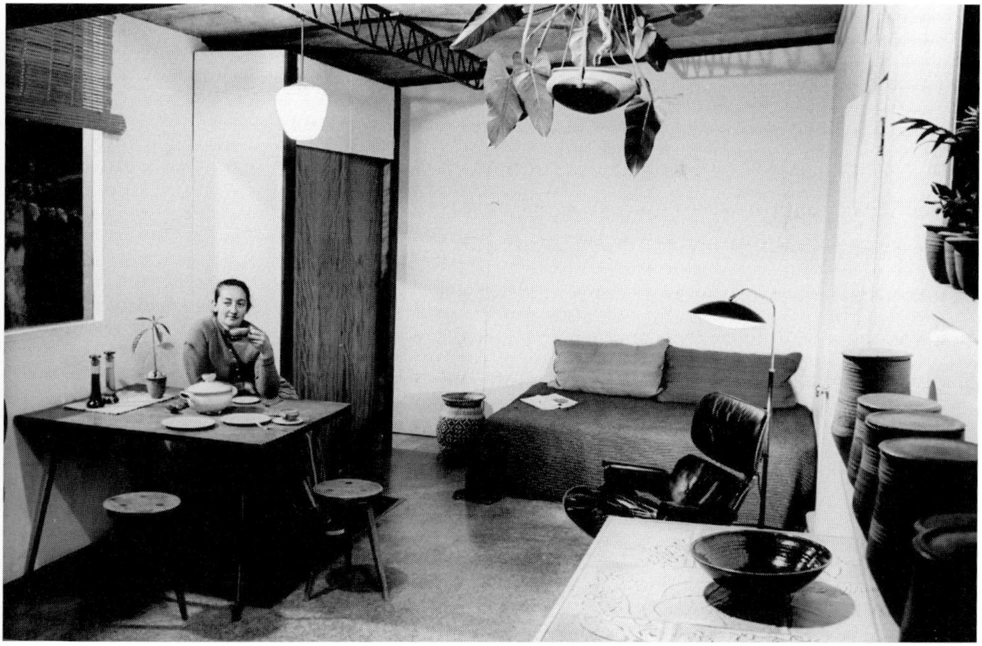

and steel trusses overhead, her spare, modernist home Le Corbusier's ideal 'machine for living in'. Beside her is an Eames Lounge Chair, which was new in 1956, a design icon as costly then as it is now, standing in contrast to the affordable handicraft marked with her own fingerprints and the three-legged stools that she had purchased from the Southern Highland Craft Guild in Asheville, North Carolina. This collision of accessories, pastoral craft and palatial accent piece, continues today.

In many cultures, urban and rustic pottery have represented opposed notions of refinement – and ended up ensconced in theatrical recreations of the peasant's lair or monarch's mansion. Cosmopolitan pots are presumed to be glazed a viscous white, their pastoral opposites to be flecked with random imperfections. If you attend a craft fair or visit an art school, it becomes clear that people still believe in this binary opposition between nature and modernization, with certain materials seen as more 'natural' than others. Yet appearances are deceiving. The rustic and the urbane are equally artful and artificial. Aesthetic differentiations are easy to mistake for cultural schisms. Karnes was considered accomplished by international sophisticates such as Isamu Noguchi and Gio Ponti, who published her work in *Domus* magazine when she was only 25. Her ceramics straddled the self-conscious pretensions to being 'primitive' and urbane.

Does Karnes's example help us with the question of whether the archetypal mid-century modern artisan laboured in a bucolic shop or a smart urban studio? A binary opposition between urban luxury and pastoral folk production haunts books on craft – as well as presumptions about who is a 'real' craftsperson. This tension and its class-based implications tugged on Karnes, a potter who was both incredibly prolific and influential in the second half of the twentieth century because she lived by selling thousands of pieces of handiwork, a feat few accomplished. From today's vantage point she embodies a paradox, both going off the grid and trying to make it as an artist. She is like the avocado plant beside her, erupting from a pot too small. Her independence matches the ideal proclaimed in that same moment by Edgar Kaufmann Jr, curator of design at MOMA, that 'modern design is intended to implement the lives of free individuals.' We still believe in such liberating creativity, expecting the contemporary craftsman to be an exemplar of self-determination.

Karnes was proud of having parents who worked in the garment industry and were union organizers, but she was glad to work alone, to not have a factory job. Growing up in a cooperative housing complex in the Bronx, she attended the High School of Music and Art in Manhattan and then Brooklyn College. After a few months as a housewife, she eloped with her teacher at the Newark School of Industrial Arts, David Weinrib, and travelled with him to Italy, then Alfred University in western New York state; then the two lived at Black Mountain College in North Carolina until they circled back to New York and helped to settle Gate Hill Cooperative, a commune in Rockland County. She lived there for a quarter-century, raising a son on her own. She was driven and territorial, in both the context of family life and the cooperative: 'I made it very clear: that's my time, just like if I went to the factory, like my mother went to the factory.' This declaration is oddly boastful and also counterintuitive – workers at factories generally aren't considered to have their own time. They cede autonomy when they punch the clock. Yet her pride is no stranger than Brancusi's testimony against the machine to New York's customs inspectors. However paradoxical her statement, Karnes was proud to be a disciplined one-person workshop.

A small tribe of mostly former Black Mountain College residents seeking counter-cultural communitas formed Gate Hill Cooperative; they included John Cage, M. C. Richards, David Tudor and Paul and Vera Williams. The utopia verged on failure and was not entirely rural. Cinéaste Stan VanDerBeek and his wife, Johanna, built the interior of their vaulted prefab home to resemble an urban alleyway and repurposed a grain silo to serve as his Moviedrome, which they imagined as a prototype to franchise. Urban commerce sustained John Cage, who when not working at music composition created advertisements for the textile firm Jack Lenor Larsen, Inc. Musicians living in Gate Hill performed in and around Manhattan. 'The Land', as they romantically called it, was close enough to civilization for imported delicacies such as the avocado and well-heeled weekend visitors who stopped by to shop – and to take away the bucolic atmosphere in a pot. John Lennon, Yoko Ono and Mark di Suvero, among others, came for picnics, parties and pottery.

In her book *Centering in Pottery, Poetry and the Person* (1963), Karnes's friend M. C. Richards popularized the notion that making pottery is an individual spiritual journey, but Karnes's own pottery and the atomization of so many families at Gate Hill suggest that craft does not automatically aid social cohesion or grow community. The pot shop was a retreat where Karnes experienced autonomy at a time when few women could achieve professional independence. She stood out at Gate Hill as the only woman other than Richards making a go of life on her own. Her work was practical – more useful than Nampeyo's – even if her choice of lifestyle might seem to have been more radical. Karnes was capable of steadily precise manufacturing: note the row of lidded jars along her wall.

Photographs from Gate Hill Cooperative reveal a chaotic social life carried on alongside diligent cultural labour. The sensibility of the potters was to actively cultivate a Japanism (*Japonisme* in nineteenth-century France) that prized *wabi* – an aesthetic of serenity. Zen philosophy spurred on Cage, the experimenter extraordinaire in musical performance who was also a mystical amateur mycologist living in a spare meditation chamber at the highest point of Gate Hill. Karnes resided down beside a stream, at a remove from the hilltop social node. The concrete block dwellings scattered across the natural setting left it unclear whether individuals were opting to live together or apart.

And the casserole? The pot on the table before her is oven-to-table ware, made for the informal lifestyle and communal gatherings. In their *Guide to Easier Living* (1950), a bible for the post-war educated middle class seeking domestic order in the new suburban milieu, Russel and Mary Wright championed such casseroles and collective undertakings that turned chores into pleasures (supposedly). Karnes infused her pots with an ingredient to make them ovenproof, an engineer's technological advice that she appreciated. To rustic charm came high-performance chemistry. If the Wrights produced pastel-glazed tableware in factories in the tens of thousands, Karnes's pots revelled in varied surfaces speckled by blushing minerals. Bonniers, a Swedish emporium on Madison Avenue and 58th Street, sold her pottery amid shaggy *flossa* weavings and Danish teak furniture – affordable luxuries. Her 'unique' wares demanded prices well above those of the Wrights' mass-produced pottery. Karnes's casseroles also cultivate an intentional austerity, even if they are purportedly social: are the pots asking to stand alone, and be seen as unique, or to meld with the pace of everyday life?

Karnes also began to work on a large scale. Commissions came for the Motel on the Mountain, a restaurant on a promontory above the New York Thruway with 41 luxury rooms, designed by Junzō Yoshimura, who had built a house in the MOMA courtyard in 1954. Karnes and Weinrib furnished the hotel with decorative objects that belied their never having travelled to Japan. They built four sinks and rooms of floor and wall tiles. Then Weinrib left, and Karnes maintained this ambitious scale with a series of strange seats. The ideals of an informal lifestyle were eroding the boundary between interior and exterior, and Karnes explored the genre of the stool that could be on a deck, patio, beside a fireplace or in a garden. Sliding plate-glass doors opened up new liminal spaces for bird baths and planters, and Karnes's seats revel in being slightly asymmetrical and biomorphic. Low and rounded, like heavy fungal growth, they are as off-putting as they are inviting.

Karnes began to make seating, usually in pairs, about 1958, and she turned the stool into a demonstration of her own autonomy: the seat itself sits uneasily between obstacle and a lesson in clay fabrication. The colour and thickness of the brown coils elegantly preserve the plasticity of wet clay. As a building method, the coil pot is a fundamental manipulation, a common preschool exercise. However, the novice's method becomes virtuoso performance in these stools, as Karnes preserves the coiling process, much as Brancusi's antique screw bears traces of its making. The coils are unnerving, suggestive of sagging intestines or eroding geological strata. Heavy and squat, they have handles but look unwilling to move and do not invite our touch, evoking the uncanny almost like taxidermists' transformation of elephants' feet into wastebaskets. Narrow at the base, they flare outwards, and resemble nothing in everyday life so much as the base of a toilet. On the one hand, the bucket seats slope welcomingly to match the human body's curvature. However, the seat is sliced open dramatically. The deliberate gap permits rainwater to drain out and yet also lends mystery to the interior. While the coiled base arises in organic motion, the seat is taut like a piecrust.

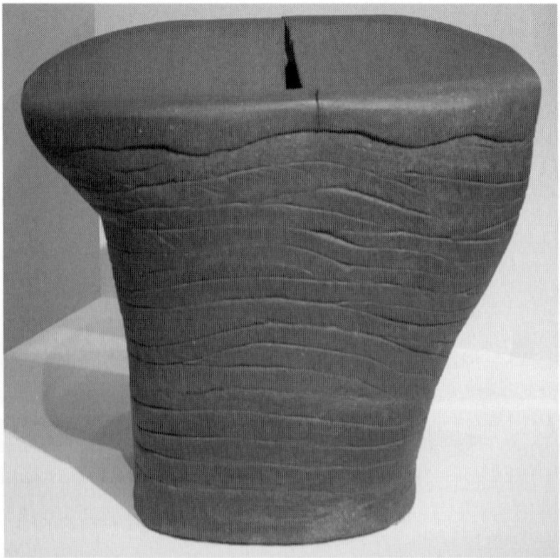

Karen Karnes, ceramic seat/stool, one of a pair, *c.* 1960s. Like the Eames stool, the curvature of the top surface welcomes multiple uses and contrasts a smooth finish against a striated body. Clay, like wood, can be tooled to achieve a diverse range in its character.

At the 13th Milan Triennale, the *Saturday Evening Post* and other mainstream media read Karnes's seating as exemplifying modern leisure. The American pavilion organized by Jack Lenor Larsen, the weaver-entrepreneur, and MOMA's Edgar Kaufmann Jr was a large white nylon tent stretched into sweeping parabolic curves: within was an ensemble

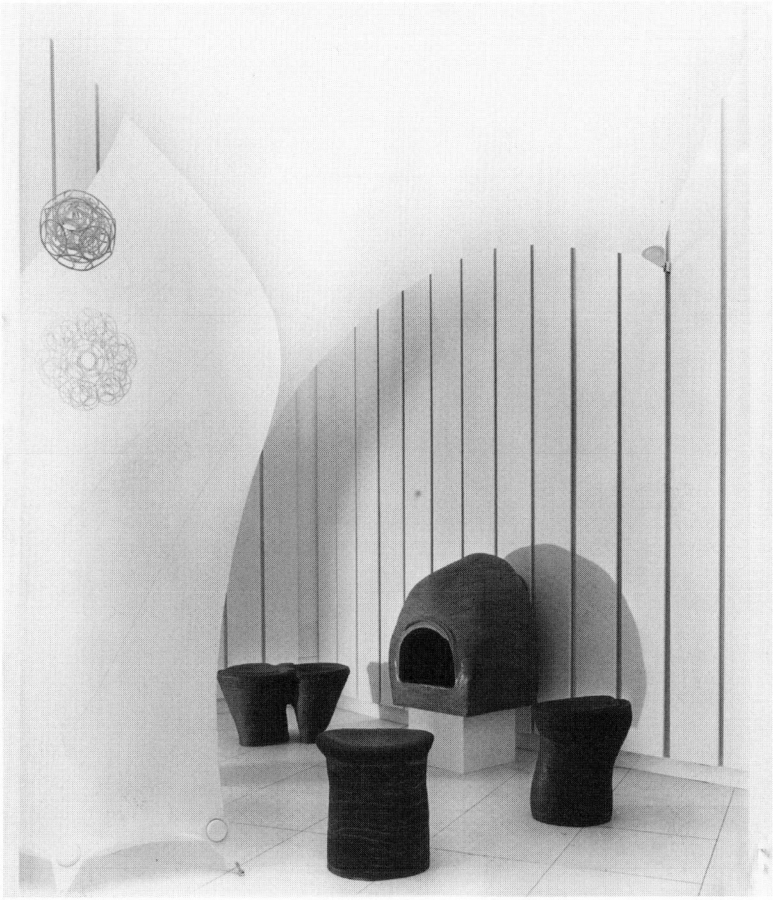

Karen Karnes, ceramic seating and hearth in United States Pavilion at the 13th Triennale di Milano, 1964. The *Saturday Evening Post* as well as *Design Quarterly* published photographs of Karnes's work, and this image of leisure as a fireside gathering remains a perennial ideal in lifestyle publications.

of Karnes's stools, one coupled like Siamese twins, clustered around her coil-built hearth. Nearby was a hammock and a Wharton Esherick music stand, also signifying the cultivation of relaxation and pleasure. Other seating included David Rowland's steel chairs stacked forty high for institutional seating, Edward Wormley's walnut chairs made by Dunbar and an Eva Zeisel tubular steel chair with a knitted seat, a 1948 prototype that had never gone into mass production. These objects celebrated a duality, the American lifestyle as an integration of leisure and work. A Karnes stool was visible for years in the Noguchi Museum in Long Island City, where it was the one work of sculpture displayed that was not Noguchi's handicraft – and where my curiosity began with a first-hand encounter. Larsen, who had learned of Karnes's work from Noguchi, acquired several of her stools for his African-inspired Round House on Long Island, which received widespread media coverage in 1964. Karnes contributed a fireplace, garden stools, sinks and tiles to the bathroom, as well as light switch plates and roof finials. In 1969, a pair of Karnes's stools were featured in 'Objects USA', a record-breaking exhibition in terms of attendance, with hundreds of thousands seeing her work in venues across the nation.

Karnes's seating indicates the potency and enigma of craft as a social tool. The stools seem to want to connect to rocks, leaves and tree stumps outside. They lent weight to the theatrical 'primitive' staged in Larsen's Round House and harmonized with the austere biomorphic forms in Noguchi's reclaimed factory. At the 1964 Milan Triennale under the white tent, they articulated the need for warmth and community in a hyper-rational world. Karnes's hearth suggests that craft is a campfire that makes people human. Her bird houses hung nearby, similarly suggesting that pottery is a tool for creating community at both an ecological and human level.

Seemingly social, Karnes's stools have willpower: they sit apart from mainstream ideals of relaxation. 'Karen's chair sits you, you don't sit on it,' notes Zeb Schachtel, her friend and long-standing patron. Karnes's fused stools suggest the act of bodies huddling together, making communitas a literal space. The conjoined form reads like a physical way of thinking through coupling and uncoupling: she began to make seating when she became a mother, when she lost a partner, when she gained a dependent. If a teapot and matching cups and saucers, a tête-à-tête set, is an eighteenth-century form to facilitate intimacy, the fused pair of Karnes stools evokes the post-war American craftswoman: counter-cultural and abandoning inhibitions, she avoids the predicament of conformity but sits on the margins of culture. If the stools suggest the fragility of human companionship and the ways material weight can inhibit dialogue and movement, they also suggest craft has as circumscribed a time and place as a walk in the woods. The biographical role of the work is intriguing: Karnes made seating in suites of two and three, beginning in the years when her marriage disintegrated up until she began her long-term relationship with Ann Stannard, when she began to make art that more overtly discarded function.

Karnes's possession of an Eames Lounge Chair, a talisman of style in 1956, provides another perspective to think through her own production of seating. The Eames Lounge Chair was an expensive commodity in post-war America, and its reclined angle similarly immobilizes the sitter. The Eames chair proves Karnes's sophistication and alters her credibility as a rustic. How could a single mother eking out a living as a roadside potter afford such a throne of comfort and emblem of the leisure class? In 2013, when I asked her how she came to own the Eames chair, Karnes stalled before explaining, 'My mother bought it for me.' Did her mother pick it out, I asked? 'What did she know, she was a little woman from the Bronx,' Karnes snapped, drawing a line about the boundaries of taste, generational limitations and independence. Whereas she seemed to believe I was questioning her originality, or intruding on her privacy, my question was really about whether seating reflects – or models – our desires as social and antisocial beings. Chairs change users and meanings as we play house. They are artefacts that make our physical desires visible, compensating for our sense of inadequacy or longing.

Below the horizon line of heroic modernist art, Karnes's seating and the Eameses' Time-Life stool provide robust sculptural undergrowth in uncluttered interiors and speak to the compartmentalization of craft as a gendered instrument and object of leisure in the modern world. Karnes desired to keep the clay 'natural' to differentiate herself and her work from mainstream culture – hence her repudiation of the Eameses' influence. She was striving to be taken seriously as an artist and live apart from the world of plastics and metals. Avoiding gilding and reflective surfaces, her casseroles and seating are arguments for communal engagement, and yet are unsure of their social inclination – whether they prefer to dine with others or sit alone.

Karnes embodies the contradiction that follows when handicraft is idealized as a personification of the maker or ideal form of labour with improved social relations. When using her casserole or seating, do we commune with each other or with her? If we believe we connect to Karnes herself, how do we negotiate her alienation from modern life? Are we falsely believing that we, too, are at a commune, building communitas from scratch? To buy a Nampeyo or Karnes pot is to express a longing to be part of something larger – and to seek a heightened individuality. Through things, we theatrically define ourselves against cultural tendencies or as part of alternative ideals and values. Brands exert this emotional force in our lives more often than craft. And when we dwell in photographs, digitally swapping on Pinterest, we paste bonds together to connect us. Materials and rituals once were such bridges. To apprehend Nampeyo's tin pot, Brancusi's screw or Karnes's Eames chair is to move beyond hagiography and re-admit the import of tactile mystery. These three archetypes exist fine in isolation but when juxtaposed they begin to argue, to reveal assumptions about gendered materials and the contextually-dependent emotional qualities of artefacts. Today, in the age of social media, we must all admit to staging slightly fraudulent self-presentations, and so we can forgive Brancusi – he did not imagine such pictures of his posturing in wide circulation. Let us move from thinking through craftsmanship in photographs to experiencing craft in person.

TWO

TODAY'S CRAFTSPEOPLE IN AN EXPANDED FIELD

Nampeyo, Brancusi and Karnes reveal that craft is an action that responds to everyday constraints and forms, reacting to the contours of economic as much as emotional forces. Great craft is neither genius operating in isolation nor a continuum. Nampeyo, Brancusi and Karnes did not make things solely 'by hand' – they used the tools around them and their agency was a responsive tooling that unravelled the logic and absurdities of their time and place. However 'unique', 'personal' or 'organic' you might perceive their work to be, their labour is most interesting as a cipher through which to understand their constructions of identity in relation to their environments. While I revere their heroism and brilliance, a tactile knowledge of an antique cider press or just about any old or new chair is equally worthy of engagement and certainly better than admiration of a photograph of them or their production.

To step away from written texts and photographs of individuals, let us embark on first-hand observation. What follows will be an eclectic survey drawing from ten years of my experiences visiting workshops and worrying over artefacts. When I teach I value site visits and direct contact with stained glass or silkworms to touch the shape of craft. Only through direct experience can we balance archetypes with contemporary craftspeople. Moreover, we can learn to admire individuals without limiting ourselves to individualistic craft. Recognizing teams of craftspeople is critical – individual genius does not explain how the world gets built. Developing respect for anonymous labour is also vital: if every lovely stone wall or bridge were signed by their authors our world would deteriorate to resemble the landscapes of contemporary American museums and sports arenas, littered with the names of the wealthy and corporate sponsors of the moment. Let us cultivate a distinct 'craft consciousness' through field work – and may you add your own local interactions to these, or at least find them ready and welcoming to a broader canon than my own limited experiences.

THE LIMITATIONS OF BIOGRAPHY (AND AUTOBIOGRAPHY)

Admiring a radiant old pine floor in central Vermont, I wonder what definition of craft might include this work. To praise flooring, not an artefact signed by Nampeyo or Brancusi, is to move away from work that bears an identifiable author. I recall being twelve when Walt Dewey, a handyman, sanded this wood floor, stripping off brown enamel paint to reveal the soft yellow pine not seen since the 1830s. Walt worked deliberately and gracefully, guiding a howling drum sander. I remember being incredulous as Walt emerged from clouds of sawdust, the floor transformed. I would not see the floor as craft were it not for him, and this realization prompts questions about the influence of biography and autobiography in shaping distinct perceptions of the craftsman.

The obscurity of Walt Dewey, his social class and rural location stand in contrast to most histories of craft. If the term 'artisanal' gives an iota of honour to beer or bread, 'handymanish' is damning in any context. He is the floor's craftsman of record in my mind, even if others were responsible for hewing the timbers and hauling them with wagons in the 1830s. He might have only sanded the wood, but he did that very well. There is the occasional vermiculated pattern of termites but no dips, divots or gouge marks. (This I know from botching the job of floor sanding and also from getting it right.) After taking the floor down with successively less coarse grits of sandpaper, the lanky 65-year-old removed his boots and socks and assessed the floor barefoot inch by inch, as he trusted his feet more than his eyes to give his work a proper reckoning – a strategy I am emulating.

It is absurd to think of a museum of craft dedicated to flooring or floor sanders or any other home renovating trade. Primarily this is true because there is little self-expression in sanding floors, plastering walls, sweating copper pipes or levelling windows. Walt Dewey's labour is at odds with the notion of creativity and being able to savour the touch of a specific individual craftsman. However, a sublimation of individuality is necessary when making a tool or prioritizing use. A floor is mainly judged by how level it is. David Pye ridiculed that our dogged pursuit of flat ceilings is in no way commensurate with reason, as they do not make us warmer, but such tooling does have an emotional influence. A level ceiling can help restore our sense of equilibrium and a wonky floor can instil psychological disorder. If we locate artistic autonomy in self-expression, the floor sander has little, but if we see Dewey as a craftsman who is driven by his own concept of excellence and is self-motivated to instil order in a disorderly world, then it is hard to classify him as a mere cog in the wheel.

We can grant Dewey a kind of autonomy if we think of him as in dialogue with the floor, the way a graphic designer makes a biblical phrase an exhortation. In calligraphy or typesetting, creativity is set on the primacy and clarity of the text or it undermines accessibility. Beatrice Warde's manifesto on graphic design, 'The Crystal Goblet' (1930), urged lettering and layout to be transparent so as to let text be read foremost. Sublimation of an artistic voice is decidedly out of fashion and not part of our expectation for uncommon craft, but it is largely the condition of commonplace craft – the great majority of craftspeople who have roofed and shod humanity.

Walt Dewey saw refinishing the floor as his contribution to the work of his forebears – it was an incremental task that began before and extended beyond his lifespan. His relationship to the house was intimate because he had grown up a few miles away in a similar modest home. Pointing to an area of the floor stained grey-black, Walt explained where a sink once stood when the four-room house was configured differently and how as a child he left the water running overnight to prevent it from freezing. This notion of the regional craftsman collaborating with the past, with the forebears of his neighbours, is another reason to embrace anonymous artisans who restore and mend. Preserving a piece of the past is the closest most of us get to experiencing a collaborative venture that is lacking in ego and ample in reciprocity.

These pine boards 12 to 20 inches in width cannot be bought in twenty-first-century lumberyards and were probably milled on a terrifying circular saw powered by the nearby stream, which fuelled a dozen cider mills – stone foundations are all that remain of these systems. Due to its age, the pine is finely grained. When the trees were felled their slow growth and girth were taken for granted. The 12-foot-long planks line up in a rectangle in the centre of the room like a raft; shorter spans run to the baseboards. Going into the basement, one can see that the house's structural beams still have bark on them; they were never fully dressed. There is no subfloor. The basement view reveals the teeth and chatter marks of the circular saw that ripped timbers into boards. Both the preparation of the lumber and the sanding were artisanal, with one craftsman working at the beginning of the Industrial Revolution and the other, Walt, in the 1980s. The craftsmen were each born in their respective middle landscape that was partly pastoral and semi-industrialized. Each used the tools of their time.

If the floor is inadvertently beautiful, does such a characterization undermine my praise of Dewey? When the planks were first laid down and nailed into place, the surface was to be covered and rendered invisible. Like Brancusi's antique wood screw, the flooring is an unintended sight of beauty. The original Vermont residents would have thought it mad, backwards and forgetful of winter weather to expose the grainy wood; they would have preferred carpet or accepted any covering, paint or oilcloth. Sanding the floor and sealing it with polyurethane is a peculiar aesthetic carried over from gymnasiums or Scandinavian modernism and only started to happen in domestic interiors in the twentieth century. In the 1930s, Russel and Mary Wright invented the term 'blond wood' to describe their polyurethaned maple furniture. Today we call such floor refinishing gentrification. Each generational mode of beautification shows specific cultural ideals projected onto the built environment. Walt thought his work increased beauty and felt he was closer to his own era than the aesthetics or habits of the past, like many of us. He had an awareness of his own temporal situation as well as regional constraints, and accommodated both.

Inspecting Walt Dewey's labour prompted my respect. The words inspect and respect share the etymological root, *specio*, which is logical if one's eyes and ears operate independently of preconceived notions of the types of dignified labour. Each of us has our own figures that personify wonder – snowballing from childhood into larger, more generous spheres if we are lucky. Benjamin Franklin's father wanted him to determine his path after watching 'Joiners, Bricklayers, Turners, Braziers, &c. at their Work, that he might observe my Inclination, and endeavour to fix it on some Trade or other on Land. It has ever since been a Pleasure to me to see good Workmen handle their Tools.' These people lodge in our minds as craftspeople only through observation. Fantasy is not sufficiently gritty. My view was shaped by John Dewey as much as Walt Dewey; I came to respect working hands as a type of thinking because I watched Walt. When we witness a demonstration of craftsmanship, we don't need to know who the potter or glassblower or weaver is, we simply watch their hands dance with the material and their tools – and then we judge critically with our eyes, sure of ourselves as to whether we are seeing something merely good or really great. Most museum visitors read labels before trying to understand artwork. No spectators watching a craftsman at work look for a name tag or written explanation to measure their greatness or worthiness: we respect athletic bodies in motion.

Today, I cannot weed out Dewey as a lesser craftsman than his nineteenth-century forebears who built the house. My loss of objectivity extends to Gustave Caillebotte's oil painting of floor scrapers; those workers are no longer visible as abstract shapes and compositional forms. From my own hours dedicated to laying floors and sanding the wood, I empathize with their posture, feeling a numbness in my lower back – even if I do not count myself a craftsman. The craftsman inclines towards the material, throwing his body into his labour. I have learned about the musculoskeletal pressures of craft in being a part-time 'grade C' handyman. 'Two minutes experience teach an eager man more than two weeks teach an indifferent one,' noted Pye, celebrating the value of sensitizing humanity to craft.

The deferential posture to material is a fundamental aspect of workmanship – 'observe my inclination', to heed Franklin literally. In history we can see images of such bent people if we are alert to their acts of tooling. In Nanni di Banco's carvings at Orsanmichele or in Petrus Christus's painting of a fifteenth-century goldsmith, the artisans are diagonal men, set on edge almost like a pencil to paper. This is the physicality of craft, which one cannot sense from pictorial illusion – again, experience is the only way into accurate empathy.

We each proceed outwards from our own exemplars; only later do we borrow language from philosophers to verbalize and rationalize our intuition. Ideally, words and working definitions will not obscure our sensual knowledge. A worthwhile text on craft meditates on labour and materials and still preserves intuition. Worrying over rules such as whether the craftsman 'made it by hand' or is 'authentic', 'traditional' or sufficiently 'unique' are exercises in futility if they remain litmus tests or generalizations. Walt Dewey's view that his craft is 'good work done well' is not much different from the British Arts and Crafts architect and educator William Richard Lethaby's definition that craft is 'the well-doing of what needs doing'. I grafted Lethaby onto Dewey; I owe my belief in this definition to the handyman.

Anonymity is part of the beauty of work, but also a reason craftsmanship is underestimated. A battle cry of 1970s feminism, 'Anonymous was a woman', pointed out that domestic craft is rarely granted equal prestige to men's. Textiles have been especially subject to anonymity. The exception, alphabet samplers or mottoes embroidered or woven by schoolgirls, are rarely considered creative. Quilts, usually both anonymous and lacking in overt self-expression, are seen in a positive artistic light when they are considered representational of a regional or vernacular identity, such as in the recent celebratory exhibitions of work from Gee's Bend, Alabama. Reversing the usual fortunes of quilters, these textiles have gained appreciation while the makers are still alive, and ideally they will pave the way for other regional artisanal collectives to emerge. Even after their dramatic rise in dollar value, few connoisseurs can identify the individuals working in Gee's Bend. Is this demeaning and insulting? Yes, because there are few African Americans granted artistic identity in museums or monuments in the USA. But such a collective patterning is also the beauty of craft: no biographies could explain why the quilts of that small town are truly remarkable. The quilters were bound to vernacular forms that somehow flowed from and connected their minds and hands. The quilts can be distinguished in terms of personal styles but are powerful as a group because they evoke a specific place and time when they made something all their own. Collaborative craft signals that one person working alone cannot make a world. Again, to recuperate the words of Lethaby: 'No art that is only one man deep is worth much; it should be a thousand men deep.' In schools, students tend to observe a teacher working solo and are taught to work alone, and so it is to collective labour that we need to turn in order to see Lethaby's ideal in action.

COLLATED CRAFTSMANSHIP

A contemporary factory tour is enlightening for inspecting the ways in which craftspeople are still necessary tool builders no matter how far automation advances, and to think about the ways humans have worked more momentously and with more meaning together than apart. Many narratives about craft simplistically situate artistic labour as an individualistic operation; rarely is teamwork a focus. As a result, identifying when the assembly line is a craft endeavour – an epiphany I gained on a tour of manufacturing – has become a consuming interest of my fieldwork. The system of divided labour, where no one artisan takes a job from start to finish, has been indicted as destroying autonomy and individuality. But collaborative projects smelting gold, tending dye vats and finishing elaborate funerary garments produced spectacular and powerful achievements in skilled craft in ancient civilizations (be it Egypt, China or Peru). Regal tombs sometimes took decades to prepare. There was the possibility that a generation of contributing craftspeople might not see the finished product. Structured into sequential specialized steps, production can integrate numerous crafts. Such a network is required to produce any highly refined artefact – and especially large, complex, composite ones, like ships. At the Steinway & Sons factory, it is a thrilling drama to witness six sets of hands bending a 20-foot-long piece of laminated wood and wrestling it as they clamp it into the jig that will shape it into the curvaceous rim

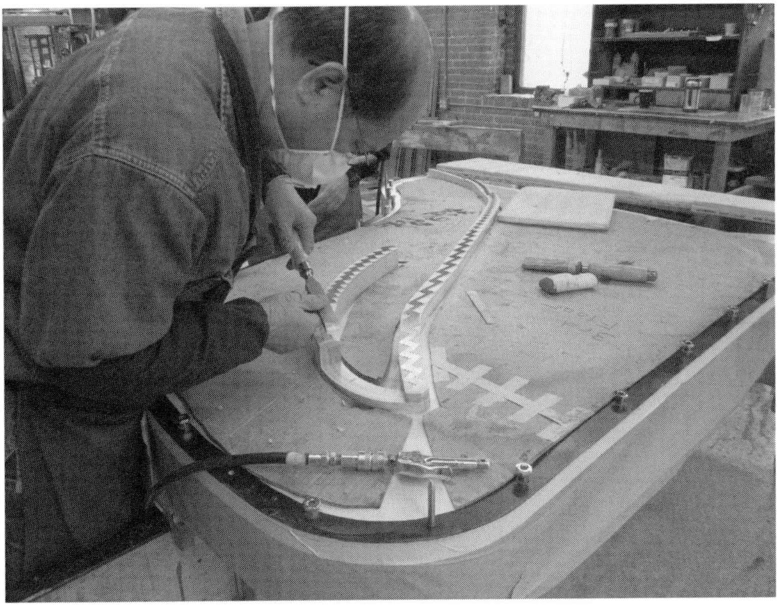

Lisheng Yu notches a bridge at the Mason & Hamlin piano factory, Haverhill, Massachusetts, 2013. No simple classification of labour explains piano manufacture, which for two hundred years has used both handicraft and mechanization.

of a grand piano. One can also follow such a piano over months as it gains guts and a keyboard to apprehend the specialization of craft at each stage, as hundreds of components are added. Instead of using the phrase 'assembly line', which implies a routine, predictable sequence, we might do better to describe this layering of expertise as *collated craftsmanship*. Multihanded-craft generates meaningfulness more readily than a single artist working alone.

In Wisconsin, touring the Kohler Company's production of porcelain and cast-iron sanitary ware, I could observe two very distinct types of labour within one plant. The automated production of cast-iron bathtubs and the manual slip casting of ceramic porcelain sinks and urinals coexist, wildly dissimilar. The automated iron furnace is fully robotic, requiring only supervision from a booth to pump out tubs. While the most banal ceramic sinks are compressed by computer numerical control, the large, heavy-duty hospital-grade sinks, toilets and urinals require

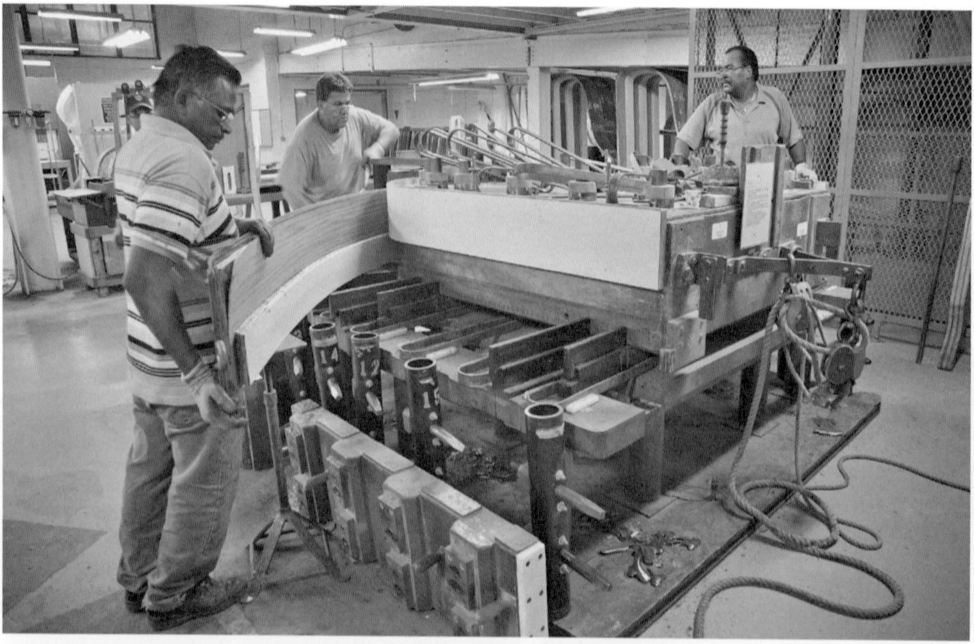

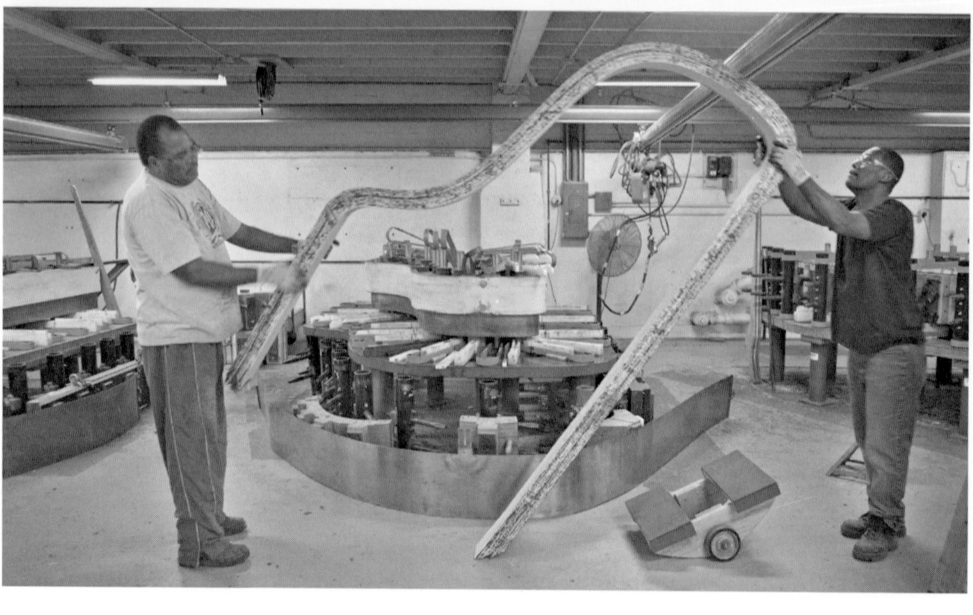

athletic craftsmanship and collated craft to cast the liquid porcelain in plaster moulds and mend the seams.

Paul Roehrig has been working at the Kohler Company for 45 years and even though he is considered one of the most highly skilled in the slip casting crew, he still describes the clay as 'dynamic' and a force he must respect in order to control. Each morning at daybreak the foreman tests how the slip is behaving and the casters at Kohler discuss the clay body and its setting time – is it softer or stiffer? Efficiency in production has increased with computerization but artisanal sentience and communion with material are still necessary. A Kohler slip caster refines the moulded ware ambidextrously, a steel shim in each hand, and then a sponge in each, to smooth seams and tidy edges. The degree of skill that the slip casters possess is reflected in their wages being the highest. Roehrig knows his dozen moulds and how they are ageing and which ones need preparatory care to coax out the clay – some need a dash of drying talc powder in one corner and others a splash of muddy water. These plaster moulds are also being replenished steadily, too, after a few months of use. Interviewed on the shop floor, these workers speak of their moulds and clay as an unruly platoon that they manage. The sign on the factory wall proclaims, 'variability is the enemy of quality,' a corporate mentality apt for the glory days of Henry Ford and his materials of choice, but this mantra is contradicted by the nature of clay. No matter how carefully processed, this material dictates the pace and success of a strictly regimented routine.

Steinway & Sons rim bending. To assemble the elegant curvature of a grand or baby grand piano, several Steinway employees corral multiple layers of maple and clamp these in a mould.

'Look at that. That's my autograph, and it's out there all over the world,' Roehrig declares, indicating his identification number stamped into the underside of each of his sinks. His ability to feel authorship in a collaborative anonymous process – a factory line of serial numbers – is rare today, when we are trained from elementary school onwards to feel the pride of authorship only if our name is writ large with a signature. Today, if more people than ever before in history have confidence that they know what art is, it is more shocking that increasingly few people seem to value work that is not individualized. Our failure to derive satisfaction from working on group projects relates to our idealization of artistry as an individual, solo endeavour. Factory craftsmanship teaches an understanding of interdependence. Moreover, factories do not inherently deskill production and produce alienation. Most of the highly skilled workers at Kohler are stakeholders, even if the labour rules out overt self-expression or if they are conforming to managerial choreography. The Kohler workers are aware of their distinct skill set: as caster Neal Henschel describes it, 'I work in a factory but it's not a "factory job".' Neal's clay-splattered arms, a cigarette in one hand, gesticulate these quotation marks. The slip casters respect the block and mould shop that gives them their tools: plaster moulds need to turn the radius at the corners in a manner that will facilitate removing the clay neatly. Each department has a grasp on when and where the path of collated craft might falter and curtail their productivity or quality.

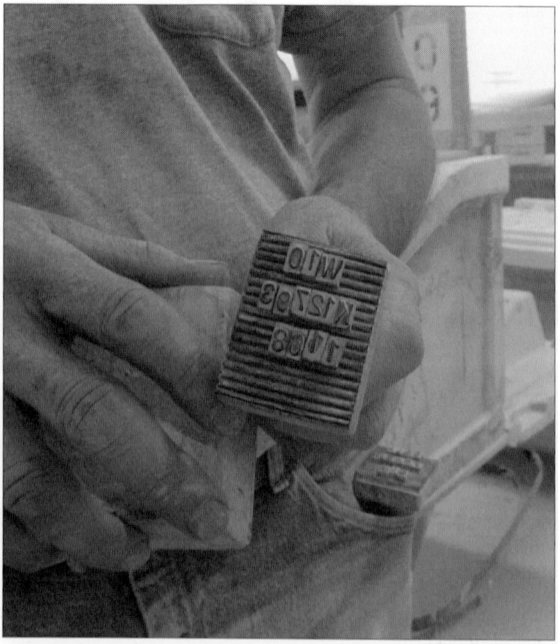

Kohler Company associate Paul Roehrig holding his 'signature' in the slip-casting department. Reflecting on the stamp that identifies each sink with an alphanumeric code as his work, Roehrig told me, 'That's my autograph, and it's out there all over the world.'

Do Roehrig and Henschel and other factory craftsmen take 'joy in labour'? The influential writings of John Ruskin, William Morris and, more recently, Richard Sennett suggest workers on an assembly line might not. In most art history textbooks, illustration of factory work is non-existent. Collated craftsmanship is depicted in the engravings in Denis Diderot's eighteenth-century *Encyclopédie*, but to generalize about the affective value of such labour seems absurd. Pathetically, Charlie Chaplin's film *Modern Times* (1936) is still cited regularly as a satire of the drudgery and dehumanizing effect of Fordist manufacturing, a punch-line being taken more seriously than a real assembly line. The academy is good at pondering Adam Smith's 'invisible hand' abstractly or pictorially, less so empirically. Solitary, autonomous labour is not de facto morally, aesthetically, spiritually or intellectually superior to the concerted skill of two-dozen hands on an assembly line whether they are making toilets or pianos. Primary schools and then colleges and university programmes, in addition to most museums, teach most of us to assume that art is made by individuals and not in a factory. In reality, manufacturing has historically sustained collated skills more often than eliminating individual expertise. Factories were built to house machinery – and all big instruments are built by collated craftsmanship.

Behind most examples of mass production – even pretzel factories – stand obscure artisanal enablers. The distinctions when it comes to

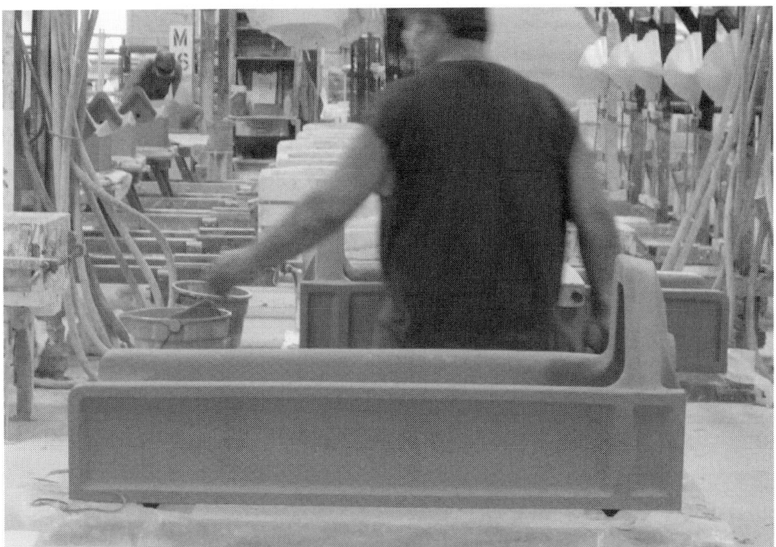

Kohler Company slip-casting department. The heavy plaster moulds for hospital-grade products have a limited lifespan and each caster knows where their moulds are ageing and temperamental and need to be pre-treated with the trick of using 'muddy water' and talc to coax out high-quality work. Does such knowledge suggest that a manufactory might preserve the 'arts and mysteries' of this particular craft better than the art academy?

buying pasta – spaghetti, ziti rigati, rotini or farfalle – might be a matter of cooking time, perhaps a nod to childhood fancy or an aesthetic taste suggested by a recipe, but a person once sculpted the moulds that make these forms. In Brooklyn, the Maldari family factory remains in two brothers' hands, and the small outfit of ten workers cuts brass into extrusion dies for pasta manufacturers – a small and highly specialized field. Only two such businesses exist in the United States, supplying hundreds of factories that engage in food production. Chris Maldari continues the hundred-year-old family business of prototyping moulds and tools for large-scale factories. Imagination is necessary to make the leap from a brass slug with a few holes milled into it to the extruded ziti. Large pasta companies don't use one die at a time but dozens of 1-inch dies, often Teflon mounted into a large disc, so that thousands of strands of linguini or lasagne noodles can be made each hour. Chris still designs new dies, for extruding pretzels and pet food as well as pasta. He takes time to tinker with each mould to find the right radius of a curve, the desired crenellation in a ridge. Cutting and milling a prototype, he keeps a hand press to test the ways dough passes through his die, gauging its shapeliness. One snack food took more than eighteen months to develop. After research and development, or 'tinkering', as Chris calls it, a design is then repeated digitally, through state-of-the-art CNC milling. But one hundred years ago, the tinkering extended to making several copies of the same die and filing each by hand. The initial steps for making a die remain relatively unchanged.

D. Maldari & Sons, pasta and extrusion die, brass with Teflon insert. While pasta production is a large-scale enterprise carried out in numerous locations by thousands of employees, macaroni die manufacturing remains a specialized, highly skilled activity pursued by only a handful of small workshops. The relationship between the visual appearance of the brass die and the extruded pasta can be a sculptural surprise.

As Chris Maldari shows off some of the brass dies that his family had made over the decades, my inability to guess the resulting shape from the extruding press is increasingly challenged. The company makes novelty items for alphabet soup as well as Disney characters. To pursue the invention of new forms of pasta might seem flighty, but the company's archive of hundreds of glass canisters, each with samples of their work, documents four generations of metalworkers – artisanal labour – realizing each new form. Their museum of pasta is a quaint room but breathtaking as a profusion of human skill matched to the whimsy of desires. It might seem a contradiction that careful tooling results in standardization and mass production, but the sequential shift is not new. For centuries, gourmets and novice cooks alike have savoured artisanal pasta and expected whatever batch they bought to be consistent for cooking times. Standard measurements were the basis of trade, necessary for inter-factory production of yarn for looms, paper for books. Mechanical consistency had a place in human habits long before the rise of agribusiness.

One example in the Maldari archive that exemplifies the theme of humanized mechanization is their pasta in the shape of a radiator. The *radiatori* was conceived by the Maldaris' father, Ralph, and could only have been invented in the last hundred years, when centralized heating made these cast-iron appliances into novel domestic fixtures. The pasta is made with one, two, three, four and five flanges. If the Maldari museum of extrusion dies mostly reflects mass culture, such as noodles in the shape

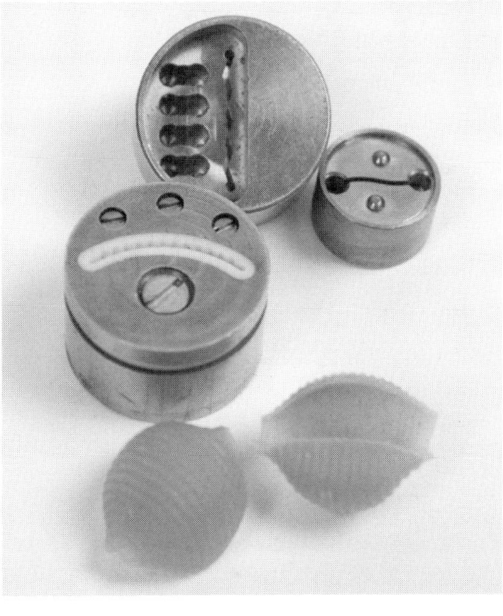

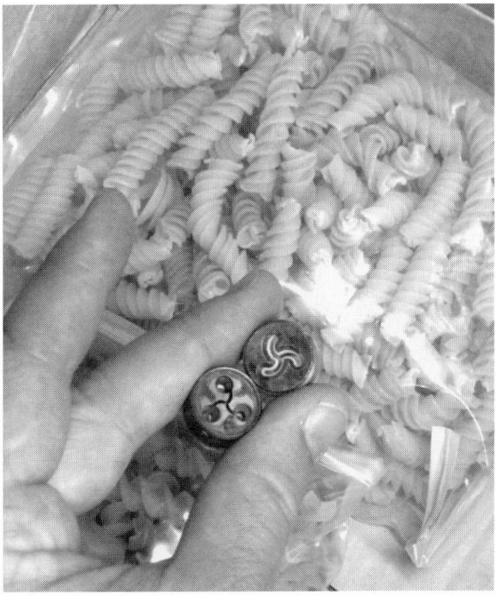

of Mickey Mouse, the *radiatori* arguably expresses the zeitgeist of collated craft. To eat *radiatori* is to commune with the fabrication of cast iron – and to taste central heating and the art of plumbing as a cosy, mouth-watering phenomenon. The banality of modern life transforms into a new beauty. No one at Maldari sees this design as proprietary intellectual property. Chris Maldari's signature or artistic identity is not asserted or memorable in any box of pasta. When the *radiatori* is eaten, it will likely be thought of as the product of a small gourmet shop, if it is considered to have a maker at all. An educated tongue might taste it as a delight, but otherwise it is merely an instance of the underfoot, unacknowledged craft that shapes our world.

THE PLEASURE OF ANONYMOUS ARTIFICE

To lift a cup that one has not touched before is often like shaking the hand of a new acquaintance: quickly, one gauges a sense of compatibility and the possibilities and limits of pleasurable engagement. To discover craft that is responsive to one's own human wants, needs and pressures, imaginary and invented, is to feel fully alive – and so there is good reason not to praise dead heroines and heroes of existing and established genres, materials and canonical types. Reacting to the contemporary moment is essential to keeping craft a process of invention and what it does so powerfully – act as a mode of self-invention, often for both maker and user. A consideration of two craftspeople who have worked in industry anonymously for decades highlights the enigmatic phenomenon of stasis and responsive skill adaptation. Their limited autonomy and individuation is worth weighing in relation to our prevailing belief in craft's tendency towards obsolescence.

Twenty years ago, Rita Floyd and Kevin Millward were demonstrators in the Gladstone Pottery Museum in Stoke-on-Trent, Staffordshire, a heritage museum that celebrates the five hundred years when the area's six towns were known with pride as 'the Potteries'. Rita showed visitors how to make ceramic flowers. Kevin demonstrated the potter's wheel. They were exemplars of 'living history' – which made sense when the trade was still alive in Stoke-on-Trent. They entered the Potteries in a period of decline, employment having peaked in the 1940s. Prior to being museum demonstrators, Rita worked for more than three decades building bone china roses, daisies and carnations and other radiant species in factories, while Kevin trained in an art school and then worked for several years as a production potter for a garden tool company, among other brief ventures. Apart and together, they personify the fragility of craftsmanship and are worth identifying and comparing in order to revise how we might ponder the preservation of skill and respect the unidentified anonymous artisans still at work across the globe.

To watch Rita create fifty distinct types of flower is to admire the structural elegance of biodiversity and the simplicity of dedicated specialization. If the isolating phenomenon of factory expertise seems undesirable, it is often necessary. Moreover, it is worth noting that several manufacturers have told me that employees often do not want to rotate through distinct tasks; many like a steady routine and the feeling of mastery. Rita's hands began to memorize floral patterns at age fifteen, when she apprenticed among a table of older women and began to get paid by the flower. Calculate how many of her flowers are strewn across the world: she averaged between 420 and 480 each day. Being paid by the piece increased her pace of production. None of the thousands of flowers made by Rita to adorn paperweights or table centrepieces bear her name; instead, the firm of Adderley or Coalport was stamped upon them.

Of course, the factories did not want self-expression when the order was for a dozen camellias; the idea of anonymity is that flowers should resemble prime bouquets. In the Gladstone Museum, Rita demonstrated

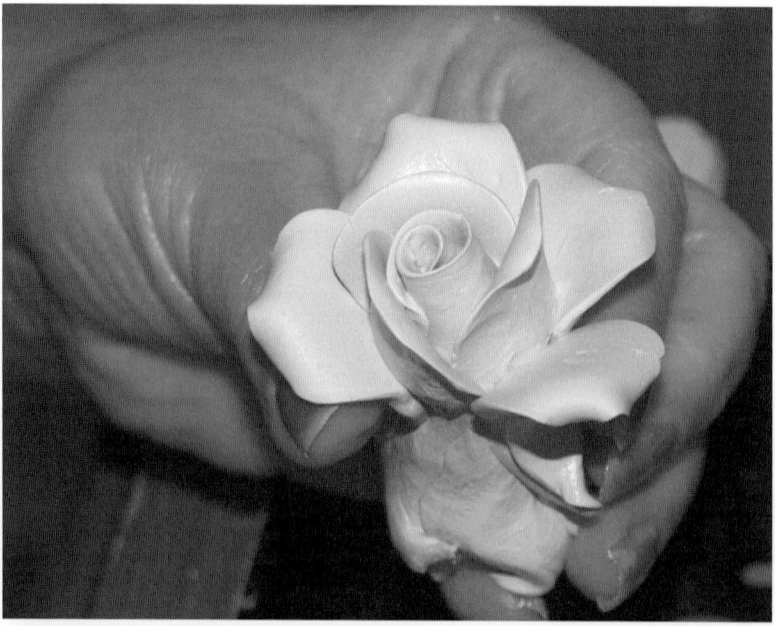

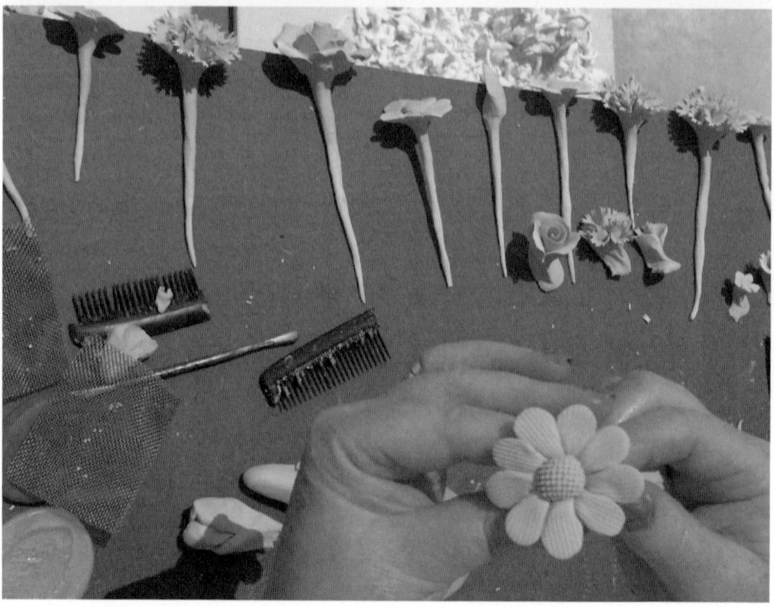

Rita Floyd making bone china flowers in Neil Brownsword's performance-installation *Re-apprenticed* at the Ashmolean Museum, Oxford, 3 December 2016. To make the pattern for the centre of the daisy Rita uses a piece of wire mesh; to make the petals and several other flowers she uses plastic combs, each specific to a form. Rita's four decades of work for numerous firms means that her flowers, all unsigned, are greater than or equal to the eight thousand ceramic artisans working in manufactories in the United Kingdom today. There were approximately sixty thousand when she began her career in the potteries. Brownsword is committed to repositioning Rita and other highly-skilled factory workers as unrecognized 'national treasures'.

making one rose a minute out of clay, each the size of her index finger. This specialized craft flourished for two hundred years, collated alongside the painters and modellers and other artisans. Six pence per dozen flowers was her initial rate. After several years developing her skill, a dozen flowers took about fifteen minutes to make. No matter how facile she makes the work appear, her crisp and springy narcissus or carnation is not easy to recreate.

Rita's manual creation of a daisy is a nuanced operation. She pinches, pulls, combs and pinches five more times. Each stroke is seemingly related to pastry more than pottery. The head of the daisy is pressed against wire mesh. The petals of the carnation began to be made using combs only in the 1960s, and prior to that a faceted nail was the major tool. The flower makers themselves invented the use of combs – a way to increase production rates. The floral sprays should be seen as sculpture; that is the finished form they took, ending up on a mantel or in a china cabinet. There is a soothing rhythm to Rita's movements and yet when one looks at the product, doubts creep in. The flowers exude enforced good cheer, and their uniform vitality can be anxiety-provoking to eyes more accustomed to seeing roses in half-states of maturation and death. Although Rita is wonderfully conversant and edifying about the processes of the potteries, her work has no overt, autonomous function. Whereas a cup thrown on a wheel seems to hold some independent existence regardless of surface decoration, Rita's flowers recall a very specific stylistic era, the rococo. She makes a pure form of applied ornament that relies on another form to serve as scaffolding. Universities might begin to value her skill as one worth incorporating into a curricular project – such as a short-term venture to present at the Chelsea Flower Show – but her mastery is almost the antithesis of where academic fine art curriculums or home furnishing trends are heading. Single-material exploration is rarely considered a worthwhile or enduring lesson. The rococo is anchored in *ancien régime* excess and valuing useless work simply as beauty. If Rita's work fits a faux Louis XV Las Vegas hotel or, in more measured dosage, the ironic decor of a boutique selling architect-inspired teapots, such as Droog or Jonathan Adler, it falls outside what we consider self-expression or conceptual craft. None of these shortcomings dims Rita's craftsmanship. Videos of her at work will linger as pieces of living history and testimonials of the precarious ways that we build and then discard crafts and, more disturbingly, craftspeople. The factories that employed her are no longer in operation.

Rita proves that we need a better conception of craft that encompasses her work – and other skills that are invented and discarded as manufactories come and go. Her closest contemporary parallel might be one of the young Jingdezhen women who painted the 100 million porcelain sunflower seeds for the artist Ai Weiwei to fill the Tate Modern's Turbine Hall in London in 2010: that was a grand gesture, an absurd pop-up assembly line of manually skilled china painters regressively tasked with repetitious gesture. Until we reach a more generous outlook on how to preserve craft, stream Rita into your home and try to make some flowers yourself, and look upon her as the remainder of the thousands of anonymous, highly skilled artisans who once adorned millions of homes with ceramic floral sprays. Those glazed porcelain flowers will never fade or wilt.

In contrast, Kevin Millward drifted into the Gladstone Museum for a brief spell as a demonstrator and left because of his restlessness and desire to be self-employed. He juggles contract work for firms and selling his own ware with occasional teaching. Millward's hands are remarkable because of his skill but also the breadth of his output – small-scale artisanal production and large industry rely on him. Millward is fascinating because his obsolete skill has never been more applied to tangible goods and yet never garnered less respect. His prototypes for mugs and plates are reproduced in the hundreds of thousands. When I first met him in 2013, he was keen to walk through the Portmeirion outlet shop in

Stoke-on-Trent and identify each piece he had made – or is it designed? Or is the right term 'potted'? To dispel my disbelief, he showed me his iPhone, which was loaded with images of unfired green ware in his studio that matched the Sophie Conran line on display – the same rippling wobble was in all the pottery. The reason for my shock was not that I had imagined that Portmeirion's work was actually made by Sophie Conran, daughter of Sir Terence of Habitat and Conran Shop fame. I had not envisioned her at the wheel, centring 5 pounds of clay as the muck splattered about. A jaded consumer, I had guessed incorrectly that behind the Conran branding effort was a committee of marketing specialists and focus groups that imagineered these well-branded commodities by sending a digital file overseas to outsource production – and that the potter's marks were probably simulated. A historian, I mistook the potter's wheel to be obsolete. But twenty-first-century technology has not displaced the wheel or the individual potter as a resource. Millward lives in a bucolic hamlet outside Leek, near Stoke, and his wheel-thrown pots are sent to China to be copied – slip cast in moulds with all of his texture and his imperfections intact – and then shipped back to be advertised online by Bed Bath & Beyond as tableware 'with a nod to Japanese serenity and a wink to English eccentricity'.

Kevin's workshop confounds because his artisanal skills are visibly resolving a myriad different artistic identities, giving shape to both corporate lines of ware and small batches for studio potters who advertise their work as being made with 'a personal touch'. Whose expression and self-expression we see is difficult to sort out. Apart from the wobbly ware marketed under the Sophie Conran label, Kevin supplies sleek teapots to Portmeirion if it needs a more refined shape. Other jobs include making trays for a robotic system to feed people with quadriplegia, bespoke mortar and pestle sets for gourmets, rustic French jardinières and, perhaps most strikingly, mugs that are retailed at the Covent Garden market and elsewhere as another artisan's limited-edition wares. Whether the mugs are imbued with an individual's personality or a committee's is also complicated to disentangle. If uniqueness is being subcontracted out to Kevin and he works as an alternate craftsman, he doesn't mind remaining anonymous so long as the customer pays. As he sees it, his success lies in his manual handicraft, eye trained in figure-drawing classes and, most of all, his ability to 'put any genre on'. His sublimation of his own ego might not seem to be a skill to many, but it is – and once was a traditional part of being a craftsman.

Inhabiting other aesthetic sensibilities and being efficient at the potter's wheel are virtues Kevin realizes were once commonplace in Stoke but are now rare. Such assets have been dropped from the art school curriculum as well the factory. He taught at universities but has found that students perceive him as a contractor, and that they were not interested in an apprenticeship or in learning techniques so much as realizing design schemes by relying on him. His virtuosity at potting is such that when

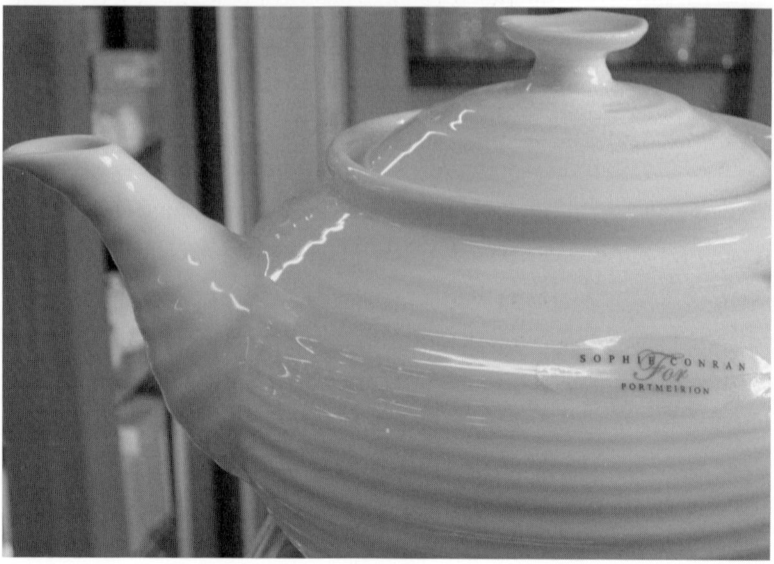

Sophie Conran for Portmeirion teapot, in the Portmeirion outlet, Stoke-on-Trent, 2012. Despite the widespread assumption that the potter's wheel is an obsolete technology, Kevin Millward made the prototype for this teapot on the potter's wheel and now it is mould-made and cast in the thousands. Millward is a 'ghost potter' working for large-scale manufacturing in the 21st century.

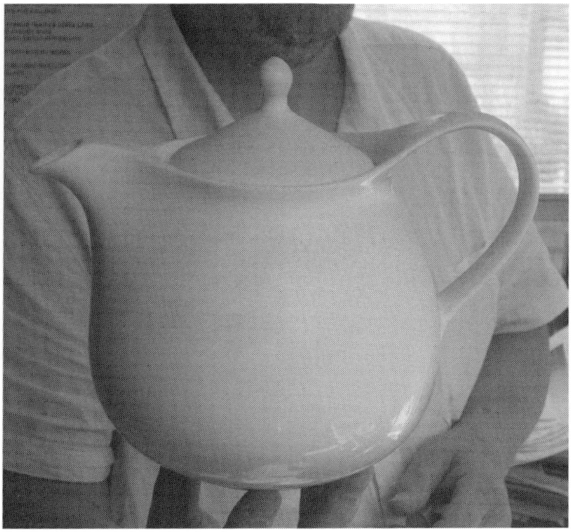

Portmeirion Liquid collection teapot, manufactured *c.* 2009 in Kevin Millward's studio, Staffordshire. Millward's fluency in clay means he can produce work in any style that a patron requests. The successful realization of a design, especially a translation from a two-dimensional plan into a three-dimensional object, requires thinking about creativity and self-expression in nuanced ways.

one of the most outspoken champions of handicraft, Emmanuel Cooper, was asked to pose in an advertisement for a wheel, he asked Kevin to throw an enormous bowl on the wheel – Cooper's own skill not lending sufficient hyperbole to the advertisement. Millward showed me several styles and lines that he copied for studio potters to fulfil their orders. He throws fifty mugs in one hour – speed and consistency that make his hands highly sought after. Kevin understands that he cannot necessarily throw precisely like another potter because their physiques might differ, but he knows he is more proficient at being his clients than they are.

Kevin proves the potter is economically viable in our age of digital artistry that loudly applauds the gadgetry of 3D additive printing or CNC subtractive processes. Corporate designers generate three-dimensional designs in a computer program such as Rhino, taking a day and nearly a thousand dollars to print out one pattern. He shows me a finished prototype, a yellowish thermoplastic object, which could not be moulded because the corners had too sharp a radius; he made adjustments to the form by quickly casting it in plaster. In the development of a new line of merchandise, a marketing department might reject the proportions of a shape or want various slight adjustments to be attempted and tested, so to employ Kevin Millward to make a hundred prototypes on his potter's wheel is still more efficient and economical than to use the latest digital technologies.

Millward still makes his own work, too, and looking at it one can see why Portmeirion's director of design selected him to realize Sophie

Conran's tableware. He declares his own work 'wibbly-wobbly pots'. The pottery does have more emphatic hand marks, like a bowl with indentations knocked in when the clay is still wet. Compare his own mugs to the ones he threw for Portmeirion to reproduce: both have a conical body. Millward's own is squat with a wider foot. Portmeirion's Sophie is more photogenic but tapers so much that it's tippy. In Millward's view, the Sophie mug 'looks right but functions poorly'. It works best when solely viewed on the Web. The handles differ more, as his is an extrusion – an eighteenth-century method of producing standardized tubes of clay – that he imprecisely joins, tearing the tube open visibly on the thumb rest. On Portmeirion's Sophie, the pulled strap handle resembles a puffy ponytail on an adolescent cheerleader. Portmeirion pottery is purchased online often, so looks rate higher than touch as a priority in marketing. Millward is supplying Portmeirion with what it wants – what he calls 'a diluted version of bad 1960s pottery' – and the skilled potter knows he is dumbing down his handicraft. He made several variations and disagrees with Portmeirion's choice but also understands that the decision wasn't

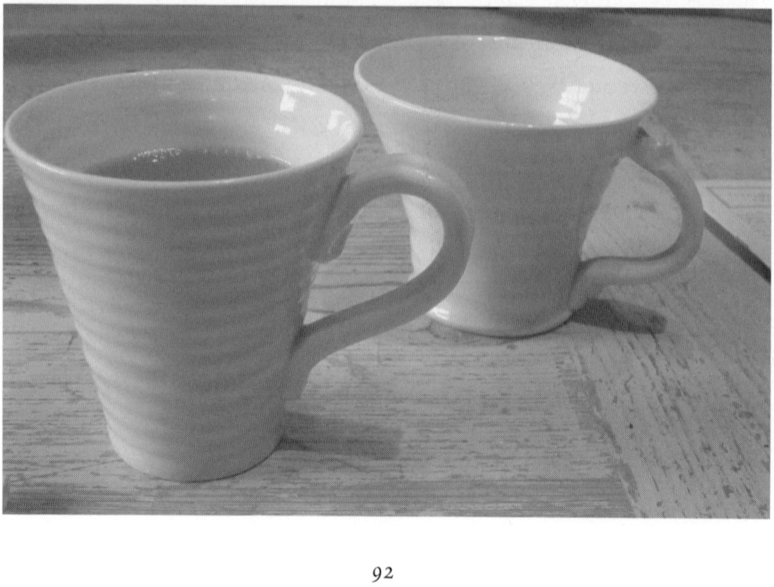

Sophie Conran for Portmeirion mug, left, and Kevin Millward's mug, which was wheel-thrown with an extruded handle, right, in Kevin Millward's studio, Staffordshire, 2014. The close proximity between these two drinking cups in terms of style explains why Portmeirion sought out Millward as the artisan who could best realize their designs. They are both examples of craftsmanship, differing mainly in their scale of production and numbers of authors.

his to make. But he recognizes his choice probably would have proven less successful in the marketplace. His own design for an extruded handle is a sophisticated tactile subtlety, a detail that is probably lost on many users and is impossible to mass produce by casting in moulds.

The Sophie teapots are crowned with wiggly lids, an idiosyncrasy to give the consumer a visual sense of tactile engagement and the pot a strong personality – but whose? Millward remembers his instructions from Portmeirion: 'add a bit more wobble to the knob'. The plates stack and fit our industrial lifestyle of dishwashers but have eccentric lips that droop. It is noteworthy that when the line debuted in 2006, the work stream was outside the factory's comfort zone. At the garden party to announce the new line of manufacturing, marketing was ahead of production. When the press caught its first glimpse of Portmeirion's Sophie Conran line, they ate off a dozen matching sets of luncheon services that Millward himself had thrown on the wheel. Yet no one wrote it up as handicraft; it was deemed a new industrial design. Millward's proficiency is such that his pottery is consistent enough to appear to be factory-produced. When the tableware was met with intense interest and an award, Portmeirion expedited the shipment of Millward's prototypes overseas to have the pottery copied and produced en masse in China. Proud of his work on the Sophie models and of his ability to 'put his business hat on', Millward is resolved that 'No one would buy it if it had my name on it,' adding that the product carries in it four crucial components: his craftsmanship and sense of form, the art director of Portmeirion's savvy marketing, Sophie Conran's own sense of form and style; moreover, perhaps most important of all, the Conran name, an English regal provenance that is the contemporary version of eighteenth-century aristocratic approval, such as Wedgwood's association with the Duchess of Devonshire or Sèvres with Madame de Pompadour.

Virtuosic potters once aimed for standardization and visual coherence. Does Millward's pottery for Portmeirion confirm David Pye's warning that 'the danger is not that the workmanship of risk will die out altogether but rather that, from want of theory, and thence of standards, its possibilities will be neglected and inferior forms of it will be taken for granted and accepted'? These attempts to cultivate sentimental associations in household goods are age-old strategies, and Pye's fears are warranted, but shoddy workmanship is nothing new: it is not standards that we should invest in but genuine education in handicraft.

A man with a sense of humour and scale in the world, Millward is irreverent towards studio potters who speak of the 'handmade' with moral superiority and the self-assurance that such a thing exists. His potter's mark can be contrasted with that of the English potter Edmund de Waal, whose austere cylinders thrown on the wheel are exhibited in massive shelving units – recently to critical acclaim at the Gagosian Gallery, New York City. If de Waal's initials are impressed into the wet clay on their sides – visibly artsy signatures – Millward's blue rubber stamp, 'Handmade in England', is out of sight, on the base of his own mugs. Millward thus emulates mass marketing even as he asserts the role of the human potter. His name is mentioned nowhere in Portmeirion's publicity – hence my initial doubts of his authorship. Yet his labour is somehow his own, while his identity is malleable and susceptible to role-playing and reinvention.

In a so-called post-industrial economy, highly educated and skilled manual workers remain active, denying the obsolescence of craft as they submit their virtuosity to corporate goals. They are pleased to re-enter the factory reclassified as consultants – once they were mere 'mechanics'. Yet the academy has systematically dismantled the programmes on which they studied. And factories no longer train apprentices in Stoke-on-Trent. Rita and Kevin embody an enormous population of non-replenishable resources that we have normally never considered 'craftsmen'. Skills assembled over several lifetimes of incremental and collated labour are easily lost in a generation.

The role of craftsmanship in our society is fragile and there is danger in preserving it artificially as well as underestimating the vitality of ancient skills. Millward is a rare occurrence, an anonymous craftsman identified through oral history. The great majority of craftspeople making baskets, chairs, glass, jewellery and pottery will remain anonymous. The ultimate challenge to you, the reader, is to search out and applaud the anonymous handicraft that is in your own local context, under the hood of a well-oiled machine or inside the tent at your local carnival.

Virtuosic anonymous craft has always existed in greater volume than authored and signed self-expressive craft. Anonymous craftspeople in manufacturing will outnumber craftspeople operating individual workshops – and probably always will. And women have historically outnumbered men in factory employment. One can state with certainty that there are more skilled hands in factories making pianos today than there are individual studio craftsmen able to bequeath such skilled instrument manufacturing to the next generation: the piano has always needed several skills and materials joined together.

So how should we cultivate future craftspeople and craft consciousness? It is high time to expand the honorific to be less of a distinction given on the basis of class or status. For Paul Roehrig, Chris Maldari or Rita Floyd it is merely their work; they don't grandstand and call themselves artisans. Schools, museums and aesthetic movements have inadvertently ossified craft, making it a static thing. Historically, craft has developed in response to demand, inventing itself anew wherever and whenever there was patronage. Feeding cash to summer camps and cultural institutions might appear to be a way to support handicraft, but in those workshops there is as much routine production as in any tedious factory. Invention in craft and responsiveness to social need cannot be taught; it must be found. Responsibility to social needs can be taught – and should be more often. A more empirical, directly sensuous and sensible recognition of craftsmanship as it exists today is vital, urgent and still worthwhile.

We have now worked through archetypes that are pinned onto refrigerators and above desks as exemplars, and also through the messy present context, to demonstrate that there is no overriding continuum in craft history; a linear genealogical history sounds good but when set in motion often produces blinders or canonizes individuals. The practices of these archetypes should not be emulated but their responsive attempts at tooling are worth considering in terms of temporal sensitivity. A craft is always in flux.

THREE

ORGANIC OR INDUSTRIAL? WEAVING CANE AND WELDING STEEL

The sense of an opposition between artificial and natural materials is a pervasive worry in craft. We misread materials as metaphors for the authentic and phony. Surely chapters One and Two shuffled between numerous ways of handling wood and ceramic and emphasized the subjective qualities of tooling and workmanship. It is easy to label materials like rattan and willow as 'organic' and 'natural' and to categorize welding tools (such as the electric arc and oxyacetylene torch) as 'industrial' and 'artificial'. But such binary conclusions are misleading; vegetable fibres and metals have both been bent to human whim for thousands of years. Instead of reiterating the tired cliché that craft is about 'truth to materials' like some Victorian Arts and Crafts reformers (and many a twentieth-century Brutalist architect), or the ethical mission of 'working in natural materials' like my childhood friend John Christopher, go to IKEA or some other furniture warehouse and sit in one of the many variations of chairs with steel frames and seats of caning or woven vegetable fibres. The Swedish company sells a squat rocking chair, the Gullholmen, designed by Maria Vinka, a steel frame encased in a weave of coarse banana leaf; and the Karlskrona, a chaise longue of bamboo and rattan designed by Karl Malmvall. On whichever chair you choose to sit, bounce a bit in order to ponder the integration of materials and enjoy the intermingling types of elasticity. Focus on feeling the

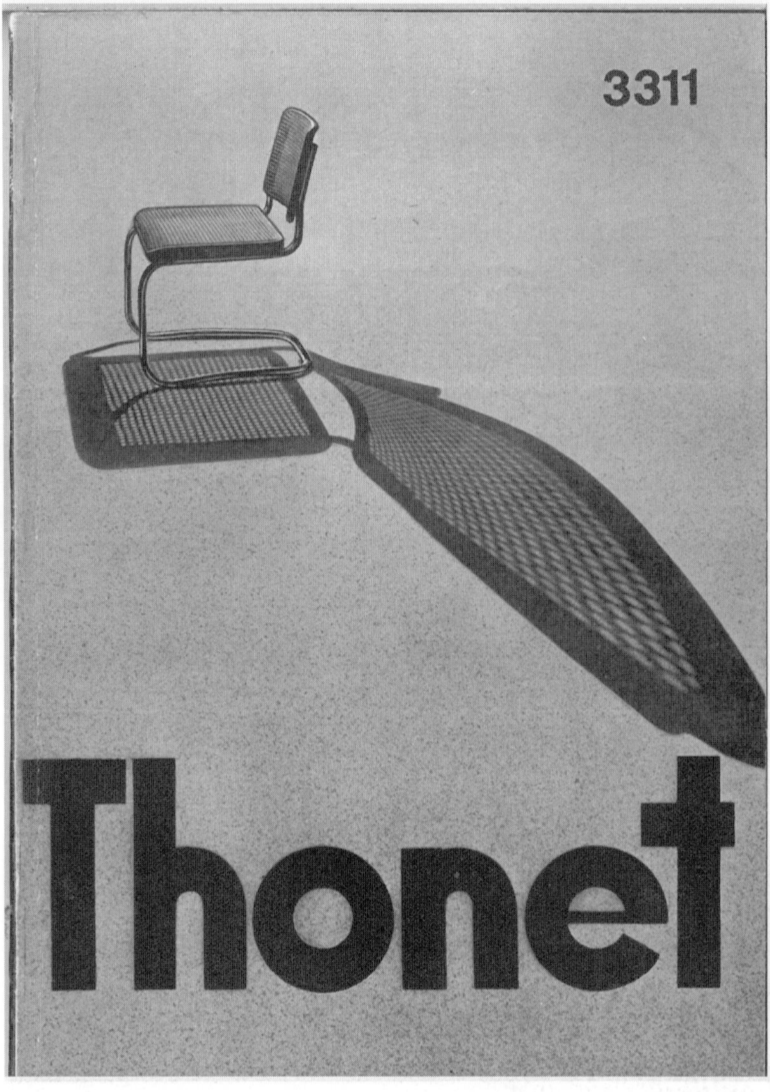

Thonet catalogue (#3311), November 1933, with cover image of the B32 chair designed by Marcel Breuer. One of several cantilevered steel chairs designed in the 1920s, Breuer's was expensive handicraft that Thonet turned into a successful avant-garde accessory. Now marketed as the S32 by Thonet and as the Cesca by Knoll, authenticated versions of this iconic design are artisanal and more expensive than ever before, while reproductions that use woven rattan sheet and cheaper chroming techniques sell for one-tenth the cost.

IKEA PS Gullholmen, a stackable rocking chair designed by Maria Vinka in 2002, banana fibre woven over steel, manufactured in Vietnam 2002–present. If craft is often identified as unique or a 'limited-edition' run of production, the consumption of folkloric furnishings often hinges on more superficial material attributes. By advertising the 'handwoven' quality of the banana fibre and its sustainability as a resource, the IKEA catalogue speaks to specific contemporary desires.

tension between steel and vegetable fibre: they are woven of Vietnamese and Indonesian fibres according to the plans of Swedish designers. The support of a supple steel skeleton and the network of interlaced fibres parallels the anatomical suspension of the human body and its mixed materials of muscle and bone, ligament and tendon. This global mixture epitomizes the complex reality that Western furniture has been made of exotic materials for hundreds of years.

Ancestry of the IKEA seating can be traced back to the tubular steel chairs designed in the late 1920s. At the Bauhaus, Marcel Breuer made a 1930 design, the B32, which remains a best-seller and 'icon of design' and twentieth-century modernist aesthetics because its spare structure – a seemingly single bent tube of steel – seems impossibly daring as a way to cantilever the human body with a minimum of support. One's body bounces in the chair, with its two legs that curve underneath like runners; your legs are free to swing underneath and your backside can respire through the rattan. The form seems to turn fellow Bauhausler Paul Klee's notion of drawing as 'taking a line for a walk' into a material experiment.

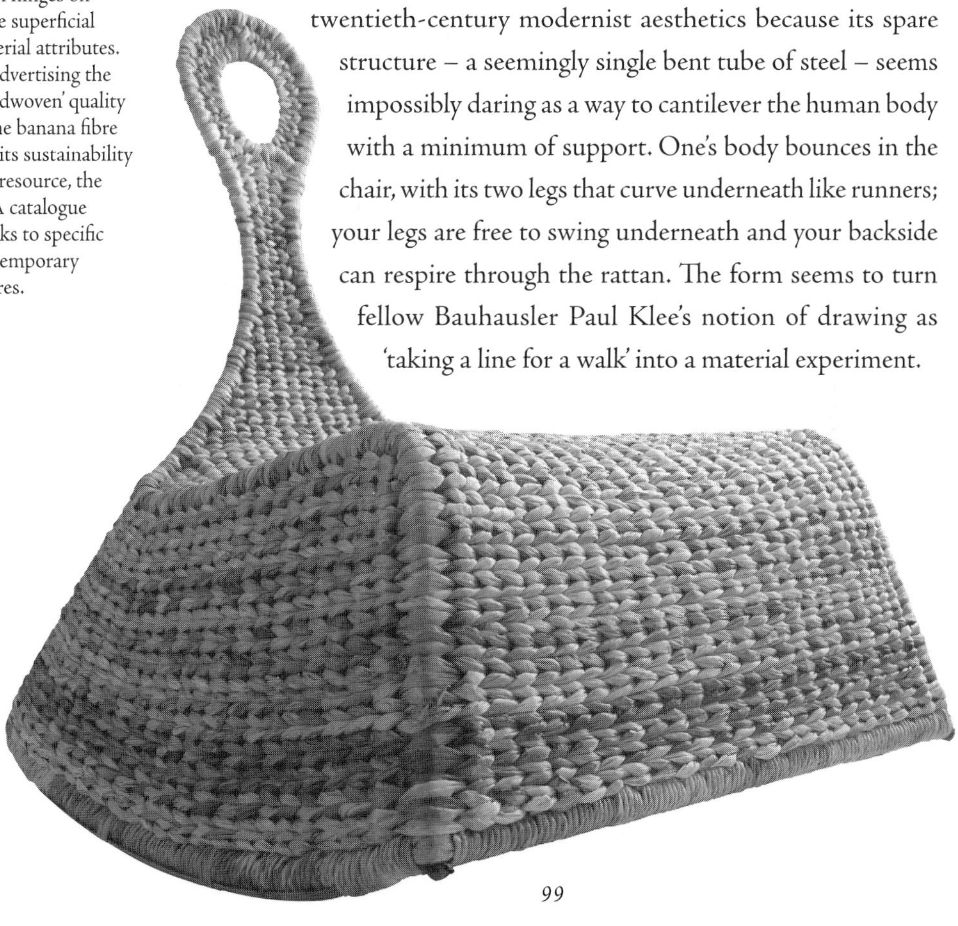

The enduring beauty of Breuer's chair might be precisely that it sustains the tensions between the limits of artisanal craft and the properties of its materials (rattan and steel). The union of materials illustrates the subtle ways in which ancient physical properties are continually reinvented. Both materials have qualities to exploit – there is no inherent tendency. To make Breuer's chair, vine and ore must be refined beyond recognition. There is no criterion for ascertaining whether the materials are 'authentic' or 'inauthentic', 'natural' or 'unnatural': we cast these subjective perceptions onto materials. If the seat of the B32 you have is sagged or torn, it is likely one with machine-woven cane. At its origins, Breuer's bending of tubular steel and superficial plating were the more costly parts of production, but today's mass-produced version is made using all shortcuts. Many unlicensed versions of the Breuer chair are annually produced in the hundreds of thousands. When the first versions of the B32 were made, the frame was a piece of plumber's craftsmanship, expensively nickel-plated; the rattan was manually tied into the wooden frames strand by strand. Today, labour-intensive caning by hand is expensive and steel and plating are more affordable, inverting the economic constraints of 1930.

Breuer's insight that these two materials – cane and steel – could become a sum greater than their parts can be traced to the Bauhaus philosophy and practice of building in teams and also, perhaps more specifically, to his earlier collaboration on chairs with Gunta Stölzl (1897–1983), before she became the head of the weaving shop at the Bauhaus. For a unique experiment on what is informally named the African Chair, the two students made a pseudo-tribal wooden throne with five feet, and Stölzl wove its wool upholstery directly onto the structure. Youthful (they were only in their early twenties), Breuer and Stölzl intentionally executed a naive romantic idea of craft that still looks slap-dash today, almost a century later. Perhaps the partnership taught Breuer something about the complexity of textiles and upholstery as structural components. The collaborative experiment foreshadowed Breuer's syncopation of disparate materials. If the success of the B32 is often credited to the Bauhaus being a hothouse, Stölzl's role as a catalyst – and the importance of weaving as an intellectual model – deserves to be revisited.

If Breuer's subsequent chairs seem to epitomize the Bauhaus's 'machine aesthetic', the school's in-house art historian, Sigfried Giedion, saw the steel in relation to the delicate ribbons in Celtic ornament, noting that 'the tubing flows in an endless line, as in the Irish interlace.' Breuer was the prodigy of the director of the Bauhaus, Walter Gropius, who deputized his student to be its youngest master. When Breuer took charge of the furniture department, he took to heart Gropius's call for 'old craft workshops to develop into industrial laboratories'. Stölzl would be made head of a studio too, although her department of textiles would struggle for recognition. In it she celebrated manual weaving. Stölzl believed that 'only work at the hand loom allows the kind of latitude for an idea to be developed from experiment to experiment until it is defined and clarified.' She gained her title herself, when she crossed out 'student' on her identification card and, in her own cursive hand, wrote 'Meister'.

For all these reasons – the authenticity of nature versus industry and the gendered distinctions of weaving versus welding – make the B32 a good place to worry over craft. We wear blinders if we categorize the use of steel as innovative and a rattan seat as traditional. Tubular iron chairs and bed-frames have existed since the 1840s. Moreover, in 1926 Breuer knew that Mart Stam, a Dutch architect living in Berlin, had assembled a chair using threaded pipe. Rattan seats dated back to the seventeenth century, when Europeans absorbed the idea and material from China, and in 1925 Thonet's bentwood café chairs with rattan were considered as modern a chair as any (and Thonet had been making them for more than seventy years). The B32 is not only significant for its 'design'; the material matters: the cane weaving in a high-quality Breuer chair might be a product of undervalued labour, but it was made with skill and it has endured longer than any other version of upholstery on a tubular steel frame.

If the African chair exemplifies generative collaboration within the Bauhaus, Breuer's tubular steel furniture crystallizes the school's competitive contentiousness, for Gropius expected the patent to be the school's to monetize. Chafing at the implication that furniture was less than art, Breuer compared his chair to a painting. In contrast, Stölzl accepted her supporting role when she wove others' designs, probably because she had precious little choice. The school would soon be riven by politics, too: Breuer would not fall on his sword for the left-wing socialism that Stölzl championed. He left the Bauhaus eager to achieve autonomy in 1928, whereas she was forced to resign in 1933 after marrying a Jewish architect and losing her German citizenship. Craft and design split along lines of gender and national identity and the power of body language: seats remain thrones while wall hangings must struggle harder for respect, even if they resemble paintings, the forms of art people tend to worship most freely. Steel somehow stays central to Bauhaus mythology, and weaving is marginalized.

Breuer conducted multiple trials before settling on this upholstery. He cited his Adler bicycle as his inspiration for the chair structure. When he began to design steel chairs he bought extruded tubing from the Mannessmann Steel Works – the same material his bike was made of. His first designs had seats and backs of waxed cotton canvas called *Eisengarnstoff*, or 'iron yarn', a shoelace-like material. Solid seats and backs did not reveal the arc of legs underneath. In 1925 his B5 combined steel with wicker, and in 1928 Breuer tried rattan. Christopher Wilk, curator at the Victoria & Albert Museum, calls the B32 'masterful' because 'the caning made the seat and back transparent.' Only the rattan version extends the airy quality of the cantilevered tubing. The union of materials still has weaknesses: place a knee on the seat and it will rupture the rattan; most plating shows signs of corrosion due to humidity. Breuer's B32 has an anthropomorphic quality – a system of material husbandry. Steel and rattan, bent and sprung, rely on tension.

When Thonet manufactured the first assembly-line rattan B32 in the 1930s, it was a limited production – handicraft. Reissued by an Italian firm in the 1960s, the B32 was renamed the Cesca (after Breuer's daughter) and has been by far his most popular design. Breuer himself valued the flexibility of the B32 enough to deploy it both in his own dining rooms and in business offices. His equally famous lounge chair, the model B3 Wassily, named after Kandinsky, forces a user to lean back and cannot be used at table. But the B32 accommodates many postures and permits someone to exit from either side gracefully, and can even catapult us upwards when we abruptly need to stand. In the early 1970s, Knoll began to make thirty thousand Cescas a year, so the chair was no longer handicraft but still seductive.

The Breuer chair shows the strange plight of basketry: both the skill and the material are taken for granted. Because it has become an iconic 'masterpiece of modern design', it is hard to imagine the B32 as being handicraft originally, prototyped by a plumber. However, if we overlook today's cheap copies with machine-woven cane seating and weak tubular steel, the B32 still can be experienced as a complex fusion of diverse flexible materials and remains influential.

In our contemporary landscape, Maria Vinka's Gullholmen woven out of banana leaves is a successor as both high design and global handicraft. IKEA advertises the chair as 'handmade', and it is, in Vietnam: artisanal labour is only affordable if procured from a developing country. Most weavers of the Gullholmen also are part-time farmers, a balance of agriculture and the assembly line not unlike a nineteenth-century Shaker community. The Gullholmen is specifically designed to fit a tiny apartment in Stockholm and also stack economically into an overseas shipping container. The flaring base makes it child-friendly, near-impossible to overturn. Vinka envisioned the form as a way to 'stimulate several different senses'; a rocking chair, it is potentially therapeutic. She also explains her pleasure in selecting banana leaves as upholstery: 'I think it makes the chair even more beautiful and nice to sit in, knowing that it's made of a waste material.' The shape remains curiously Swedish, even though its resonances are global: it relates to the spoons of the Sami people carved from birch tree burls. One sits in the ladle, and the tapered backrest is like a handle. Hidden inside is the steel, a pivotal infrastructure as it is in our buildings and bridges and ships, but still a material lacking in domestic warmth, despite Breuer's attempts to transplant the dentist's chair and laboratory aesthetic into the modern home. The Gullholmen proves that craft remains desirable and in demand: we still grope for a way to be in touch with the vegetal world and bring it into our living rooms as reassurance that we have not lost complete touch with the organic world. More informal than the B32 and in step with our current idea of a living room, IKEA's furnishings prove that exotic vegetable fibres are easily assimilated into the modern environment: they are chameleon-like in their ability to accommodate high-tech or low-tech environments.

ARE ANY MATERIALS NATURAL OR ARTIFICIAL?

The contrast between steel and fibres – be they rattan or banana leaf – highlights differences of material origins and preparation. There is no comparable ground zero between vegetable and mineral. Weaving begins in the bush, proceeding from the ground up, as it always has, with the initial harvesting of fibres. Soaking, sorting, splitting are steps towards producing semi-finished raw goods. But rattan is not identified as cane until peeled, split, shaved, soaked and woven. Welding, on the other hand, begins with the acquisition of standard shapes of mild steel from

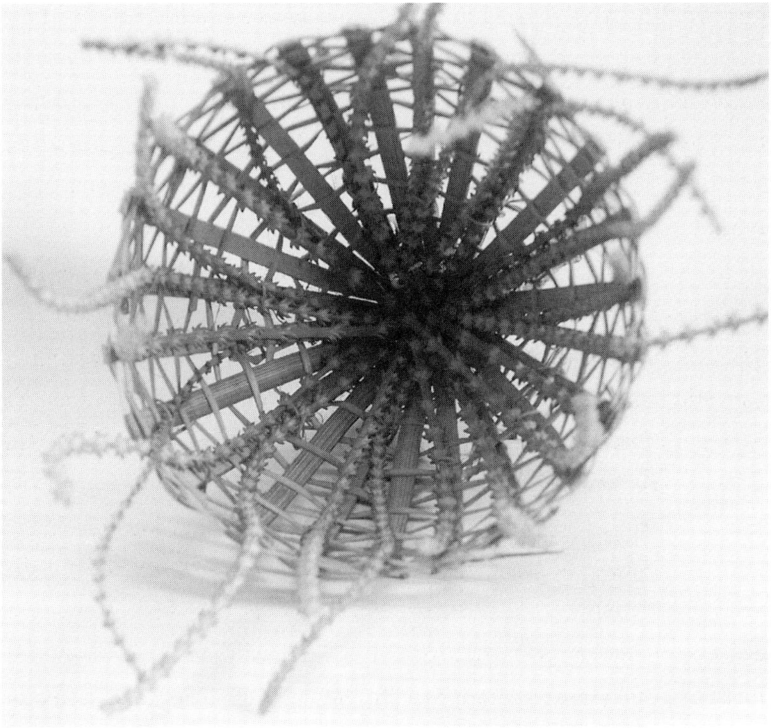

Sangtam Naga artistry, conical fish trap lined with thorny calamus, *c.* 1900–1920, collected from Nagaland, India. The combination of the thorny and refined rattan reveals the material's potential for dramatic transformation and reinvention, and myriad species of calamus serve countless other human uses, from food to roofing.

a factory's distributor (unless one harvests junkyard debris). The steel is routinized, and the vegetal fibre is too, transformed beyond recognition, even if it remains more susceptible to humidity or fire. In craft, there is often the expectation that a raw material be worked, tooled and manipulated, but also be authentic or not falsified. The ways that parts of our chairs – bamboo and rattan – still feel alive are beautiful but misleading sensations.

The idealizing of 'natural materials' is appealing but more evasive than ever before in our Anthropocene era of massively disrupted ecosystems and centuries of invasive transplants – and yet remains sacred and pivotal to most definitions of craft. It seems impossible to describe activities like mining, smelting, puddling and refining iron as 'natural', although of course people have been at them a long time – so long that it seems strange to call these actions unnatural or inhuman. Rattan is a rough, thick, thorny vine before being skinned and soaked so that its siliceous outer layer can be cut into polished strips – but it is often soaked in petroleum-based fuel in order to preserve it and eliminate insects. How 'natural' are materials that depend on such extensive refining?

Two quite distinct conceptions of nature emerge as a cultural *idée fixe*: nature is rude and barbaric and simultaneously redemptive and purifying. As western Europeans first discovered the East and West 'Indies', their taste for mahogany and porcelain as well as rattan grew. These materials and many others, especially silk, cotton, new spices and dyes, came to symbolize domestic refinement of the exotic. The materials remain charged by colonialist imperialism. For centuries, handicraft has been a sort of oxygen pump bringing either refined delicacies or untrammelled rustic charms into Westerners' interiors. Both these conceits linger on today. Imported shawls and embroidery are valued as evidence that pre-industrial production survives seemingly uncontaminated by modern life. A complex notion of 'nature' tantalizes twenty-first-century craft, when a walnut burl bowl, sisal and jute placemats and a gilt ruby chalice might stand side by side on a glass table, supplying a modern room with textures from somewhere vaguely otherworldly – somewhere pure and refreshing. Just as eighteenth-century consumers savoured quaint accent pieces, we still do now, even if domestic furnishings like woven cotton table runners are purchased from big box stores where they are obviously not singular. It is worth noting how the tiers of the marketplace define craft distinctly. Craft is inherently touristic; material you're meant to experience as a holiday from the quotidian – and especially away from the factory assembly line.

Today, craftspeople and craft advocates alike use the phrase 'living materials' to signify 'nature'. This strange conceit is a subtext underlying much twentieth-century craft. Raymond Williams suggested that a 'personified idea of Nature' serves as a counterbalance to 'first, an obsolete or corrupt society, needing redemption and renewal, and, second, an "artificial" or "mechanical" society, which learning from Nature must cure.' These binary oppositions, especially when embodied as a steel rod and rattan weave, remain vital to our understanding of craft. The supposition is that by weaving a basket, a process with all the violence of a disciplinary action, 'nature' is seemingly retained.

We ask a lot of baskets: that they carry us back to the rude loins of uncultivated wilds and also preserve organic vitality as they are cut, shaved into modular units and twisted and knotted into patterns. We expect the craft artefact, like the craftsman, to navigate the difficult course of being natural in a way that is superior to impersonal industrial production, and see it as a route to becoming more human, too. Can the artefact walk this tightrope of being refined but not too refined, a product of art and worldly knowledge and yet still naive?

The etymology of the word 'nature' has these meanings in it, naiveté and indigeneity, and these characteristics contradictorily demand that a thing can be lacking cultural affect and yet physically embody a local culture. The mute basket might yet articulate that it is the great sieve that enabled the first farmers to winnow their chaff, to keep their seeds safe from the jaws of fellow hungry mammals gnawing their way through winter in the night. And yet the pursuit of basketry has kept humans digging like pigs for spruce roots and sorting through swamp grass for specific lengths and thicknesses of fibres, no better than birds assembling nests.

The American basket-maker-artist John McQueen articulates this precarious threshold: the desire to be of nature but not quite in it. As he sees it, 'my baskets still have the tree in them, the bark, the bug marks.' However, he also articulates the anxiety that the pretension of art overwhelms inherent and natural material beauty – a hallmark of craft discourse. 'The object of art', McQueen writes, is some thing or some place that 'the basket must reject . . . even when inside, it secretly entertains it . . . A basket must be careful. In such a state it could become unravelled.' McQueen is gentle where others have been dismissive or dogmatic. The problem is not in craft becoming too useful, but bearing more affect than it can support.

This ambition to engage refinement yet not become trapped in pretensions strangely parallels the myth that craft is on life support. Over-refinement, industrialization and commercial degradation threaten, and heroic artistic individuals save the day – not a manufacturer, design, tourist-consumer or factory. This romantic story of craft imagines it as eternally endangered. That is usually how Nampeyo or William Morris are depicted as protagonists. In craft, the dial of refinement is carefully set to a specific tolerance; there needs to be some pretence to art, but not too much. To be a lawyer-turned-blacksmith making medieval strap hinges at the dawn of the twenty-first century is an acceptable recuperation of folklore and virility. However, to forge massive public installations in steel might be going too far from the anvil to be craft, implying that unwritten codes of material and institutional hierarchies still exist. Basketry, 'gathered from nature', is sometimes looked at sceptically when it becomes 'sculpture' with no apparent connection to function. Basketry is strangely more susceptible to respect when imprisoned or frozen

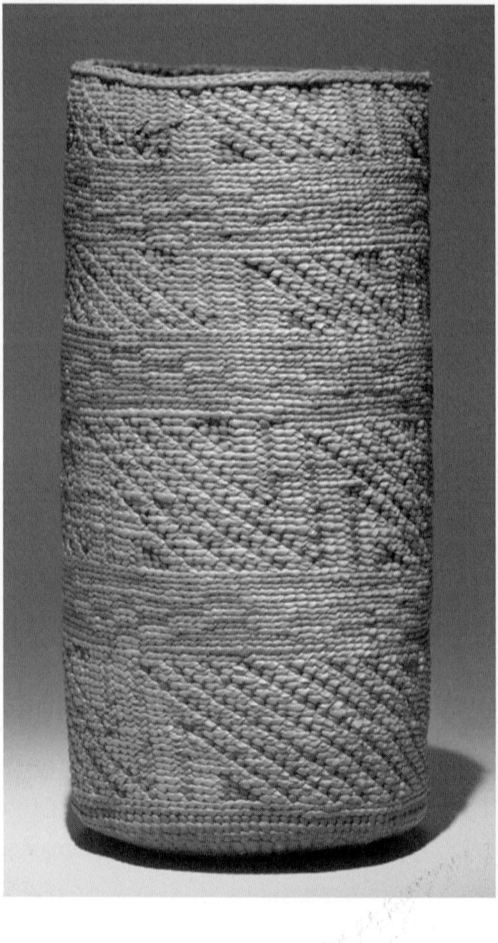

in time as heritage ritual or recreated historic agricultural implement. Willow work, for instance, is preserved as French national identity at the École Nationale d'Osiériculture et de Vannerie in Fayl-Billot.

Baskets are more exciting when they connect humanity to its environment, to its pace of life. Once upon a time, rattan and willow epitomized one or another *terroir*, evoking the sentience of a specific ecology, but that was a prehistoric era. Now they have been cultivated nearly everywhere. Samuel Colt, known for his namesake guns that dazzled nineteenth-century Europe from London to St Petersburg, procured over a hundred skilled German artisans and seedlings of *Salix viminalis* (basket willow) to be employed in Hartford, Connecticut, in the 1860s, and his Colt Willow-Ware Works was productive for only a little over a decade. In seventeenth-century England, John Evelyn noted the unmitigated expansion of willow as a recent phenomenon – it had been imported from Flanders only a hundred years earlier:

> baskets, flaskets, hampers, cages, lattices, cradles, the bodies of coaches and wagons, for which 'tis of excellent use, light, durable, and neat, as it may be wrought and cover'd: for chairs, hurdles, stays, bands, the stronger for being contus'd and wreathed, &c. likewise for fish weirs, and to support the banks of impetuous rivers: In fine, for all wicker and twiggy works.

Tlingit artistry, drinking cup, northwest coast, North America, before 1824, spruce root, grass, dye. 6½ x 3⅛ in. (16.51 x 7.938 cm). Successive ownership as this cup journeyed from the northwest coast to Hawaii to Massachusetts suggests watertight basketry was once prized as evidence of human ingenuity, and weaving savoured as a technological wonder.

Today's loss of biodiversity does threaten basketry, such as the disappearance of river cane, once indigenous to North America. Certain Cherokee basket-making traditions cannot be continued. And examples of cultural hybridity are only increasingly inevitable. Honeysuckle, an invasive species from Japan, now thrives across North America. If Gullah coiled baskets from the Carolina coasts reflect the dislocation of African methods to North American soil, and Cherokee baskets are now made

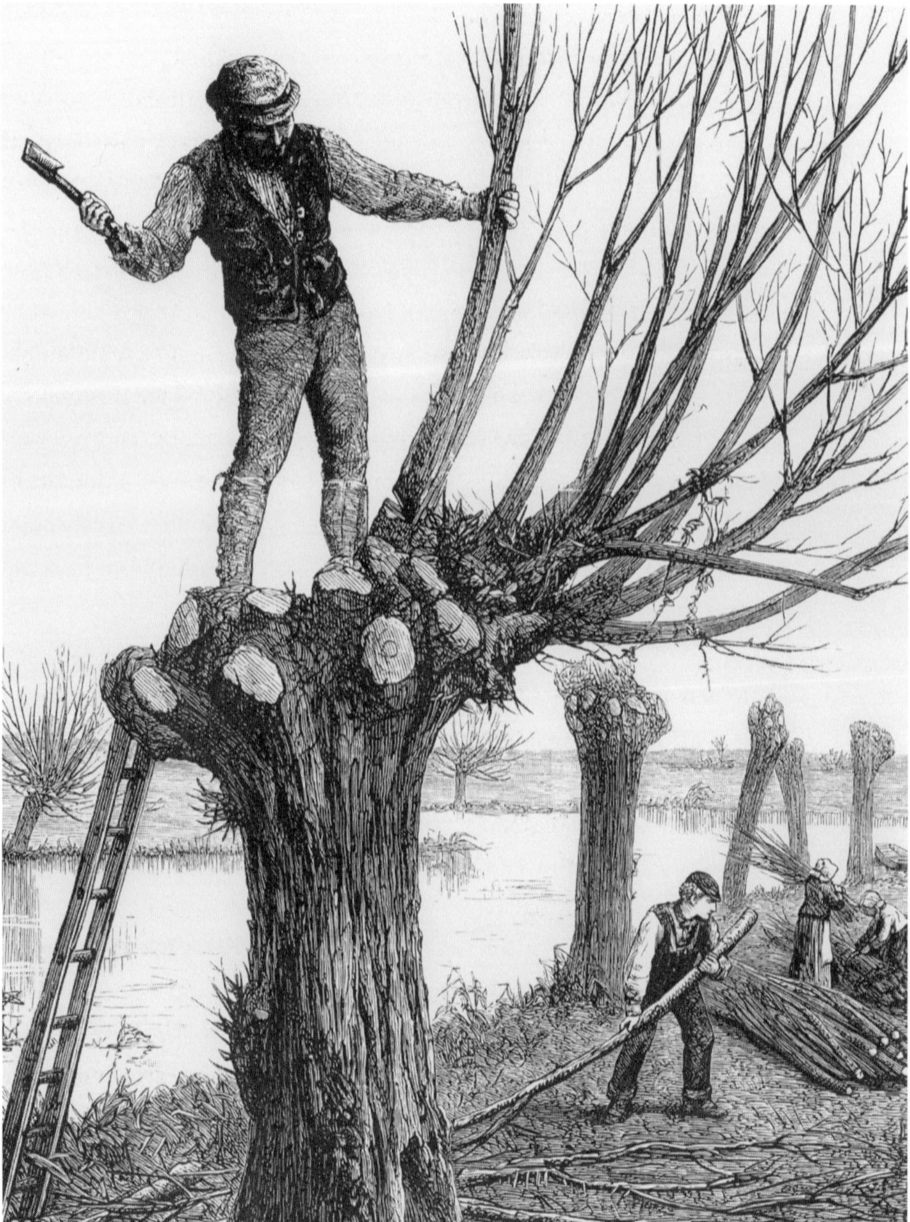

out of honeysuckle, then there are ample reasons to stop measuring baskets against any notions of ethnic purity or cultural authenticity. We impede craft unnecessarily when we categorize it as from one specific vernacular. Perhaps the notion of an 'honest basket' is itself contrary to the nomadism of the world, the tidal pulls of migration and the pulse of diasporic cultures. Ancient materials, such as willow, rattan and bamboo, continue to be used, but warehouses store these 'natural materials' and operate on an industrialized scale, much as immense fields of whale baleen were common in nineteenth-century stockyards. To chart the use of specific materials like osier, the cultivated willow, *Salix purpurea*, alongside 'foreign' imported ones such as rattan or cane reveals a web of global transportation at least four centuries old. For these reasons, it is prudent to stop thinking of basketry as either 'natural' or stable.

Humans have acclimated to steel and become alienated from the forest floor – one more reason we fail to value Breuer's rattan in the B32. Basketry is too ancient to measure, while acetylene welding is just over one hundred years old, but the techniques illuminate our notion of time and tendency to categorize craft. Oxyacetylene tanks and torches were novelties in the shipyard and turbine factory in 1900. Was such metalwork comforting or tantalizing in 1899 when in *Heart of Darkness* Joseph Conrad described the horizon from his ship in the Thames as 'sea and the sky welded together without a joint'? Modern industry served as a becalming metaphor for imperial vision. As early as the 1840s, on an Arctic expedition through 'wonderful works of nature', a young literate blacksmith, C. J. Sullivan, described the passage as akin to being inside 'a Steem engine in a large factory'. Today, there are certainly greater numbers of people who feel more comfortable explaining steam engines' pistons than judging the distinctive strengths of twined and wicker basketwork. The developed world, maybe even the entire globe, is fundamentally more in touch with the arc weld than the tree root.

Henry Robert Robertson, *Polling the Willows*, engraved by W. J. Palmer, in Robertson, *Life on the Upper Thames* (1875). In harvesting the willow every seven years, the stumps, called pollards, were considered visible signs of the industrialization of wickerwork – a far cry from today's notion of a landscape altered by manufacturing.

If basketry is sometimes regarded as a natural or bucolic activity, when scaled up it provokes fears about environmental degradation; signs of labour have been seen as blemishes on the landscape for centuries. H. R. Robertson's *Life on the Upper Thames* (1875) describes the variety of public opinion when the pollarding of willow trees occurred every seventh year: 'By many people they are considered at all times unpicturesque – a view we personally do not share. On the contrary, they seem to us to harmonise perfectly with the gentle current of the Thames, its lazy barges, and smooth, low-lying meadows.' William Paulgrave Ellmore's 1919 essay on the large-scale production of willow preparation on the Thames describes disruptive modernization, specifically the wrought iron brake, which enabled branches to be peeled at a faster clip. Ellmore saw willow work as a system lurching from small workshops into an immersive scale of industry:

> The first thing that strikes a visitor, on approaching the scene of the rodstripping, is a hum of merry voices mingled with the ever-recurring musical 'ping' of the break: the shape of the instrument is not unlike that of a very narrow jew's-harp, and folly accounts for its resonance. The strong aromatic smell of the fresh peelings is probably what will be next noticed, as the air is quite laden with what is an agreeable, if slightly pungent, odour. The recently peeled rods, thousands of which stand everywhere about, look very attractive in their pure whiteness, fit, indeed, for a child's cradle – the actual destiny that awaits not a few of them.

Ellmore noted that the most advanced tools were 'iron breaks faced with india-rubber', an improvement contingent on colonialist imperialism – another type of harvest on yet another continent. When and where craft begins to resemble industry – or ancient artisanship – has been debated and remains subjective.

In considering a length of willow or half-inch-round stock steel, the foolishness of our contemporary habit of labelling some materials and spaces as 'smart' becomes clear. The tension of a willow basket, when hugged, is audible in its creaking and flex, and its combination of lightness and strength is magical. Just how smart would it be to use biodegradable bowls and have more of our furniture made of springy rattan and less of it made of foams that off-gas formaldehyde or steel on which we scrape our shins? A basket is unbreakable in any normal bear hug, yet defenceless against a sharp corner of steel. It can last a lifetime lingering on a porch or be reduced to kindling after mere hours in the average express delivery truck. The osier's length foretells its use, such as the circumference of a basket.

Once cut, a willow stave is only good for certain jobs. Too-short lengths of willow are useless, but Lego-sized pieces of mild steel can be assembled into sturdy rods. It is miraculous that an 8-foot length of steel can be cut into 2-inch segments and welded together, and that the process does not weaken the steel. A willow branch might be said to embody predestination; it is what it is and once broken remains so always. But steel actually resembles the mythical phoenix in its capacity to be remoulded and reborn from ashes. Is this comparison hyperbolic? Or does it seem nonsensical because materials are simply incommensurate ecologies? Carcasses of the B32 and other facsimile reproductions are common on city streets, garbage usually, because the seats are torn and the chrome flaking. A rekindling of basketry could mend this waste and bridge this mental rut – if rattan caning were more commonly practised.

Comparing the roles of these techniques in educational systems is also instructive. Why is welding part of vocational or university education with dedicated facilities, whereas weaving basketry is rarely taught? Whereas a welding class tests for proper joinery, if twining or coiling or plaiting are taught in a fibre class it is for textural variety and emotive association.

Basketry falls in and out of the edges of a curriculum while automotive technology is a mainstay in the vocational system and design academy. If there are basketry courses, they often meet our gender clichés: retired white middle-class women make historical replicas in rustic getaways and young women pour their angst into self-expressive wall-bound fibre art in urban art schools. In our own era, the dominant issue of sustainability has so far failed to revise curricular content or academic conventions – even though basketry would seem poised to benefit from a 'green' curriculum. If our carbon footprint is truly a concern, the field of basketry would be ready for a renaissance. What prevents willow from replacing reams of paper, crayons, tempera and acrylic paint? It is worth realizing that basketry is relevant and intellectually fertile in order to challenge such entrenched habits. High school students might be equipping their bicycles

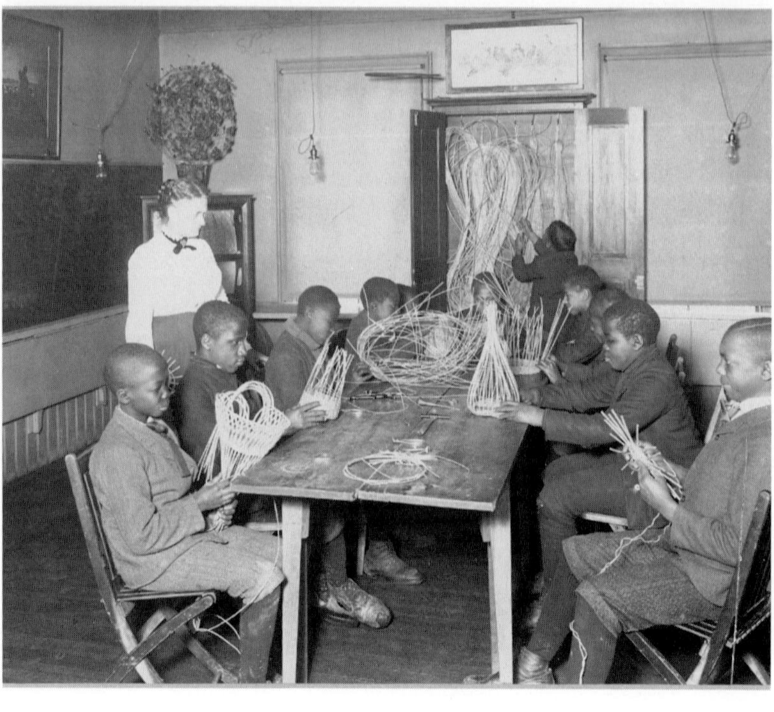

Basket-making class in Neighbourhood House, Cambridge, Massachusetts, *c.* 1903. The problematic history of basketry as a disciplinary activity imposed upon targeted communities according to class, race and ethnicity, in some cases selectively training blind people or prisoners in the vocation, is shared by many developed nations.

with handlebar baskets and panniers after growing and harvesting willow in abandoned lots, if we took the craft seriously as an avenue of inquiry.

The institutional identities of these crafts relate to economics and ethics as well as our sense of nature and culture. In the early twentieth century, schools aiming to acculturate Native Americans to Christianity, capitalism and second-class citizenship used basketry skills to take economic advantage of tourism. Craft was a way to assimilate and yet essentialize the nature of these peoples' cultures. Basketry was also taught to the blind, the orphaned and imprisoned, perhaps as a way to make them useful but also as a way to keep them manually trained, tied to low-earning jobs. Basketry has rarely been seen as a path to a brighter future.

In fact, weaving rarely appears futuristic. We have no books on futuristic baskets; they remain as emblems of primitive society. It is a perverse (or at least paradoxical) assumption that the baskets of greatest value are ones that symbolize an idea of 'nature' more than the drive to 'culture'. Curiously, we have many films with futuristic welders; watch *Star Wars* again and you can catch scenes of the Wookie, a hairy humanoid-ape named Chewbacca, arc-welding his spaceship's innards. Sparks from the arc welder are still photographed as futuristic and high-tech when they are ancient and manual activities. And basketry is gendered and regarded as nostalgic. Why?

THE ARC OF WELDING STEEL

No matter how industrialized, metal is finicky; it bends, buckles and drifts when heated. It might not seem alive, but its structure remembers heat and stress. Steel might sound modern but was made for thousands of years – by feel, not by scientific method. In the twentieth century it became homogeneous and standardized according to international guidelines for specific tolerances. Working with steel and iron was fetishized and romanticized long before Marcel Breuer and the Bauhaus gave it sex appeal with reflective plating. And working with metal has long been depicted as a heroic job of industrial brinkmanship – and a manly one, in contrast to the association of basketry with women.

The painter Joseph Wright of Derby glamorized the muscled smith working at the forge, and the poet Henry Wadsworth Longfellow praised 'The Village Blacksmith' just as the Industrial Revolution centralized such labour into factories. The art of the blacksmith – always among the most industrial of the crafts – has risen and fallen historically over the last thousand years, yet has rarely been regarded as a genre of fine art. Armour and weaponry have been praised (as have their descendants made by engineers and metalshops for Richard Serra and Barbara Hepworth). In the twentieth century, the welder was seen in a similar light to the blacksmith: a man working solo amid flying sparks, subduing steel with a speed heretofore unknown. But the welder was not a professional, hobbyist or sculptor until the twentieth century. Paradoxically, the rise of welding made the blacksmith appear more traditional but also gave metalworking an updated image. Breuer negotiated this issue of craft and skill in industry. He famously went to the Junkers aeroplane manufacturing company in Dessau to try to get his first chairs made, but had to use a plumber as the factory did not see the experiment as worth their time or energy.

To speak of metalwork as a craft with any accuracy, specific techniques and metals must be recognized and defined. The blacksmith hammering wrought iron, the factory artisan casting iron and the artist arc welding are each associated with craft in their own way. Yet the standardization of steel threatened craft. In contrast with modern mild steel, wrought iron has a more varied body, so it is easier to consider a living material. Each batch from different areas of the world has a distinct melting point and set of structural properties. 'The craftsman can compensate for differences in the qualities of his material,' wrote Cyril Stanley Smith, one of the great historians of technology, arguing that historic alloys had constitutional complexity. The artistic smith 'can adjust the precise strength and pattern of application of his tools to the material's local vagaries', unlike the welder of mild steel, who Smith saw as deskilled. As James E. Gordon sees it, 'Steel, especially mild steel, might euphemistically be described as a material that facilitates the dilution of skills . . . Manufacturing processes can be broken down into many separate stages, each requiring a minimum of skill or intelligence.' These two historians praise the manually intensive process of creating a wrought iron billet – like kneading dough, creating both an internal grain and increasing its elasticity – but both saw welding as an inferior skill.

What we call welding today is generally conceptualized as an additive process, perhaps similar to gluing, but the technique has older meanings that describe hammering and coaxing wrought iron into an overlapping joint – called a scarf – to achieve integrity. Whereas wrought iron can be given distinct character in parts of its body, steel and cast iron tend to be homogeneous. Any large gates that are more than a few hundred years old have variety – some parts might be spongy and others diamond-sharp, depending on variables such as the carbon content, quenching and other forge techniques. A surfeit of carbon in cast iron makes it brittle and unsuited to be worked on an anvil but also more resistant to the stress of heat. Cast iron is useful as a factory column or stove of any kind: it has strength under compression and retains heat evenly. Comprised of cast parts bolted together, cast-iron architecture required little skill to assemble and was the first prefab architecture to travel thousands of miles – to where it was entirely unsuited to the climate. A forge, in contrast, retains its identity as a birthplace of flexibility and power.

For the twentieth-century sculptor seeking to close the gap between the atelier and factory, welding was one obvious choice. Modern artists who chose to work with steel, like Breuer or his fellow Bauhausler László

Moholy-Nagy, were regarded as trailblazing. The welder's torch illuminated automobiles and skyscrapers. The modern acetylene torch, stick welder and electric arc technique assumed roles as tools exemplary to the zeitgeist. Even though welding was a democratic art form founded upon distance from the traditional academy, the tools quickly became part of both vocational education curriculums and the art school by the 1950s. Welding illustrates the tendency of the crafts in the twentieth century to sidle up to fine art methods and approaches, or perhaps travel in their wake, too swiftly, in pursuit of respect. One could interpret welding in a great many ways: as novel because of its obsolescence or as nostalgically related to the blacksmith or as contemporary. That the tool – or the craft – could be seen as both an extension of industrial processes and a practice unencumbered by history, yet stable as a gendered pursuit, suggests the complexity of craft.

The first welding of steel work to be recognized as significant cultural labour was that by Julio González and Pablo Picasso. (The great artist, not the tradesman, is invariably cited as the superlative innovator.) Picasso made some fifty sculptures in 1930–32, working with González, who himself had gained exposure when welding in a Renault factory during the First World War. González had soldered and brazed on a small scale before. The American David Smith gained skills welding when employed at a Studebaker automobile plant in South Bend, Indiana, but only added it to his artistic toolkit after seeing Picasso's work. In the 1950s, Anthony Caro and numerous other sculptors made welding their primary medium, and by the 1960s welding classes proliferated, easily entering the fine art curriculum. 'Welded steel' became a recognized artistic medium. It seemed to tie the artist's work to the DNA of speed and machinery, modernity's twin emphases. Welded steel seemed more authentic – and perhaps more naturally American – than bronze or marble. Yet there are some unanswerable mysteries: why was steel more popular than plastics or more novel metals like aluminium? Welding also became imbued with romanticized working-class identity. There are many ways in which this technology has been turned into cliché.

The Industrial Revolution created new distinct identities in trades and art schools, making the blacksmith seem ancient and the welder modern. And welding was as disruptive in organized labour as it was in fine art, craft and design. The United States government's Labour Relations Board struggled to adjudicate disputes among boilermakers, blacksmiths and machinists as these three groups questioned who was more skilled and therefore deserving of higher pay. Herbert Lahne, working for the Labour Relations Board, published an essay empathizing with 'The Welder's Pursuit of Craft Recognition' (1958). 'Most government agencies have concluded that welding merits recognition as a craft' because it required an apprenticeship period, Lahne asserted. But the government flip-flopped on whether the technique should be elevated to the level of skilled or semi-skilled production.

The populism associated with welding was full of paradoxes. In 1951 the exhibition 'Direct Metal Sculpture' in New York City claimed that the 'direct' execution constituted no less than 'a reunion of the artist and the artisan' – utopian rhetoric once used in the Bauhaus, too. Many 'fine artists' in the 1950s saw a 'more personal and intimate means of expression' in welding than in figure modelling; the Bauhaus partnership with industry and anonymity was not considered as salutary as an individual appropriation of factory tools. Instructive texts claimed that modern welders worked 'without a preconceived idea of the limiting possibilities' because they had dispensed with moulds and casting. Several of these books began by rejecting the cast bronze statue by Giambologna as a point of departure. In contrast to the Renaissance icon, welding was seen as 'free of academic cliché'. Suzanne Benton even praised it as suited for women, as the technique 'needs no brute force like the blows at the blacksmith forge'.

While the rise and fall of welded steel coincided precisely with the aesthetic of modernist abstraction, blacksmithing was of little to no importance to modern artists, who saw it as a traditional craft. Ironically, the golden age of American artistic blacksmithing came in the twentieth century, when automobiles numbered in the millions, and not in the Colonial era. The immense monumental infrastructure of the nineteenth century – its bridges and trains and steam engines – warrants praise, but architectural ornamental work flourished in the twentieth century. Just as Breuer left Hungary for Germany, Samuel Yellin (1885–1940) left Poland for America at the turn of the century. By the 1920s his workshop had more than two hundred men forging decorative ironwork for wealthy universities like Columbia, Harvard and Yale, as well as for banks, churches and private estates across the country. Yellin's immense floriated French Baroque gates adorned the monumental institutions of the first half of the twentieth century, whether Georgian brickwork, Renaissance Revival marble, Gothic or Neoclassical limestone. Today, more people have looked at Yellin's ironwork than at the most famous Abstract Expressionist paintings of the twentieth century, but his name is obscure: when he is recalled it is as a craftsman, designer and entrepreneur, rarely as an artist. While his work was not overtly stylistically modern, his eclectic oeuvre and the scale of his output could only exist in the twentieth century.

Yellin was aware that his work was desirable because it contrasted with the industrialized and mechanical world of the time. He worked hard to impart a patina and texture of hammering to the stock units of wrought iron with which mills provided him. To make round bars on his gates, Yellin used 'a one-inch square section . . . forging it as near to round as the human eye can measure. The bar will possess the quality of hand wrought craftsmanship and be far superior to . . . any machine-like perfection.' Yellin and his shop were consciously exposing the signs of manual labour on refined industrial products, taking the finish off modern

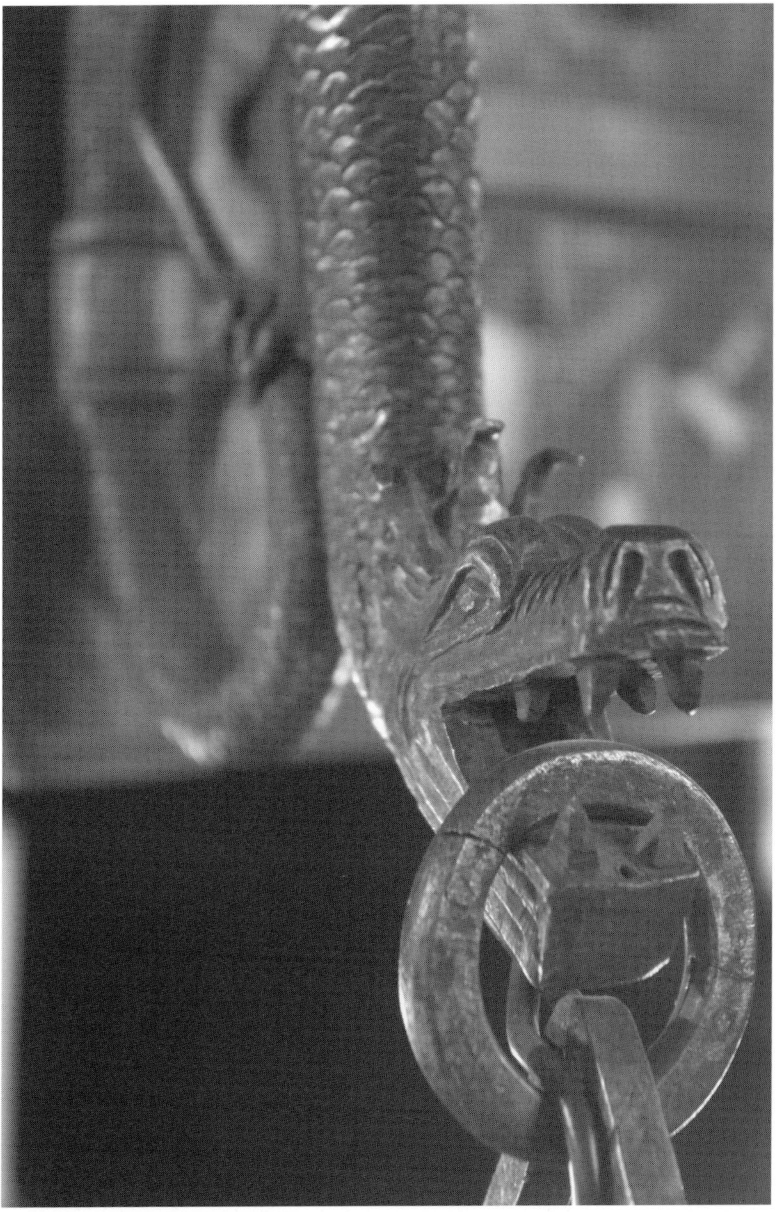

Samuel Yellin, wrought iron chandelier, *c.* 1911. The plasticity of iron and steel extends to the ways it clothed modern American capitalists' homes and institutions in Renaissance finery. Such cultural adaptation and appropriation is compelling to consider in regard to Yellin, a Jewish-born Ukrainian-trained immigrant who arrived in Philadelphia at the age of 21 in 1905, and the fanciful dragons in his depiction of the voyage of Christopher Columbus for the Daughters of the American Revolution. His firm also decorated the Washington National Cathedral as well as St Patrick's Cathedral in New York City.

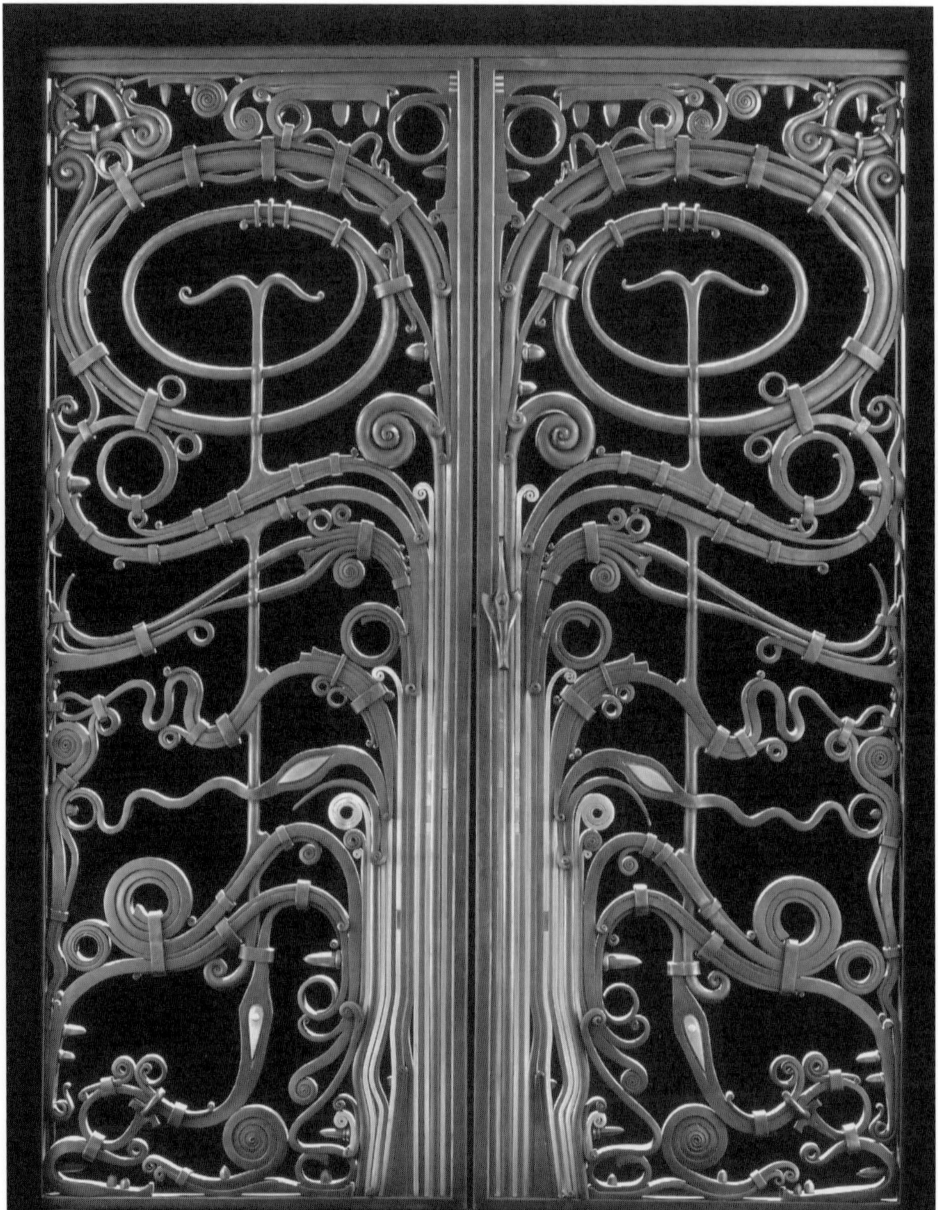

Albert Paley, portal gates for the Renwick Gallery, 1974–6, forged steel, brass, copper and bronze. Commissioned for the Renwick Gallery, Smithsonian American Art Museum, Washington, DC. Paley's gates and jewellery with biomorphic tendrils in this phase of his career mine the tensions in our associations with materials as artificial and natural, as had earlier Art Nouveau decoration by Victor Horta and Hector Guimard. Paley regained for metalwork the visibility and recognition it had in Samuel Yellin's commissions, but as an independent object more than an architectural accessory and ornamental necessity.

stockyard goods to imbue them with the romantic hammer marks that modern aristocrats and corporations appreciated.

Of the thousands of commissions that Yellin's Philadelphia shop made, many have a mixture of repetitive formulae and inventive flourishes. His workshop made full-scale preparatory drawings, and while they hammered out remarkably consistent stylized gates, the blacksmiths were more idiosyncratic and ambitious. Following prescribed proportions, weight and style, the skilled members of Yellin's team were also encouraged to creatively invent with zeal and vigour within those parameters. The rhythmic ornamental patterns, surely tedious at times, demanded precision. But the most grid-like mechanical design, such as a tight Greek fret, became vital when the iron was athletically propelled by a skilled eye and hand.

Francis Whitaker, who trained in Yellin's Philadelphia shop and lamented the demise of blacksmithing at mid-century while celebrating its late twentieth-century revival, passionately argued that

> Iron has a strength no other material has, and yet it has a capacity for being light, graceful and beautiful. It has this capacity – but no desire. It will do nothing by itself except resist you . . . All the desire, and all the knowledge of how to impart this desire to the iron, must come from the smith.

Whitaker compiled *The Blacksmith's Cookbook* at the age of 79, excited by the new practitioners in the early 1970s, such as Albert Paley, whose monumental forgings – an 80-foot fence at the Hunter Museum of American Art in Chattanooga, Tennessee, and portal gates for the Renwick Gallery in Washington, DC (1974) and the New York State Capitol building (1980) gave artisanal metalwork a novel visibility. America had a second golden age of ironwork that was something like a fusion of Yellin, Picasso and Breuer.

The large-scale revival of ironwork at the end of the twentieth century offers a window into human–material intersubjectivity, or what we describe, in shorthand, as 'taste'. The reclamation of blacksmithing began just at the time when American steel production plateaued at 150 million tons per year, and coincided with the founding of the Artist Blacksmith's Association of North America (ABANA). Paley was training as a goldsmith at Tyler when he and his teacher, Stanley Lechtzin, set up an experimental forge – and then they participated in ABANA. For Lechtzin, the project was part of a life of constant experimentation, but it was only a brief hiatus from precious metals. Lechtzin is known for using computer design or electroforming, not an anvil. For Paley, the technique was a release from precious metals and dismantled his artistic inhibitions. Paley became known for his iron tendril forms reminiscent of Art Nouveau. Unlike Whitaker, he felt, as he noted in a 1982 interview, that

> iron was plastic, it was fast, it was expressive, and . . . very exciting . . . and then I would go back to the jewelry [where] the plasticity, say, in silver and gold is very, very resistant and when you forge it or you move it, it moves very slowly.

The divergence in these descriptions of empathy and antagonism towards metals reveals the human subjectivity of craft. Materials and tooling resonate differently in each generation.

Blacksmithing today is considered a vital craft and has more institutional support than basketry. Today, steel can be forged on an anvil and with a furnace, but one needs to add flux, and the home-batched steel has a more limited tolerance than wrought iron in terms of malleability. Since its first meeting in 1970 of a dozen metalworkers in Lumpkin, Georgia, ABANA has grown to include more than five thousand members. Anti-establishment impulses and nostalgia converge in the blacksmithing revival – and these are enabled by post-war affluence. The blacksmiths might make horseshoes, but they drive automobiles. The resurgence of craft was fuelled by the counter-culture of Woodstock and going 'back to the land' as well as more conservative sources of funding at living history workshops in Colonial Williamsburg, Old Sturbridge Village and the Shelburne Museum. The recuperation of blacksmithing was driven both by antagonism towards corporate America and the desire to re-enact the Emersonian myth of self-reliance. Paley remembers being heckled in 1976, while presenting his work at ABANA: 'We're here to talk about blacksmithing; we don't want to hear about this art shit.' Blacksmithing seemed liberating because it was considered a means of bypassing 'artistic pretension' – a strange echo of the support for welding a few decades earlier. Although ABANA is not as antagonistic to the fine arts as Paley's memory suggests, the ambivalence towards pretensions that John McQueen so elegantly articulated is deeply ingrained in many genres of craft.

More recently, welding has assumed an even more overtly theatrical role as a form of spectacular craftsmanship in the work of Tomáš Libertíny, who used the tool in a performance in Miami in 2009 at the fair Design Miami/Basel. Based in the Netherlands, Libertíny often turns the art of fabrication into the theme of his work, such as building a beehive inside a plaster mould so that honeybees unwittingly create a vase over ten days. In Miami, Libertíny made a continuous bead of welding that resulted in a 3¼-foot-wide mushroom-like shape he called *Weldgrown*. By using a foot pedal to control a motorized rotating positioning table and an arc welder, he put the tools of a fabrication shop to an unprecedented level of purposelessness: there were no pieces of steel to connect, only a weld that was slowly built up. Mounting the positioning table in a vertical orientation, Libertíny stood still, layering weld upon weld. He slowly built a cylindrical form, as if working molten metal on the potter's wheel. He did this while on display, wearing goggles and a leather coat to protect him from the sparks – the latter an advertisement for his sponsor, Fendi. The hybrid act combined and transformed two historic craft methods, welding and throwing pottery, utterly repurposing these types of tooling into a virtuosic and impractical performance. *Weldgrown* flares and gently swells, a void but not an actual container. The graceful curve of the weld line relies on a modicum of manual dexterity. Beforehand, Libertíny presumably synchronized the speed of the turntable's revolution and the arc welder's spool of wire, two variables that determine the rate of accumulation as well as the texture of the weld, making it resemble a dry bead more than a wet puddle.

In the hands of Libertíny, craft becomes theatre and welding fair game for anyone to use. If *Star Wars* shows a simian Chewbacca welding – a fusion of the primitive and the technological – Libertíny imbues welding with equal romanticism. They tap into machismo and the glamour of sparks flying from an anvil. Instead of design as a prototype, Libertíny makes what academics call *provotypes*: material provocations that

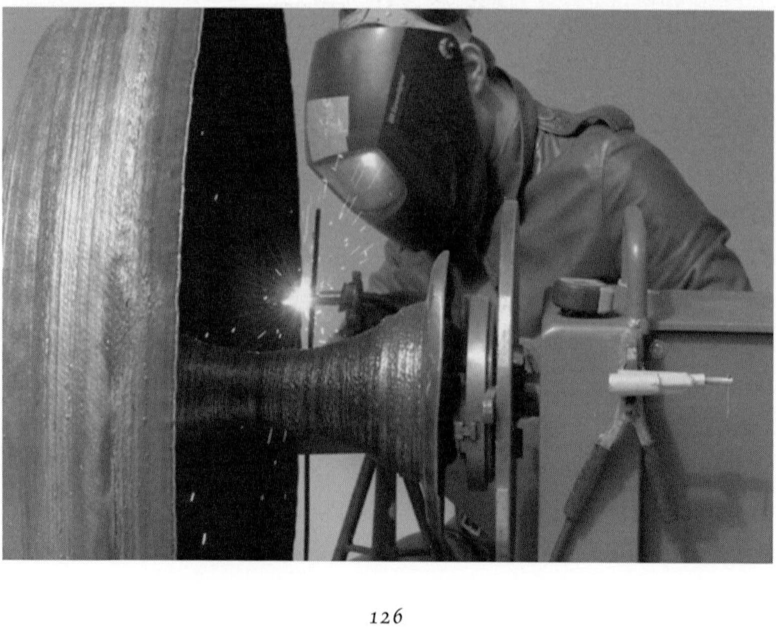

Tomáš Libertíny, *Weldgrown*, 2009, stainless steel. The spectacle of the heroic craftsman has emerged episodically and for the fair Design Miami/Basel, with sponsorship by the fashion brand Fendi, Libertíny recalled the welder, an artisan specific to the twentieth century.

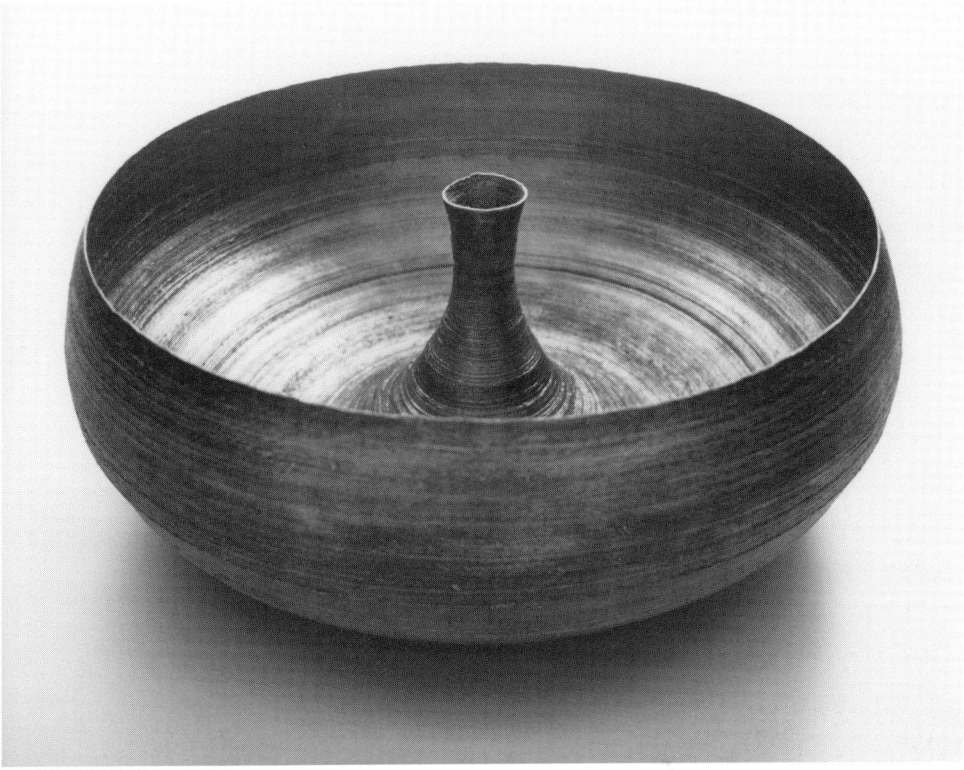

Tomáš Libertíny, *Weldgrown*, 2009, stainless steel. The *Weldgrown* forms, like Paley's work, stand as autonomous artefacts, but with a self-awareness that they are records of a performance.

intellectually challenge the system of mass production. To christen the arc-welded object with an organic title directly addresses our psychological anxiety to distinguish the natures of vegetal fibres and steel. Libertíny is evidence that welding will keep cycling through artistic identities, becoming creative or predictable in alternative contexts. The material and technique are prone to appropriation and have no fixed meaning. If welding and steel can assume the identity of a dainty artisanal delicacy or the flavour of crude punk rebellion, can basketry do the same? Or is plant matter too organic, a liability that prevents such free-ranging association?

WARPING WILLOW AND RAISING CANE

Becoming a generic action has not been good for weaving; the verb has become imprecise. How can we use the same word for coarse rope braiding and yardage of cane mesh? A century ago, the Aleutian ryegrass baskets (that seduced Ed Rossbach, among others) were twined tightly, eight hundred superfine stitches per square inch. Examples of these and of watertight drinking cups made with vegetal fibre linger in museums as lost knowledge, literally tantalizing living craftspeople – out of reach of even the most seasoned expertise. Such inventive and virtuosic realignment of vegetal fibre was a universal precondition for civilization, but our collective degeneration in basketry is real and measurable. Increasing first-hand appreciation is a necessary preliminary step to averting total alienation from our past and our plant life – and yet there are almost no places where such great basketry can be touched and only a few instances when baskets are celebrated as mechanical or artistic genius.

Contortionist shrubbery that lived modestly on the forest floor and now inhabits the domestic jungle of the closets, bathrooms and cupboards of our world, baskets are worth reviewing as commonplace pieces of complexity. A taut bamboo or wicker basket occasionally used to catch breadcrumbs or soiled laundry is nothing less than a wonder of physical geometry and basic engineering principles. Once upon a time, such a utensil was a prized possession. Imagine giving thanks to the methods of twining and coiling and binding reeds, vines, wood fibres and palm fronds as you clutched a basket and fishing net, wore clothes made of those materials and slept on a woven mat inside a thatched reed house. Basketwork preserves seeds, catches fish, gives shade and swaddles babies – a myriad tasks. Twining and tying together vegetal fibres enabled the birth of agriculture and fishing, laying the basis for the advent of Culture.

Rudimentary botanical strings once bound all aspects of human lives, and woven fibres can still be awe-inspiring in their intricacy. They can assume any form and combine to assume the incredible strength we now think of in relation to metalwork – basketry has been a means of making armour or even vessels in which to boil soup. A simple twisted repeat can add up to seating that supports the weight of an adult human body. Hammocks astonished the Spanish exploring the Western hemisphere. Rattan bridges still span rivers in remote interior valleys in Indonesia, more practical than steel to cope with annual flooding. In the Netherlands, dykes are still being made out of bundled willow: the centuries-old large-scale manipulation of the environment has found no modern replacement better than traditional fascine mattresses of bound twigs. Systematic use of willow remains central to the preservation of Holland's land. And if there is any singular artefact that can elegantly articulate a symbiosis between a healthy society and planet, it is a willow branch that might steady the weather wilding of storms and surging oceans.

If a fascine mattress seems more daunting because of its scale than intricate joinery, then try to think through multiple fibres on multiple axial planes in one small utility basket used anywhere in the world in 1800. To trace the patterns mentally is more difficult than to emulate Paul Klee's line taking a walk on a blank sheet of machine-rolled flat paper. To circumnavigate a well-made basket slows one's hands and eyes. Over time, baskets reveal all their complexity – their skin and skeleton are one and the same. Following thin splints across a basket is less like fingering a river on a map than it is like tracing an imaginary stream that bobs above ground and below, rolling in and out of sight. The most ingenuous of artefacts, baskets reveal their construction, hiding little to no information about how they were made. While many craft materials are celebrated as natural, and many are likened to the human body – a swelling pot being akin to a belly, a chair standing on legs – the bones and muscles of baskets are tangible, on the surface. If trees resemble sleeping giants, baskets are exposed nerve tissue, alert and responsive. Moreover, baskets have circulation: they respire. And an immense feasting bowl 3 feet wide has the intimacy of a robin's nest because one touches intention and human agency in each stitch. With all these vibrant characteristics, it is worth asking at what point a basket's natural material might wane in importance and a mechanical or industrial character become more prominent. This question hinges on whether we see basketry as a prehistoric remnant or as the origin of human industrial art.

At the end of the nineteenth century a basket craze, a self-diagnosed 'canastromania', seized on the preservation of baskets as an indigenous industrial art worthy of preservation and re-enactment – mainly by women. Experts discerned two types of baskets: the sort that reflected continuity with ancient traditions and modern degenerate ones. As Marvin Cohodas and other scholars have shown, there was a peculiar racialized way in which the 'primitive, aboriginal woman' was seen as a source of good basketry, but modern aniline dyes were considered ruinous to Native American traditions. George Wharton James, a leading connoisseur who promoted this pseudo-scientific view, considered basketry decorated with European imagery or shaped in forms to emulate imported metalwork or ceramics to be 'spoiled by vicious imitation'. 'It would be a calamity to Indians and whites alike if the industrial art of basket making were allowed to die out,' lamented James's *How To Make Indian and Other Baskets* (1904), urging Anglos to make Indian baskets, too. Among the Pocumtuck Basket Society of Deerfield, Massachusetts, and in leafy utopian summer arcadias such as Chautauqua, New York, affluent Anglo-American women gathered to make and admire their own baskets. James told the story of one woman challenging the degree of authenticity of another, who defended her basketry as 'Indian' on the grounds that 'I made it myself.' Making one's own basket was equated with cutting through the bureaucracy of civilization – James applauded the pride such amateur Anglos took in craft. This DIY spirit remains one of the attractions of all handicraft today. Basketry especially appeals as a retrieval of prehistoric culture – most 're-enact' historical models; few workshops aim to create new fusions suited for modern applications or made with industrial materials. Telephone wire baskets are made in 'developing economies' more often than elsewhere. Contemporary eyes see 'playing Indian' as culturally insensitive but, in keeping with the nineteenth century, many still see the art of basketry as apt for women. In reality, basketry is as neutered as a grid and was not historically gendered in many cultures – especially if one thinks about the immense range of things made.

Basketry is a type of textile and can be analysed as a structure with a warp and weft. The fundamental techniques of basket construction are coiling, twining and plaiting, each of which describe an orientation for the structural undergirding that is stationary, which we call the warp. The weft rotates in and out of it. If a warp of willow osiers is running vertically, then the basket-maker might twine the weft fibres around these rods and finish by tidying the uneven edges of the warp in a binding. In coiling basketry, as in coiled pottery, the structural rods spiral horizontally and each successive band is gradually sewn on to the previous one. A warp running horizontally might be comprised of many discontinuous but overlapping pieces, carefully integrated to maintain an even tension and thickness.

Words like 'bench,' 'bowl' and 'belt' assert the function of support, but the utility of a 'basket' is painfully unclear. The now discredited adage that 'form follows function' is especially ridiculous in relation to basketry, as culture and commerce – subjective human whim and inflexible ecological constraints – dictate its forms. Basketry baffles intellectual frameworks and defies cultural categories: A woven mat might lie on the ground, turn into a roof and then serve as a throne. Humans once designed fish traps to suit specific stream currents and the size of distinct prey. Such baskets reveal the depths of human communion with the environment, documenting knowledge that took hundreds of years to accumulate – and only a decade to lose.

Might a tree dictate the form of a basket to its maker? Perhaps. Some call the thin strips of material the 'weavers', as if to add confusion as to who is the maker and wherein agency lies. Is it the tree or the grain of a specific tree? And if humans split the wood and select the grain, a standardized character of any species is difficult to identify. Working in oak, one hews and then froes a quartered sapling or tree into billets a finger thick. Learning a tree's character and useful components in the course of harvesting it, the weaver determines which interior pith to discard and what type of basket it might be possible to make. Ash separates into billets a particular way, by being mauled with another log. Honeysuckle is simmered in a pot and then skinned. A specific harvest schedule varies with each of these plants, as does the proper humidity and drying time. The width and suppleness of each splint dictates the gradient of the curved walls and the acuteness of a radial turn. Moving from a square base to a round shoulder, or vice versa, demands limber timber. One begins to search for words that physically match the complex geometry more than the bland term 'weave' ever might. Musical words such as 'imbricated' and 'catenary' offer panache, yet the complexity of a pattern rotating in space tests our spatial imagination and verbal agility. Mapping a basket requires keeping many lines in one's head. How abstract the basket seems, and how exhausting it is to conceptually delineate the complex intersections of material and time! Yet we usually categorize basketry as a hobby more often than a conceptual exercise. So ask yourself: exactly how conceptual might a basket get, how far might it stretch your brain?

Baskets are spiritual and soulful graph paper. Before an axonometric drawing, a mimetic representation of three-dimensional space, came the warp and weft. Can we visualize a world of houses and containers without right angles and corners – a curvilinear spatiality that for us to experience would be stranger than any existing science fiction fantasy? Maybe only basket-makers can do that. Baskets have always been conceptual pathways through space, place and time, marking birth, death and regrowth both literally and metaphorically.

Basketry is pure technology, pure engineering. What did technology originally mean? The invention of rope and knots of masticated fibre lashed together the earliest societies, providing both subsistence and dwellings. The adaptation of either an S-twist or a Z-twist – the direction of these fibres – remains a regional mystery. To follow Elizabeth Wayland Barber's scholarship, string can be thought of as a device that 'conquers the earth' by surveying it as well as harnessing clothing to our backs and lashing together communities. In preliterate societies, complex geometries were known by hand and stored in the head, and transmitted tangibly in song or oral lesson. No basket-makers ever made preparatory drawings or blueprints until the twentieth century. The forethought of gathering and preparing raw materials in advance of the actual weaving is both abstract and predetermined.

'A conceptual form of art . . . means that all of the planning and decisions are made beforehand,' wrote Sol LeWitt, describing his own artistry but perhaps also basketry. The decision of which fibre to harvest is made only after a basket is imagined. Ornamental patterns, the tightness of the stitch and the scale and weave: each aspect is predetermined when the material is prepared, before the actual weaving begins. 'This kind of art is not theoretical or illustrative of theories; it is intuitive, it is involved with all types of mental processes and it is purposeless,' wrote LeWitt, delineating a provocative portal between conceptual art and craft. In fact, standing inside a room of LeWitt's graphite wall drawings might be the closest non-weavers come to immersing themselves

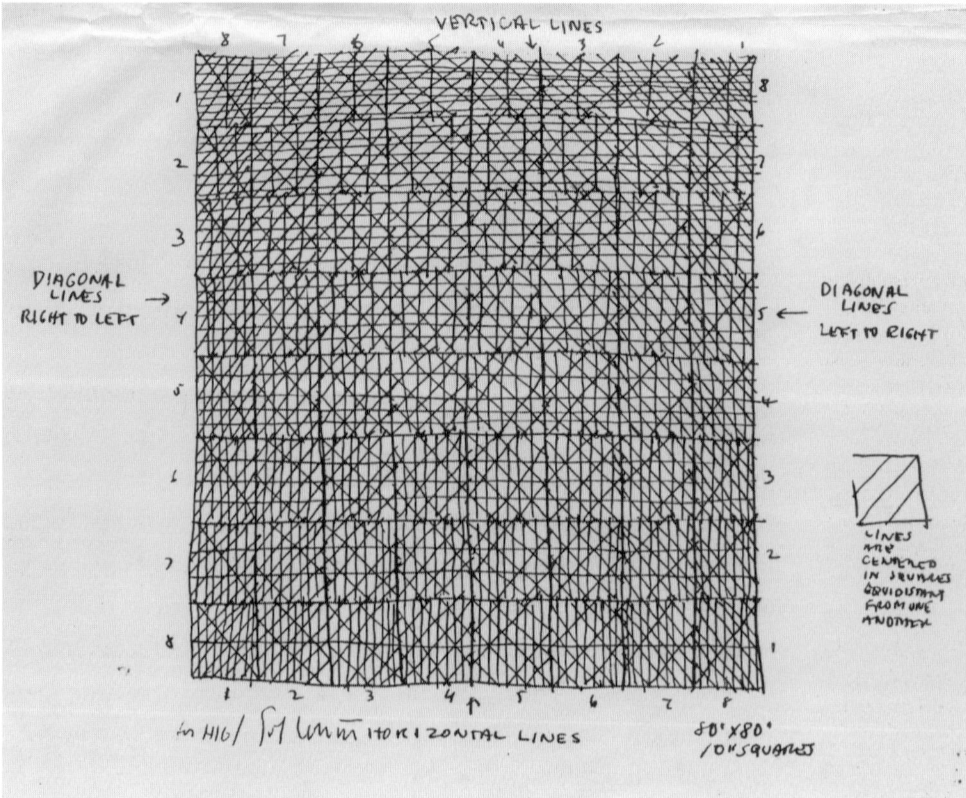

in the linear gestures of a basket. His demarcation of 'all combinations of two lines crossing, placed at random, using arcs from corners and sides, straight, not straight and broken lines', simultaneously fractures and integrates orthogonal white cube galleries. The white latex paint or bleached paper buried under LeWitt's lines resembles rays of sunlight; his basketry is predicated on such whiteness. More recent contemporary immersive environmental basketry includes Janet Echelman's aerial webs and Patrick Dougherty's swirling thickets, but neither of these implicate viewers in spatial decision-making to the degree of a LeWitt line drawing. The success of these drawings is to learn a specific room and to

Sol LeWitt, instructions for a wall drawing, undated. The immersive wall drawings of LeWitt, with 'all of the planning and decisions . . . made beforehand', remove gesture and illustration but not intuition from the act of creation. Like a basket-maker who has gathered and prepared willow, sedge root, bulrush root, black quail topknots and red woodpecker crest feathers in advance of the actual weaving, LeWitt committed to a line pattern and specific wall size and scale. Unlike LeWitt, the basket-maker's form was never committed to paper but was purely in mind and hand.

actually feel the measurements of spatial increments in a manner that is closer to music (and basketry). But it is much easier to make a LeWitt drawing with a pencil than it is to coax cane or willow into an arc: the girth and softness of the graphite is predetermined and routine, flat sheetrock walls are passive.

George Kubler declares that all tools and art can be categorized as planes, solids or envelopes in *The Shape of Time*. However, basketry might be the one genre that can be all three at once. What is a woven sieve used to refine cornmeal or separate hulls from seeds? It is a vessel, yet functions as a porous plane and yet is perforated. It hovers between an open and a closed structure. Basketry slides between opaque and translucent envelopes, transparent solids and invisible planes.

Kubler's desire to make connections in South America across indigenous and Spanish cultures called for more inclusive and fundamental descriptions of art. He realized many ancient artistic methods were incongruous with the shibboleths of modernism. Modern architects praised three formal concerns: revealed construction, modularity and transparency, but failed to appreciate the behavioural qualities that made baskets meet this criteria with greater poise than their concrete and steel buildings. Basketry fulfils these readily in most instances. Great basketry realizes the modernist ideal of creating both construction and ornament simultaneously, so that pattern is intrinsic. The ornamental patterns on most baskets differ from those on vessels made out of metal, glass or ceramic, where applied decoration is usually a second finishing step after the creation of form. Although basketry exhibits the prized qualities of modularity and transparency, too, there is no existing defence of the medium on these formal grounds.

The idea of the 'honest' or 'authentic' basket is one made of locally sourced vegetal fibres. Authenticity is, moreover, expected to connect to traditional tribal lifeways. A modern work of art is considered honest when a painting keeps the colours flat and non-representational or a sculpture does not falsify materials but reveals its composition: steel resembles steel, wood resembles wood. This concept of propriety and authenticity takes a strange turn in basketry, as most culturally hybrid baskets are considered degraded traditions. For instance, a coiled seagrass basket by Mary Jane Manigault (1913–2010) evokes the low horizon of the Piedmont landscape near the Carolina coast. The bundles sewn together by a thread-like palmetto relate to the tools of rice cultivation. Manigault and many others see their handiwork – 'Gullah baskets' – as homage to the past, a manifestation of their cultural identification with African American history, and also as a means of getting by in a tourist-driven economy. Baskets are windows into alternative cultures, other places, a phenomenon that drives some collectors to call for purity and some weavers to test out traditions other than their own.

Traditions of basketry have been remarkably discontinuous and illustrate dislocation and adaptation more often than cultural stability. The Nantucket lightship basket is another example of a cultural hybrid: a combination of Indonesian rattan and North American hardwoods, it arose as a product of whale-hunting global mariners. In the twentieth century, one of its foremost exponents was José Formosa Reyes (1902–1980), who became a Nantucket resident after serving in the Second World War and then studying education at Harvard. Reyes was born in the Philippines but attended high school in Portland, Oregon, and then Reed College. He embodies all the complexities of our itinerant populations and dislocated shrubs – and the way handicraft strategically copes with relocation and reinvention, both of the self and of ancient traditions. Reyes improved upon a tradition developed in the nineteenth century.

Chicago-born Ed Rossbach was far away from his roots when he discovered basketry while serving in the military, stationed on a forlorn Aleutian Island, but by appropriating images of Mickey Mouse and John

Travolta at the same time as he drew on indigenous cultures, he hoped to weave at the pace of his own time and culture. Rossbach appreciated the dilemma of categorizing basketry:

> At first the division of baskets into permanent and temporary appears reasonable. Then the distinction seems less clear but still a relief from the usual classification of baskets according to technique. Finally the categories seem not only invalid but deceptive and downright mischievous.

To qualify any basket as existing on a spectrum between the innovative or traditional, the useless or functional, the authentic or hybrid, the honest or false, is to make mischief indeed.

A work of mid-twentieth-century splint ash basketry in the form of a teacup and saucer is the type of hybrid indigenous craft that rarely is given critical attention. It is simultaneously dainty and quietly subversive: is it exotic or is it kitsch? It is confusing, as the cup would not hold liquid. The ash is more slender than an apple seed and yet more slippery and silken. Plaited in a one-over-and-one-under pattern, the rims are hemmed with sea grass. A Passamaquoddy weaver bent indigenous materials into one of the most regal emblems of European etiquette.

Native Americans began to mime the teacup form during the long nineteenth century and decades of imperialism and colonialism, so this is an intelligent and knowing bit of basketry. However saccharine it seems at first glance, a sense of irony bubbles up the longer one looks and thinks. Were the first of these basket-teacups trying to please whites, or was the skeuomorphic form a deliberate skewering of Western convention? This ash teacup is more closely related to postmodern-conceptual muscular contractions than to ancient tradition. It is not mere colonial degradation or a commercialization of splint production.

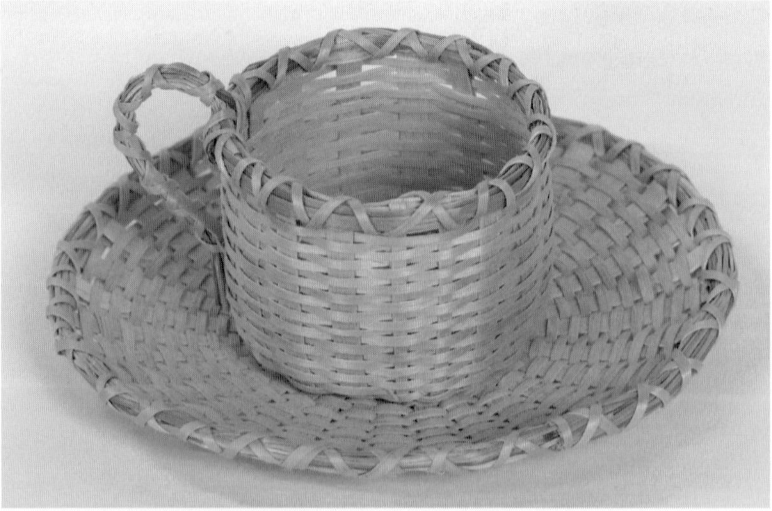

Woven cup and saucer, attributed to the Neptune family, *c.* 1950, black ash and sea grass. This deft basketry takes cultural appropriation on a quietly subversive joy ride, reversing expectations about function and cultural authenticity. While most current members of the Neptune family and other Passamaquoddy who weave customarily sign their work, this dates to a time when even the most prominent, such as Clara Neptune Keezer, did not, and their work sold roadside in shops or at county fairs.

Deciding whether to call a black ash splint basket indigenous craft or to refuse it such a label is to engage in debates that are both academic and extremely politicized. Some claim the arrival of European steel tools spurred the technique of basket-making, but the archaeological evidence is inconclusive. Coastal Maine Micmac made bark canoes and presumably wove birch long before they had access to European knife blades, but to what extent did steel blades refine their techniques? To travel back in time, obsidian blades cut ash laboriously, but all extant baskets were made using metal blades. It is impossible to attribute the origins of ash splint technology. Immigrants from Sweden and other European regions also had an impact on Native American Indian production, yet charting these influences is difficult. North American ash splits in a manner totally unlike the European species, and colonial intruders noted the indigenous technique of mauling black ash into splints as an exciting novelty, and later assimilated the indigenous technique. The fusion and hybridization of methods and styles throws into doubt the categories we usually rely on to sort out handicraft: authenticity, cultural identity and technical purity.

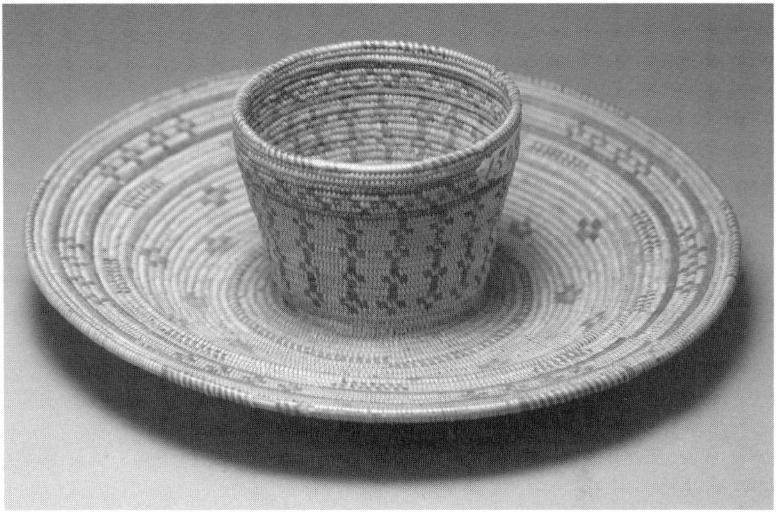

Probably Chumash artistry, plant fibre basket in shape of teacup and saucer, California, before 1821, juncus (rush) with dye, most likely martynia (devil's horns/ cat's claw). It is a mystery whether the first of these basket-teacups was made to please white tourists or if the mimesis was a deliberate skewering of the convention of tea drinking or the daintiness of imported porcelain.

The nature of ash and the complexities and contradictions of human nature run together in the little teacup.

The earliest known Native American mimesis of a teacup and saucer dates back two hundred years, to when Captain Thomas Meek of Marblehead, Massachusetts, acquired one from the Chumash in California and deposited it as a wondrous artefact with the East India Marine Society, now the Peabody Essex Museum. The pattern and the absence of a handle on the cup is thought to be the result of a Chumash artist copying porcelain imported from Japan or China. The Chumash artist wove the teacup and saucer as one object, suggesting that the maker never had the opportunity to lift the cup off the saucer. Did Meek procure it as a bit of virtuoso basketry, or as exotic, or as artistic because it aped a Western tea setting? Equally vexing is the question of whether the Chumash artist made the object to please a patron or market, or to fulfil their own sense of whimsy. Captain Meek donated other examples of virtuosic artifice that do reveal a larger social network of appreciation for basketry. He acquired a Tlingit cup that had already travelled from the northwest coast to Hawaii. The Tlingit cup was admired for being watertight, a skill that baffled many a European visitor to the Pacific coast – and a quality that made the Hawaiian owner, a member of his own people's aristocracy, also value the basket as a treasure. Despite all that we may presume about Meek, a Massachusetts sailor procuring curiosities, he was free of the phobias of inauthenticity and cultural hybridity when it came to craft. Perhaps, like Melville's Ishmael who grew accustomed to Queequeg, Meek was even free to question the validity of so-called civilized etiquette.

I bought an ash demitasse on a reservation outside Eastport, Maine, where it was labelled as the work of the venerable Passamaquoddy weaver Clara Keezer (1930–2016). She made at least eight or ten other teacups that also cannot hold liquid and seem to laugh at the very idea of formality in taking tea or coffee. Where might such a splint teacup sit two centuries from now? Is it to be interpreted as a homage to Western manners and the protocol of taking tea? Passamaquoddies still have good reason to doubt the good intentions of such equipage; they sit on a small bounded reservation with ocean access privatized and many local resources stripped from their use. In California, hundred-year-old Pomo baskets of sedge fibre, dyed bulrush, willow, clamshell beads, black quail topknots, red woodpecker crest feathers and vegetal cordage are encyclopaedic relics of a long-gone environment, codices of endangered natural resources. In one hundred years, depending on how the ash tree fares against the devastation being wrought by the invasive emerald ash bore, there is a chance that a Passamaquoddy teacup will only seem like a frightening testimonial to the Anthropocene. Keezer was certainly confident, weaving dozens if not hundreds of such ash splint teacup and saucer ensembles over the decades and blessing each subsequent generation that perpetuated the craft and even a form that she had, in a manner of speaking, made 'hers'. Keezer's outlook on craftsmanship as a cultural commons seems particularly enlightened and generous – unlike the long-standing Western museological habit of qualifying and quantifying authenticity in Native art.

Both plants and cultural constraints do not stay still but become airborne and change. Perhaps basketry is like pokeweed seed, which needs the scarification of a trip through the intestine of a bird to germinate and even then can lie dormant in soil for fifty years before maturing. Might the twenty-first century see basketry flourish now that modernists have buried it for a century? Surely baskets lead one to jest if Western civilization has yet to act civilized: the woven teacup articulates the fragility of both ecology and humanity at once.

Julia Parker (b. 1929) is another modern Native American basketmaker who is most often regarded through the lens of race and ethnicity. She is rarely simply seen as an artist. She performed as a Native American Indian on salary, working in Yosemite National Park for most of her adult life under the auspices of the United States Parks Department as a living specimen that represented the past. Deborah Valoma has written on the emotional depth of Parker's journey and the long way she travelled as an orphan to strenuously reclaim her cultural heritage after an education focused on assimilation. She turned basketry into performance and also a purpose in life. Born in Marin County, California, she married into her husband's Paiute culture and then slowly began to absorb the traditions of Mono Lake, on the eastern side of the Sierras. Her husband's grandmother, Lucy Telles, one of the most prominent Native American basketmakers of the first half of the twentieth century, lived in Yosemite and took Parker on as an apprentice. Telles's supersized baskets extended the Yosemite Miwok tradition and won prizes, notably at the A Century of Progress International Exposition, commonly called the 1933 Chicago World's Fair. To consider Telles's work in relation to that exhibition's (smug) title makes sense in that she was a pioneer and innovator, as self-aware as any artist of the twentieth century. Like Nampeyo, discussed in Chapter

One, Telles was a virtuoso who recuperated a range of basketry methods from multiple cultural groups, including Yosemite Miwok and Mono Paiute. Julia Parker continues the self-conscious process of integrating disparate and fragmented bodies of practical knowledge, from coastal Pomo as well as Telles. If Telles attempted to surpass the scale of traditional forms and add high finish, Parker works more quickly, with more of an aim to touch upon metaphorical and historical functions.

Parker speaks eloquently of the satisfaction she derives from making baskets, even though she knows that the forms, such as a winnowing basket for sifting acorn nuts from shells or a fish trap, are obsolete tools from lifeways that she never even experienced herself. Just as Parker has an awareness of having been on a stage 'playing Indian' and wearing costume to please audience expectations that she resemble a stereotypical Plains Native American, her work recreates historical models. Parker has also worked to conserve the area's traditions and maintained her sense of humour as visitors from around the world question her biological heritage. Her basketry has an immense range, of which she is justly proud:

> I am probably one of the only Native American weavers in California that knows all the different kinds of styling, stitching design, fiber, and all that. There are women that weave, but they stay with one tribe. I have broadened out. I worked with the traditional women in the Yosemite Valley and on the Mono Lake side, as well as with traditional women throughout California ... Washoes, Shoshones, Karuks, Yuroks, Yosemite Miwoks, Paiute, and my own people, the Kahaya Pomo. So I am always thinking about these things. I am thinking about how they would have put that basket together, and I am trying to preserve it.

Parker outlines the slow steps by which she learned to listen to willow, then redbud, sedge root, soaproot and bracken fern root, as well as a willingness to run against classical models and use string and beads as she wishes. She has two redbud bushes that she visits on alternate years, and stresses her slow learning curve. More than any other type of basket, she enjoys making windowpane-twined willow storage baskets, a loose-knit, seemingly utilitarian open weave that is, in her own words, 'real crude'. 'They are quick baskets. They are throwaway baskets,' she states, expressing joy that she is defying assumptions that her work should have a high finish and somewhat impishly thumbing her nose at connoisseurship. In most of these 'throwaway baskets', the willow is not scraped and the brown basket is intentionally less refined. Parker's 'crude' baskets are curiously contemporary in that she invokes utility but is more concerned with transmitting the metaphor and memory of basketry.

MATERIAL MUTATION AND RE-ASSOCIATION

Only physical work reveals the limits at which craft is susceptible to re-invention as industry, exotic species and also as a gendered activity. If William Morris declared his distaste for modern bridges by claiming that 'There never will be an architecture in iron,' today it is hard to find anyone who fails to find beauty in grand rail bridges created before 1940. A muscular and meaty iron and steel lattice that traverses a ravine or waterway looks admirable for its rugged endurance and as a metaphor for bridging chasms of seemingly insurmountable social and cultural differences. Rivets the size of babies' heads defy our ability to imaginatively recreate the labour or construction. When an ordinary manufacturing skill becomes obsolete, it begins to resemble craft. Would Morris also have grown to admire them had he lived long enough, or did he find the rows of pollarded willow trees along the Thames in nineteenth-century

England ugly, too? The art historian Michael Baxandall argued that bridge building articulates an inexplicable sense of subjective discovery, a genius that is not in any one brain and only accomplished by hundreds of hands. Bridges are psychological breakthroughs as they make us reimagine our landscape, defining an interval as a crossing, land as a bank, as the provocative architect Christian Norberg-Schulz noted. Determining the nature of resources is a human and emotional process – no material character is innate or true, and there is no clear distinction between when manufacture seems industrial or quaint.

Craft is a deeply subjective and highly charged term, and our range of answers will always be specific and rooted in our cultural associations with particular materials and tooling as well as the zeitgeist. People will continue to wrangle over these discrepancies, with some materials and environments appearing less natural and others more human because they are cultivated – with generational taste flip-flopping in response. Surely we all can agree that an awareness of materials and discernment of the differences – steel from iron, willow from cane – is a preliminary precondition for defining craft in any nuanced manner.

Today, finally, in contemporary art schools, there are growing numbers of women welding and blacksmithing – though only very recently: proof that institutions and fields can change. (Today, equipping sculpture studios with sewing machines is also a recent development, so perhaps willow and ryegrass will soon creep into greater visibility too.) But in industry, skilled

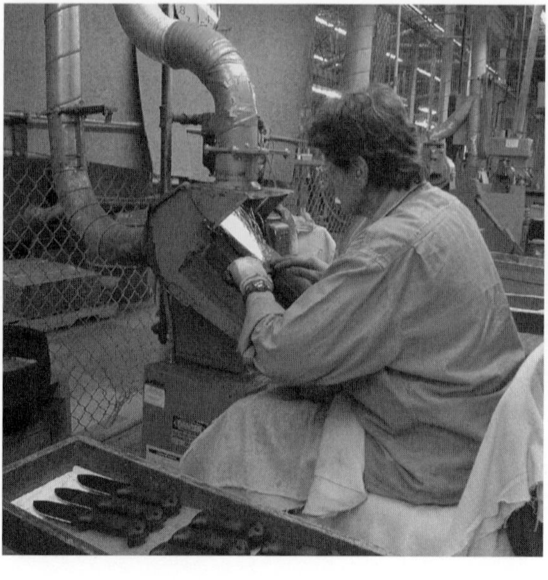

Connie Chapus honing a knife blade at CUTCO Corporation, Olean, New York, 2010. A visit to this cutlery factory proves some are more precisely *manu*factories – the skilled hand, *manus*, is still needed right beside robotic production – and Chapus upends many gender assumptions about who 'mans' a grinding wheel.

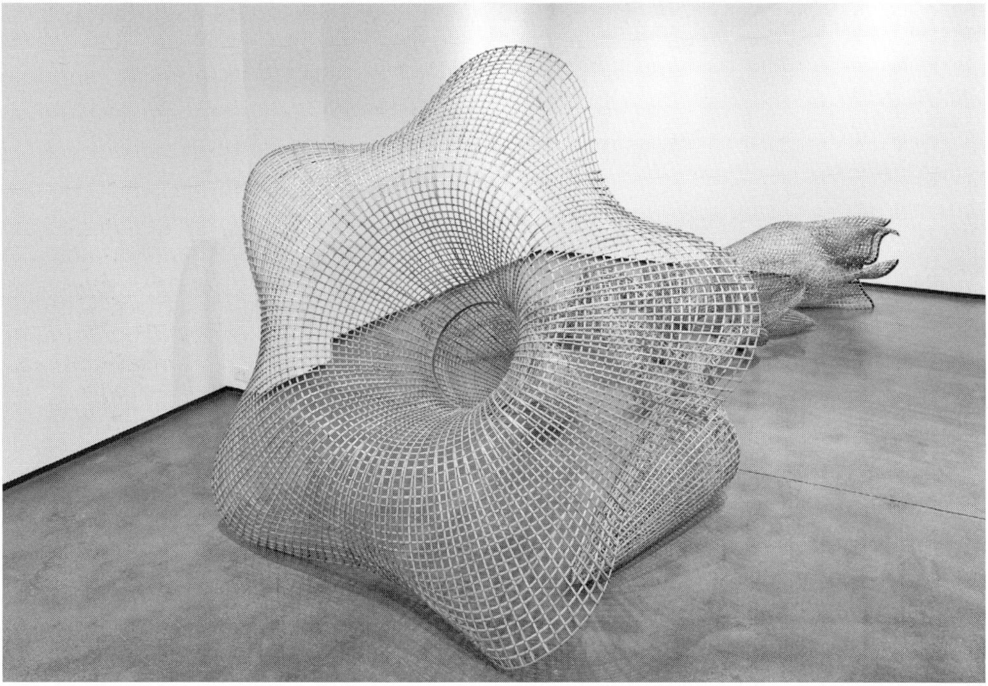

Sopheap Pich, *Morning Glory*, 2011, rattan, bamboo, wire, plywood and steel. The rise of a global artist such as Pich, who has shifted from his training in the fine art material of oil on canvas, gives rattan a new level of visibility that one can only hope extends to a re-evaluation of the status of other basketry in our cultural institutions and homes.

women work with metal. A day's visit to a cutlery factory proved to me that some are more precisely *manu*factories – the skilled hand, *manus*, is still needed right beside robotic production – and Connie Chapus, sharpening Ka-Bar daggers at CUTCO, in Olean, New York, upended many gender assumptions about who 'mans' a grinding wheel. For several students who accompanied me, establishing eye contact with Connie and others in the manufactory proved that craftspeople existed, and our conversation shifted to thinking about sustainability in human terms. To discover workers taking pride in industrial workmanship challenges our generalization that an assembly line exists only as an alienating phenomenon.

Becoming more mindful of Connie the knife-grinder, perhaps we can consciously alter the ways basketry is characterized as gendered, exotic or a specific rudimentary stage of technology. We must cease to narrate

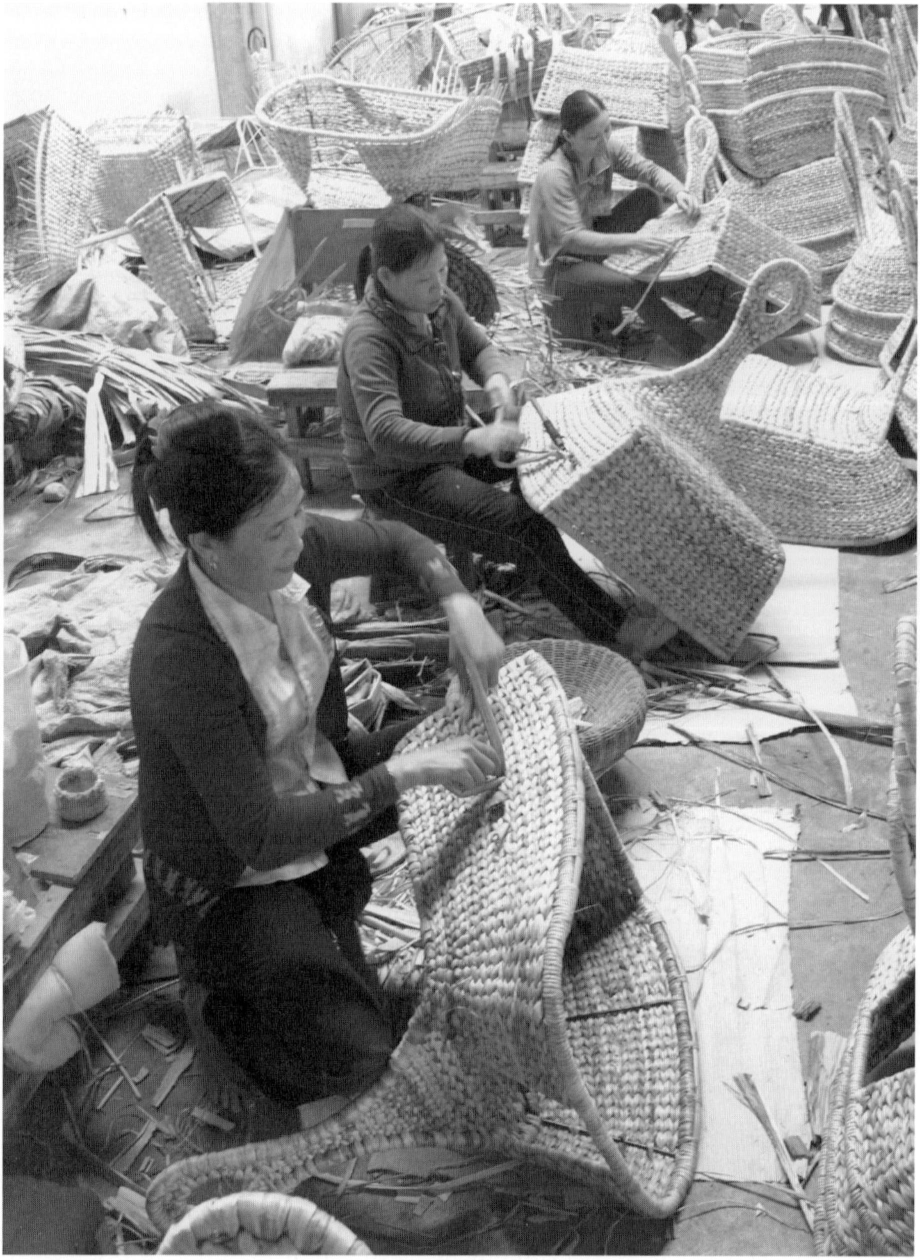

Weavers, Vietnam, 2014. A significant amount of training and skill goes into weaving IKEA's Gullholmen chair, handicraft as advertised, available at a remarkably affordable price (U.S.$69.95 or €59 in 2016). If the chair is the latest instalment in a long history of Southeast Asia providing the West with rattan and bamboo furniture, Vinka's design is peculiarly of our time as the seating is stackable and scaled to maximize the use of the interior dimensions of a standardized shipping container.

civilization's historical progress in terms of metallurgical innovation and move out of silos if we hope to experiment as nimbly as Marcel Breuer and Gunta Stölzl. To get in touch with what might next become craft, we must self-consciously upend the existing hierarchy of materials and privilege sinuous vegetal fibres and supple grasses.

The recent ascent of the young artist Sopheap Pich (b. 1971) is a telling final story about the intersection of basketry with art, wherein both gender and craft play out in more predictable ways: this story is a warning. Pich studied oil painting at the University of Massachusetts and the School of the Art Institute of Chicago before returning to Cambodia, his place of birth, to find his métier. He began to exploit bamboo and rattan – what he calls the 'basic rural materials of agriculture'. His elegant sculptural version of a fish trap, *Upstream* (2005), is a literal enlargement of an existing tool, only increased to five times its original size. Being 10 feet long, humans become the prey, unable to imagine a utility. The conical lattice structure of bamboo, rattan, metal wire and copper tapers inward as it rises vigorously, with three smaller woven structures descending inside, almost like droplets cascading inside a bottle, sequential in size. If the overall conical form stands upright and taut, the three interior forms suggestively articulate the tug of gravity. The task of funnelling fish into bottlenecked traps is an ancient device; Pich's sculpture lures humans alongside without actually letting us in. While most viewers are probably unfamiliar with the design of the trap, it was near universal across the continents in the era before plastic. And yet, today, the form has little to no recognition; both the contemporary bamboo and rattan workmanship and the antique tool are read as exotic. Pich's version only came into existence in our contemporary moment, as global contemporary art.

Critics revel in the rustic associations of Pich's adaptation of jungle fibres as 'traditional'; his materials associate him with the peasantry and vernacular construction methods of his birthplace. Much is made of bamboo these days, including bath towels, floorboards and coffee filters – all regaled as environmentally sound because of the speed with which the plants grow. However, a closer look at the production of rattan and bamboo is warranted. Pich's rattan is mostly cured in the conventional modern small-batch way, which is to immerse it in hot diesel oil. This prevents the rattan from drying out, increases its flexibility in the short term and kills insect infestations. That such a process results in a finished product that we regard as 'natural' exposes the problem with identifying meaning solely in materials and not the conditions of their production. The processing of materials becomes a lens through which we evaluate goods as craft or as industrial product – and the image of bathing rattan in hot diesel oil staunches our sense of communion with nature.

Pich might be a good artist, but it seems wrong to fall into contemporaneity and see him apart from the historical substrate of craft as well as the complexity of Western museums and fine art. Craft is the engine within these art works. But historical fish traps from wherever – Norway, Brazil, Vietnam and so on – have greater beauty, as they were driven by necessity and environmental empathy. The phenomenon of celebrating a metaphoric fish trap while being too ignorant to identify the function of an actual trap proves how fine art fosters alienation more often than it aims at lucid communication. Rattan can be a measuring device for broader swathes of real time, space and human sentience.

Lastly, Pich also reveals the painful way that craft is art's generative partner – almost its wife. These have a gendered power relation. We applaud the art as a singular achievement but fail to discern the more complex agency of craft. The basket-maker who is a man is more able to gain recognition as an artist. This is not Pich's fault but results from our own inability to look inside the manufactories where many women as well as men weave IKEA furniture and baskets and our lack of awareness that such skills can be lost more easily than gained. The status of basketry in our cultural institutions and homes reveals the ultimate hubris of not only what many call 'art' but what many deign to call 'civilization'. To truly examine a basket is to grapple with the ways that we gender cultural labour and police production. There is immense potential growth latent in a twined twiggy thing – artistic, functional and economic – and I hope we live to see futuristic basketry as a human endeavour, not simply as a metaphor for the digital network but as a reinvestigation and cultivation of human skill and plant lore. There are not enough forests and too little gas, coal and oil fuel for us to continue to consume at the pace of the last twenty years but, as John McQueen likes to tell his students, 'there are enough twigs for everyone.'

Twigs will endure, but skills expire when patronage lapses or war becomes a greater priority than culture. Who will document the weaver making the Gullholmen chair, or will such production remain the 99 per cent of craft that is overlooked, unrecorded and institutionally rendered invisible?

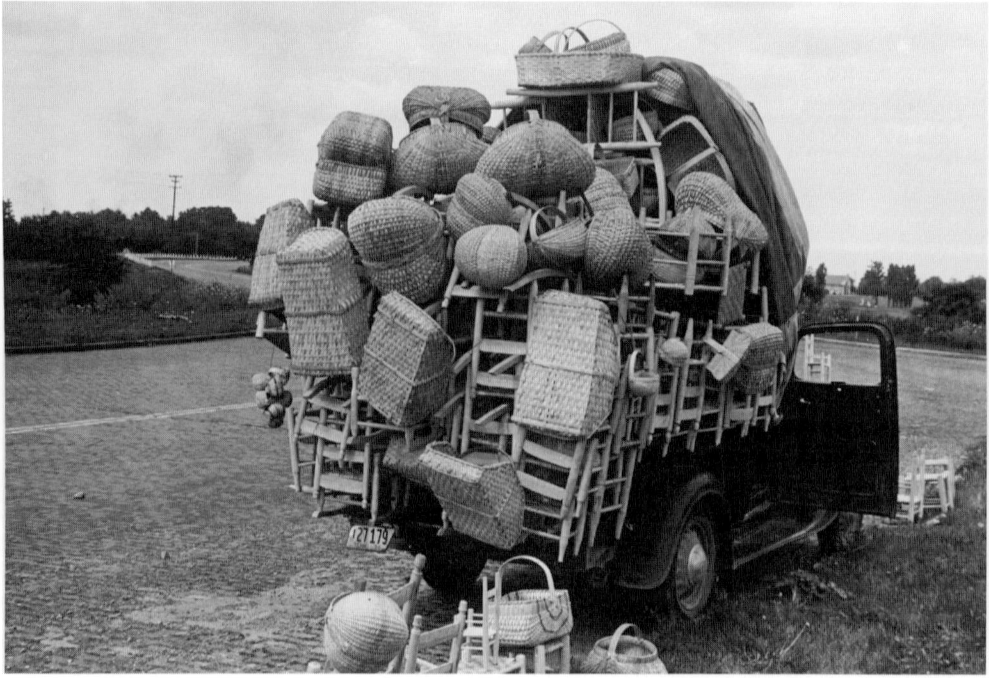

FOUR

WEAVING AS A MAGIC CARPET RIDE

To finger the enchantment of fabric, trace the pattern on a complex rug – a design with an archway or arabesque – and induce your mind to travel to that 'elsewhere'. Entrancing prayer carpets evoke portals to imaginary homelands, and such rhythmic refuges have been a reliable respite from everyday life for centuries. This meta-migratory capacity of textiles is especially potent because fibres are themselves global journeys. On the most elegant Brussels tapestries, patrons demanded Grenadian silk and specific colours that drew distant resources into immediate reach. Today, a rug might connect us to silkworms in China, a scarf to sheep in New Zealand, or denim to fields of cotton in India. Blankets and bedding give warmth and stability to our homes and yet are also the lightest and most portable of all possessions, the stuff that travels farthest from its origins. By feeling textures for their stories, the complexity of a weave becomes a hybrid map of both the real and fantastic. A twill, satin or plain weave is composed of patterns, and each geometry is a distinct landscape.

Ben Shahn, *Truck of Basket and Chair Peddler, Route 40, Central Ohio*, c. 1938. This roadside image captures the nomadic quality of basketry and weaving. How many hours of labour are in those goods and how far have they travelled from their places of origin? The marketplace, often blamed for the degradation of vernacular craft, is also a necessity for it to continue.

This commonplace phenomenon of orientation (layered with disorientation) begins with our clothes and extends to our bedspreads and tablecloths and flags. Cultural mapping lies latent in textiles, waiting to be discerned. Mosul, Calcutta and Damascus might seem like exotic destinations, but appear less so when we know these cities' names live nearby in

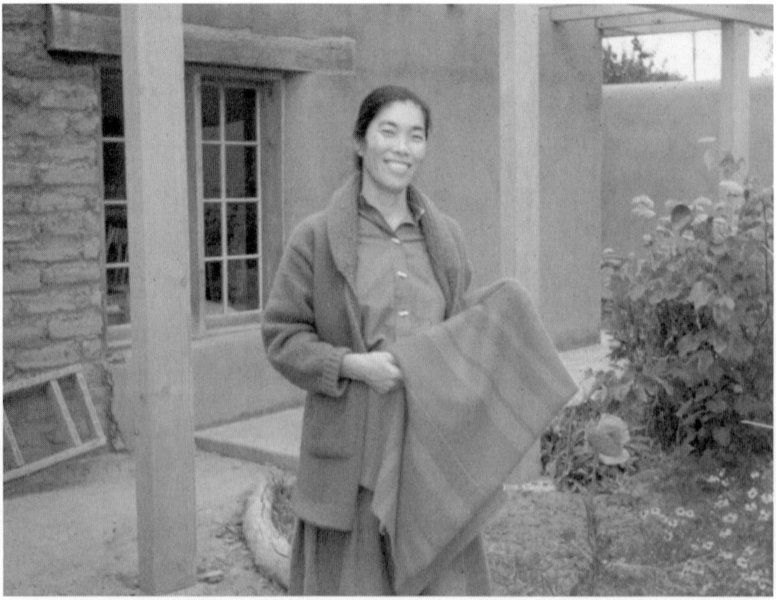

Alice Kagawa Parrott, 1968. Photographed in the garden of her adobe home in Santa Fe, far from her birthplace in Honolulu, Alice absorbed the regional traditions of the Southwest, self-consciously incorporating indigenous dye methods into her work as a weaver. Should we applaud her audacity to venture beyond national and cultural boundaries and traditions or see her self-invention as cultural appropriation?

our terms for domestic furnishings: muslin, calico and damask. Mapping a weave can become a magic carpet ride, literally and metaphorically.

When the weaver Alice Kagawa Parrott (1929–2009) moved to New Mexico in 1956, her leap across cultural boundaries was a quietly heroic act of self-invention. She began to buy coarse wool from local Navajo to spin her own yarns and to gather marigold blossoms and peach leaves to brew dyes – strategies that intentionally disconnected her work from modernization and helped her establish roots in an adopted home, far from her birthplace in Honolulu to Japanese-born parents. Her life fuses two narratives usually considered mutually exclusive: she was the classic stranger-who-came-to-town, moving into a centuries-old adobe house in Santa Fe, and yet she continually travelled to foreign cultures and embraced alternative traditions not her own.

Alice accomplished this odyssey of place-making and self-fashioning through weaving. She made and sold clothing and pillowcases that were evocative of several ethnic and regional identities – Mexican *huipils* and Japanese *hanten* jackets. As she wove, ponchos and serapes became visible in haute couture and at counter-cultural gatherings, from Woodstock to civil rights marches. In addition to her cottage industry that employed weavers to produce yardage, she wove large, unique 'wall hangings' (to use ungainly fine art parlance) that were displayed as fine art. Vibrant orange, magenta and mustard yellow hand-spun yarn connected Alice Kagawa Parrott to diverse global traditions and also made her personify Santa Fe.

Alice Kagawa Parrott grew with the town as it reinvented post-colonial indigenous arts as its civic identity. Santa Fe advertised itself as the 'City Different' in the 1920s, exploiting its numerous architectural layers and cultural fusions, a mixture of Native American, Spanish and Anglo-American influences. Victorian architecture that did not fit this official style was 'pueblofied' to match the three-hundred-year-old Palace of the Governors, which became the town's first museum and a living archaeological site in 1909. Alice arrived when the Museum of International Folk Art opened in 1953; shortly thereafter the Institute of American Indian Arts was chartered in 1961. Alice drew strength from her heterogeneous context. Artists, art colonies and patronage cultivated an exotic image. The painter Georgia O'Keeffe moved from New York to New Mexico in 1949, and later on came Agnes Martin, who befriended Parrott, in 1967. The ancient pueblos were compelling alternative cultural resources to mainstream America.

Santa Fe became a fantastical escape as well as a source of authenticity. More corporate creative types came as well as counter-cultural ones. For example, Alexander Girard, the chief designer of Herman Miller's textiles and one of the most successful designers of mid-century modernism, renovated a three-hundred-year-old adobe house in 1953 and amassed in it an extensive collection of folk art from global sources, especially Mexico and India. Girard designed modern themed restaurants for elites in New York City – most importantly the La Fonda del Sol in the 1959 Time-Life Building, a pan-Latin venue advertised as an 'atmosphere reflecting all the color, folklore and gaiety of our neighbors to the South'. (In the office suites overhead, Eames walnut stools were similarly situated as extracultural surprises.) At the Rockefeller Center restaurant, *mole poblano* was served 'hacienda style' in bright-coloured dishes by waiters attired in striped and chequered ponchos, vests and adaptations of a bullfighter's *traje de luces*. Girard's attention to detail included designing the buttons on the waiters' jackets and matchbooks. He also shaped the dining experience at The Compound on Canyon Road in Santa Fe, where decor matched table linens and menus with a more rustic version of the 'hacienda'. The ceiling was a quilt of swatches of 'Navajo weavings'. This phenomenon of packaging cultural authenticity held promise and posed perils for consumers as well as artists like Alice, who wove together international threads at a smaller scale.

Did Alice 'go native' or did she discover her real home in Santa Fe? Arriving in New Mexico after graduating with a Master's degree from the Cranbrook Art Academy, she grafted herself into a vernacular culture, just as the Navajo had a thousand years earlier when they transformed from nomads into residents of the Southwest, adopting weaving technologies from the older Pueblo. Alice's use of indigenous dye methods and non-Western forms of dress were acts of cultural appropriation, but were so respectful that her work can be regarded as preservationist. The cultural environment and landscape informed her craftsmanship, and her weaving gave Santa Fe an identity as a place where folk arts converged in a non-hierarchical melange. Alice invented a new homeland where cultural infusions from her family and educational background could intersect with New Mexico's breadth of traditions. She also turned from formal training as a hand-weaver of casement cloth to make clothing (and fashion) that transmitted social identity and signified cultural messages.

The neologism 'craftsteader' might be apt for a weaver, potter, jeweller or blacksmith who struck off on her own in late 1950s America – and saw labour-intensive practices like the loom or potter's wheel as a means of identity construction. The trend was economically viable because of post-war American affluence, automobile tourism and the surge in university art education. The twentieth-century concept of colonizing small workshops in semi-rural locations like Santa Fe was driven by social idealism as much as aesthetic and economic freedom. A belief in self-reliance and self-determinism extended from artistic agency to building intentional communities, as individuals like Alice Kagawa Parrott and Karen Karnes defied social expectations about gender and class and pioneered new identities their parents had never imagined. By opening her shop to her local community and, in her own words, labouring at 'the right unhurried pace', Alice embodied a specific American artisan's ethos, a preference for homesteading – or craftsteading – in an alleyway or along a rural byway just outside institutional frameworks. To some of her critical peers, she lacked ambition by settling for small sales on a modest scale. But perhaps her intention was not to build a career so much as a home.

Parrott's engagement with indigenous Mayan and Navajo textiles was a commitment that went beyond style. She grew a new community as much as a business, adopting two children, one Navajo and the other half-Navajo and half-Latino, with her husband Allen Parrott, fostering art education in public schools and developing an appreciation for the Guatemalan and Mexican textiles that went beyond superficial appropriation. Parrott's loom exemplifies a 'locational aesthetics' because she was not simply manufacturing things with her hands but creating an imaginary cultural space that allowed her audience to travel with her as she outflew the categories of art and identity. She knotted together temporal gaps and closed chasms between ethnic groups. The term 'relational aesthetics' has become popular in art-speak to describe artists whose primary concern is community engagement, but locational aesthetics – the power of textiles to prompt the feeling of being 'homeward bound', or alternately of exotic travel – is a much older material phenomenon that is arguably more psychologically revealing of humans' intent to cope with displacement through artistic production. Weaving in particular and textiles in general can be potent ways to fashion individual identity and a sense of belonging.

The location of Santa Fe provided her with a craft heritage, and her artistic aim was to merge into this regional cultural identity. If the Navajo gained new social and economic roles as well as mythologies in the eighteenth century when they adopted Spanish sheep and began to weave wool, so too did Alice fashion a novel persona as a local artist. When the city rebuilt its opera house as a modern structure with open-air seating in 1965, it commissioned her to weave uniforms for the ushers, making her loom a visible and enduring part of Santa Fe's larger civic image. Her ponchos in bright colours were civic decorative art. The opera still has them in storage, as they became popular and embedded in its identity. In 1998, with yet another renovation, the uniform became a kimono but in recent years it has returned to emulate Alice's style, made by a local shop that views itself as her protégé. Alice Kagawa Parrott bridged numerous arenas, connecting performances of *Madama Butterfly* to archaeology and contemporary Native American art. The psychic space of craft interweaves physical materials and artisanal bodies, and her ponchos gave the city an image as they made it her home.

Parrott's ponchos – or *ruanas* if you want to situate them as Andean in inspiration – illustrate Santa Fe's cosmopolitan atmosphere. Her traversal of ethnic boundaries was an intentional reparation and repatriation of indigenous culture. If we read it only as 'cultural appropriation' today, we disregard the fact that Alice herself was part of a diasporic culture. Her weaving was a way to repair histories of imperialism and colonization, to invent a new homeland of her imagination.

If Alice Kagawa Parrott exemplifies the expectation that craft is a search for authentic cultural alignment in a specific location, Jack Lenor Larsen (b. 1927), a fellow student at Cranbrook who graduated a year before she did, sought a larger and quite different carpet ride. Larsen, also a weaver, came closer to realizing the school's ambitions to secure prestigious monumental commissions for corporate headquarters and bring mid-century modernist 'good design' to the nation on a larger scale. His curtains adorned Manhattan skyscrapers like Lever House, as well as the nation's most grand private homes. Larsen's power-loomed textiles are in international museum collections: his was the leading American textile design firm of its type, and his team set trends in interior fabrics from the 1950s to the 1990s. He readily acknowledges that he operated with the help of fellow weavers such as Win Anderson and global entrepreneurs such as Jim Thompson and is keen to give credit to his many collaborators in his numerous publications.

If his powerhouse global brand produced upholstery and ornamented immense theatres and airline interiors, Larsen nevertheless always described himself as a weaver. He narrated his existential and emotional quest in his *Memoir of a Weaver* (1998) in intimate and direct terms: 'I don't remember a time when I wasn't seeking identity through a sense of place.' The sentiment is especially poignant if one has tactile knowledge of Larsen's first-hand journeys through Afghanistan, Morocco, Nigeria and Thailand and his historical collections of Japanese and Peruvian textiles. His books map these global traditions and his deep admiration for them. Jack entangled himself in the world's production of silk, linen, wool and cotton, integrating a dye technique from one part of the globe with a yarn from another, engaging with elite and rustic traditions and pursuing them to remarkably inventive and entrepreneurial ends. He has roamed the world as if a twentieth-century Marco Polo, conducting research in both regal manufactories and obscure desert encampments and educating many of us in the sensuous pleasures of other lands.

It is in the weave – and the marketplace – that Larsen and Parrott forged new identities. They made their own tangible crossroads in the material world and integrated multiple cultural traditions. They were not alone in seeking cultural exchange; in fact, they even prove that such a search is representative in craft, and especially textiles, in order to render the concept of cosmopolitan culture itself a tangible thing. The immense gulf between the work of Larsen, who went to live a fast-paced life in New York City and conquered it as a powerbroker of craft, and Parrott, whose quiet life in Santa Fe was no less dependent on entrepreneurial activity but operated on a tiny scale, is indicative of the space between their distinct identities as much as their distinct marketplaces. Larsen and Parrott came from altogether different backgrounds: Parrott was one of many siblings who earned money for school by working in pineapple-canning factories, and Larsen was a much doted-upon single child of a builder in Seattle. Both were in business under their own names, and both aimed to build an identity much more than just a vocation. They are alluring exemplars because they reveal the immense diversity in craft and yet they intersected in their educations at Cranbrook Academy of Art.

Cranbrook was founded in 1932 on a secluded campus outside Detroit to counterbalance the effects of industrialization with art. Intentionally not a formal school, resident artists were expected to pursue their own vocation in all the media of visual arts – architecture, sculpture, furniture, landscape design and textiles – and model professionalism for students; classroom structures were eschewed. The architect Eliel Saarinen established the curriculum and sought to integrate romantic primitivism and sleek, urbane modernization: these tendencies could be reconciled, he suggested, and all materials and techniques of artistic production integrated into a larger programme coherently through architecture. Cranbrook still is both an isolated utopia and internationally dynamic, with guests passing through and students and resident artists exhibiting nationally to great acclaim.

Larsen and Parrott enrolled to study both design and production skills in 1950: first-hand knowledge of handlooms and dyestuffs was encouraged in addition to pattern drafting and a sense of architectural placement. The academy's weaving studios, led first by Loja Saarinen and then Marianne Strengell, focused on designing window treatments and carpets to soften modern architecture's sharp edges. Finns and Swedes ran the workshops on the Cranbrook campus and enriched corporate campuses similarly situated in Detroit's ex-urbs, such as General Motors. Scandinavian design and craft occupied a privileged role in the aftermath of the Second World War as a humane, modernist aesthetic. Americans in particular, especially Edgar Kaufmann Jr at MOMA, were drawn to its independence from Continental European models. Both Larsen and Parrott learned a disciplined devotion to weaving from the taciturn Strengell, who oversaw a small student body – in these early years, Cranbrook, like the Bauhaus, had fewer than one hundred students overall, and it was known for a rigorous commitment to production and attention to materials. Textiles woven on the premises adorned the school's buildings, designed by Saarinen. Strengell worked as a consultant to designers such as Raymond Loewy and Russel Wright, and directly for manufacturers such as Cabin Crafts, Horner Woolen Mills and Fieldcrest. Her handwoven rugs and power-loomed floor coverings were in the nearby General Motors Technical Center and she also contributed designs for automobile upholstery. Robert Sailors added the teaching of power-loom weaving to the curriculum in 1940s, and a decade later, Larsen's thesis was 'Notes on Textile Designing for Production'. In retrospect, Parrott remembered feeling a bit inhibited by the 'placemat neatness' expected by Strengell, who spoke of the workshop as a design laboratory. Students tended to exhibit prototypes – small swatches or 90 inches of casement cloth – and to think in terms of economic outlets that existed in the larger world.

Larsen has written numerous books about his production and collections of textiles and yet there is no scholarship on Alice Kagawa Parrott. She worked for him briefly for a few months in New York City before moving to Santa Fe. She exemplifies a gendered stereotype – the maternal figure of craft who is sedentary and provincial, operating small-scale production within the confines of her own home. There were thousands of weavers like Parrott then, and are now, too. Larsen's firm required a cast of thousands of skilled helping hands, across cities of millions, in the age of air travel. In 1970, Ed Rossbach, another Cranbrook graduate of 1947 and one of Larsen's undergraduate teachers at the University of Seattle, described his student's journey in terms of artistic scale, commercial design and craftsmanship. Comparing Larsen to luminaries such as William Morris, the British Arts and Crafts hero, and Mariano Fortuny, whose couture made his Venice shop legendary in the first half of the twentieth century, Rossbach laid laurels at Larsen's feet. He also confessed his own antipathy to Larsen's entrepreneurial acumen. Larsen's empire-building had seemed radical and disruptive to weaving as a craft. However, Rossbach accepted that he was acclimatizing to Larsen's choice and suggested his own acceptance about the scale of industrial production as craft had changed:

> [Larsen] went to New York and invaded what seemed to me the marketplace. I thought he took the high road, or the low road, I did not know which was which. And I thought regretfully of the early pieces he had woven by hand. I recalled especially a warp across which he had dragged a brush of dye the color of tea,

> leaving a trail which moved not quite parallel to the reed. It was so restrained, so gentle, so understated – not what I associate with industry . . . But somehow, he has been able to use today's resources, whatever they are, wherever they happen to be. He is a designer in a world of technological nations coexisting with tiny nations just emerging from ancient pasts. He responds to hand-spinning and the hand loom as willingly as he responds to the technology of new machines and new materials. Matter-of-factly he moves over the entire world, using the paraphernalia of industry as well as the remnants of hand production left here and there. Everything in this mixed-up world is accepted, to become a vehicle for textile expression of this century.

This reflection suggests that the trajectories of Larsen and Parrott cannot be mapped as high or low roads or as any other simple binary opposition. Both weavers used their hands and touch in their labour. Each tapped the world's traditions to carve out a space and to find their own place. Each developed marketplaces and employed assistants. However, Parrott occupied a conventional domestic role, and several of her friends from Cranbrook found themselves in a similar predicament regarding their career options as women. There was only one Jack Lenor Larsen: he occupies a singular role as the most important tastemaker in fabrics and home furnishings in the 1960s and '70s in the USA. Yet Larsen achieved such a range in design that one could argue his abundance of styles suggests that there was no singular Larsen aesthetic. In each decade, his work took on distinct inflections. Moreover, every few years he updated his home, inevitably profiled in periodicals as a distinct new design concept. His novel melange and arrangement of artistic styles and craft objects set trends across industry.

These two weavers' searches for identity and their explicit recognition of the loom as a tool to hook into the world and download cultural patterns for reuse reveal that craft has long been a model of publicly engaged artistic practice. More dogmatic definitions might characterize Larsen's use of the power loom as a world apart from Parrott's handloom. From today's vantage, the concept of locational aesthetics establishes a framework in which Larsen's and Parrott's searches for identity can be seen as central to their weaving. It also suggests a larger conceptual way to understand weaving as a pivotal activity. Weaving was not simply a way to make things but a way to make a life, and inherently crossed the categories of art and design as a craft.

'WARP SPEED' AND THE TIES THAT BIND

Before we get more entangled in Larsen's and Parrott's specific pathways and identities, let me outline the ways that weaving should be regarded as both a physical journey and an existential obstacle course.

The intricacies of the warp and weft have no equal as a metaphor to communicate the paradoxes of craft. The orthogonal orientation between yarns running lengthwise on the loom and the fill interlacing through those yarns is a fundamental system that links ancient and modern ambitions – the integration of warp and weft is in the finery of Persian and Peruvian priests' archaeological remains as well as today's Fashion Week in Milan, New York and Paris. Textiles can materially represent cultural roots – the feeling of 'coming home' – as well as its inverse, dislocation and homelessness. Textiles make the word 'home' a tangible material place and also a portable, even foldable abstraction. Fabric is an everyday allegory of transformation. Pull on the wrong pair of pants and get disoriented; another pair is a comforting second skin.

A careful admiration of interlacing should waver between the perception of isolated strands and the expansive field of fabric: it is a mind-bending deliberation to leap from a single linear stitch to a plane and back again. Our eyes and fingers hover between identifying a fibre and an overall field, a figure and a ground. The thread and its horizon function as allegories for the human body and its geographical position. In the tension between intimate threads and the attempt to integrate with our world, no less is at stake than the question of the process of reinventing and sublimating the self. At times, we position ourselves in the here and now and yet, at other moments, fabric permits us to construct an imagined alternate temporal context for our lives. Fibre and textiles, more than any other craft process or product, are essential to our simultaneous search for self and shelter; all societies shape-shift with this craft.

The ancient philosopher Plato interpreted the loom as a metaphor for the ways social life integrates two opposing human tendencies, flexibility and inflexibility. More recently, the French philosopher Gilles Deleuze has expanded upon this by reading the fabrication of cloth as a metaphor for explaining divergent social structures. Deleuze contrasts a preference for wool felting in specific nomadic societies with the loom as a Western step towards European society's organizational control and coercive social incorporation. The technophobia in such philosophical musings is explicit and revealing; such generalizations mostly misconstrue material complexities and interpret them sociologically, sometimes even anthropomorphically. What follows is an interpretation of weaving on the loom that is less absolute in its platitudes.

On the one hand, textiles preserve much in their DNA of warp and weft, and most can be sorted out into general types of trajectories. Very few are genuinely untraceable to a specific place of origin. In a Navajo blanket, one might find the unravelled yarn of a red blanket woven in a factory on a power loom as well as pink thread that has been recarded with local wool and re-spun. A textile with a complete and developed history can be embroidered by a subsequent generation, thereby obscuring a style beyond recognition and gaining another new facade. The lengthwise threads that a loom holds in tension, the warp, can be lifted open and realigned as a horizontal infill is plied back and forth to build a pattern on the vertical scaffolding. This infill is the weft, which runs across the warp at a 90-degree angle, either by hand or in a fly shuttle. The warp and weft are a micro-topography, one that is two-sided and capable of incredible complexity – there can be floating wefts, reversible patterns and other surprises.

If the immense labour of fibre preparation is complete, then one can begin to weave, but such a precondition should not be taken lightly. On the micro level, the initial selection of fibres is elemental. One could opt to use wool, steel or jute and the same pattern would sound like an entirely distinct language. When selecting yarns, each has its own structure – these will add or diminish the tension in the weave. Each fibre has its own behavioural tendencies and resistance, so that the same pattern can be almost unrecognizable if it is very tight and then very loose. The layering of resources, or commingling of diverse matter, began thousands of years ago, when twigs, reeds, rushes and grasses were intertwined and tied together for their range in size. Specific tendencies and strengths were matched, and weavers continue to find new combinations. Plant and animal fibres might find themselves in each other's company. The details of preparing thread – such procedures as carding or spinning or the immensely complex topic of dyes – will not be covered here; it should suffice to note that each of these preparatory steps increases variables of difference in design and should make anyone hesitate to generalize about textiles.

The first step in weaving on a loom is to prepare the warp count. Increasing the number of warps per inch – the 'Ns' – creates a finer cloth. The warp is both a material and numerical commitment that determines several constraints in advance: major issues such as the final dimensions of the cloth, as well as the pattern. A careful preparation of the warp into parallel rows is essential. The warp needs to be cultivated exactingly, as a farmer readying furrows for sowing: they are primed and wound on a taut beam. They run through the heddles, sets of eyelets suspended in air, as the pattern dictates. The 'sleying of the reed' entails threading each warp through a comb-like apparatus. The fusion of warp and weft is not necessarily a homogeneous or an equal relationship, and these should not be seen as predictable; choices abound, here, too. The warp might be a synthesis of unrelated strands blended into one and might have a distinct feel depending on the ways that the thread was spun – fashioned by fingers, a spindle or with a reel.

Interlacing is a three-dimensional journey, a running and hurdling of the shuttle, the weft, tunnelling through the open warp. It is easy to focus on the weft and believe the warp is at rest, aground, but it is also in motion, like the alternating legs of a chorus line. Seen from the edge of a textile, called the selvedge, the warp is not flat during the process of weaving: it resembles a trapezoidal passageway. The space created when the warp is pulled open, the shed, is always in motion, its walls folding in and through itself as the weaver pushes down on a treadle. On a simple backstrap loom the weaver turns a stick. On a floor loom rigged with multiple harnesses and treadles, the bending of the shed follows distinct sequences of warp getting plucked up and down. While the warp is usually described in shorthand as the vertical infrastructure underlying a weaving, it can also become the visible pattern, too, and the weft can be submerged. Horizontal and vertical threads can alternate between visibility and concealment. If the warp and weft are powerful primary lines of activity and allegorical coordinates for the compass, the dynamic spatial torsion of the shed is a third symbolic space in a weaving. The shed lives on in memory, as does the motion of the beater, which can add tension to a fabric. Literal 'warp speed' is slower than weft speed. The term, invented in the television series *Star Trek* to describe intergalactic propulsion, is still powerfully seductive. It is both archaic and futuristic, as only weaving can be.

To consider textiles as complex journeys in miniature is to commune with the constituent elements of the individual threads as well as the weave. The skilled weaver extracts as much character and narrative drama from a deliberate selection of fibres as from a pattern. Each weaver has her or his own tactic. Larsen favoured the random repeat to break monotony. While there are only a handful of fundamental techniques – plain, twill and satin – variety is limitless. Invention can be a banal substitution of one material, such as goat hair, for another, or be complex in terms of the chemistry of dye and mordant. Humans' modern industrialized weaves have neither surpassed prehistoric techniques nor expanded upon them very much. We have quickened the pace of production, added synthetic fibres to the repertoire and transformed customized clothing into a rarity. In cheapening and speeding up the pace of textile fabrication, we have only weakened the depth of our commitments to textiles and their instrumental potential to be singular or transformative. It takes more than a finger or a mirror to realize the degree to which we shape ourselves psychologically through clothes.

LOCATIONAL AESTHETICS

When we step onto a rug and begin to navigate pattern, geometry and the topography of pile underfoot, a dual process of place-making and relocation occurs for which we have no existing vocabulary. Such a rug is a homing device that sends us meaningful signals to determine where we are and who we are. We absorb the same communication when touching a quilt or wrapping ourselves in a blanket. Textiles tend to travel the furthest from their origins (aside from coins). More significantly, textiles maintain direct portals between their genesis and terminus: their construction and their histories remain accessible ways to metaphorically travel.

Weavers like Larsen and Parrott might have an especially intimate connection to textiles, but it is also important to realize the degree to which all of us wrap our bodies in fabric, either to distinguish ourselves or to meld with our surroundings. Cloth provides the stability needed for shelter and the transience necessary for mobility. Fabric transforms our silhouettes and renders our salient characteristics visible or invisible, prominent or elusive. It is the capacity of fabric to assert home and homelessness, as I have mentioned, and the heightened contradiction between these two locational experiences might be one of the peculiarities of twenty-first-century denim. In pondering fabrics such as that of our own denim trousers, we can reflect that blue jeans both ground us in reality and transport us elsewhere via fantasy. As the anthropologists Daniel Miller and Sophie Woodward have noted, 'jeans seem to have taken on the role of expressing something about the changing world that no other clothing could achieve.' The presence of denim in our society is immense, and the fabric is considered expressive in numerous ways. Today, jeans somehow epitomize an American idea of informality wherever they are worn or made. A pair of cheap cotton jeans might be an amalgam of threads culled from multiple nations, just as a McDonald's hamburger is bits of ground up cows from two or more continents. Cotton from Uzbekistan, Peru, China and India might be blended together. The complex rise of global denim defies logic of place or purpose. Denim has obliterated the boundaries between work clothes and leisurewear.

Chances are the sensation of breaking in a pair of jeans is the one fundamental textile experience that is shared by every reader of this book. The ritual is as widespread as consumers, crossing all class boundaries. So can we say that jeans mean anything in particular? Although nine out of ten portraits depict craftspeople wearing jeans, these are not work clothes – these are costumes, which obscure who we are or where we are from. Today, jeans offer camouflage as well as a new type of anonymity. Denim has gained a strange affective power and social life, enabling self-deception and imaginary identity formation – arguably the most accessed dimension of locational aesthetics.

The world's largest manufacturer of denim, Arvind, a corporation based around Ahmedabad in the traditionally textile-rich region of Gujarat, India, produces thousands of millions of yards of fabric per year – exemplifying the opposite of craft for many people. The yardage is transformed into emblems of American culture – once it is sewn and riveted into a pair of Levi's or Calvin Klein jeans. A pair ranges from $20 to $350, with brand identity determining the value more often than materials or labour. Recently the manufacture of artisanal jeans has arisen in response to the overseas relocations of large-scale manufacturing. Small companies such as Raleigh Denim, started by Victor and Sarah Lytvinenko in North Carolina in 2007 with the output of five pairs of trousers a week, promote their work as almost humanitarian in scope. Their mission is 'to build the ideal pair of jeans in principle and form, to embrace quality before quantity and the humanness inherent in that idea, to be a part of the revitalization of the textile industry in North Carolina'. The global and the patriotic collide here, exemplifying the way textiles carry complex emotional and psychological values. Miller and Woodward conclude that 'The more people tried to find ways to bring these two extremes of the intimate and the global from flying apart in their lives the more they wore jeans as the instrument for keeping this simultaneity of local and global experiences.' Thus anthropologists identify denim as a coping strategy. Denim, like many other commodities, has an awkward existence, caught as it is between global networks of production and individual consumer fantasies. The appearance of craft is often hijacked for short-term commercial ends, to lay an abstract layer of authenticity or intimacy onto commonplace possessions. If these affective delusions sound trite, think again, as our emotional attitudes have genuine consequences.

If we accept that a fabric can take us on faraway journeys and also anchor us in regional identity then the emotional concept of a homeland is intrinsic to locational aesthetics. By speaking to us intimately in a tongue that affords comfort, the sensation of belonging is conjured. Raleigh Denim, for instance, deliberately yanks on the heartstrings by occupying a former mill town and seemingly recuperating the recent past. The living residents still have memories of glory days in the early twentieth century when Southern mill towns were booming. However, one of the denim company's founders was a line chef at a three-star Japanese restaurant in New York City, an experience in salesmanship that might be critical to the company's success at marketing its identity as an artisanal renaissance of Raleigh's workforce.

Building a brand identity is more about storytelling and emotional associations than actual location or authentic manufacturing methods. The magic carpet ride is inviting if it is promising a trip to the exotic or some imagined homeland – certainly more inviting than an anonymous global commodity. Handicraft is often championed as superior to anonymous manufacturing but such an opposition between the unique and the standardized is misleading. Today, most of us rely on brands and brand identity to maintain the quality and quantity of storytelling that craft in daily life used to provide. It is not the unique we crave but the signals that reaffirm our geographic location – either that we are homeward or situated in some specific place in the firmament.

If textiles have the tactile power to dispel social anxiety and disorientation, and informal denim or formal silk attire can hug us or stiffen our resolve and sense of pride, then a garment is a portable ecology by which we assert both belonging and difference. Textiles are systems we overlay on top of our differentiated bodies in order to blend into a social landscape – and at times these are practical uniforms to falsify uniformity. Often we act out of psychological need for anonymity or distinction as individuals. Clothing is the most overt and banal way to construct a temporary community – witness a political rally's field of T-shirts and baseball caps clobbered with slogans. We rely on trousers, shirts and shoes to tell us who we are and where we are; more so than street signs. At every urban downtown crossroads across the globe, billboards and skyscrapers overhead impose a visual and psychic order upon us, and increasingly one can tell one's location or civilization only by the clothes people are wearing on the street – even if most of our clothing is also made by an international conglomerate more than a local product.

VERNACULAR CLOTH

In dealing with fabrics, the concept of the vernacular is fraught, and misguided concepts of 'homespun' cloth often obstruct clear thinking. 'Vernacular' is used to describe a regional dialect learned at home, not school. In arts and architecture the term describes domestic and functional buildings rather than official monuments or imported goods. However, artefacts, materials and habits travel. Often, what is perceived to be an ancient local artistic expression is of recent vintage. Numerous invented traditions in textiles and fashion are seemingly old; many have retained their prestige even when they have been debunked. Yet romantic invocations of the vernacular are more plentiful than ever today in our era of increased globalization: we search harder than ever for authenticity in life and in things, too.

The association between craft and regional identity is unlikely to be jettisoned despite being ridden with problems. Navajo craft of weavings and jewellery are spoken of as traditional but actually epitomize modernity. They evolved out of contact with Spanish colonizers and have, on closer inspection, rarely stayed the same for more than any given thirty-year generation in the last two hundred years. We might tout Egyptian cotton but such a commodity is also modern; the ancient inhabitants around the Nile grew flax and wore linen. Italian sericulture, the production of silk, has become a local tradition in the last eight hundred years as a result of industrial espionage. Merino sheep came to live in Australia, Sweden and North and South America in the nineteenth century, and yet the branding of wool, like silk and cotton, is often wrongly regarded as a national habitual cloth. Many materials have gone on such journeys, and after three or four generations they are no longer exotic but domestic favourites. If centuries of trade were tallied, North Americans would realize that they have more reason to associate denim and dungarees with Gujarat than with Raleigh, North Carolina, or Levi Strauss & Co. But such knowledge of the past is rarely considered more tangible than our own primary experiences. The explicit power relationship in language between centre and periphery is mirrored in our understanding of tooling. We expect rural districts to speak and work in their own dialects, preserving older stages of civilization, even if we rationally understand that to be folly.

Craft is often described as vernacular expression because it has conventionally been outside the academic curriculum of fine art; this changed in the course of the twentieth century. The field of craft has largely become defined academically since the generation of Larsen and Parrott. The MFA-trained craftsmaker is ubiquitous. The vernacular is also used to describe an association with the rural arts. However, before becoming integrated into university settings, many crafts were urban. Like 'folk art', craft has flourished the same way as all the arts have, on the basis of urban patronage and trade.

'Home-grown' remains a term of affection and a perception as romantically misguided as 'handmade'. Usually the appellation is wishful thinking: locational aesthetics creates the mirage of a homeland or quaint labour conditions. Historically, most sweated labour – subcontracted piecework – has taken place in homes; the idea is that it is cheaper to spread work out than house many workers in a factory (who might organize and seek equitable pay). The pursuit of the vernacular is glorified in current commerce, as in the slogan 'Buy local'. This isolationist mentality has good intentions, but in cosmopolitan civilizations we tend to covet our neighbours' threads. It is in straying from local zones and importing fibres and dyes that we grow our knowledge of beauty and challenge insular definitions of the beautiful. 'Local' is better left as a battered bumper sticker slogan than held on to as a principle or fundamental guideline in craft. Today, we might yearn for a locally made piece of furnishing but for centuries to groom with exotic accessories was a more typical human habit. In ornamenting our homes and bodies with folkloric craft, we are not different from pre-capitalistic tribes that generally have favoured the unusual and rare adornment over locally available or widely accessible plumage.

THE HOUSE THAT JACK BUILT

Jack Lenor Larsen's genius in spotlighting handicraft is often acclaimed in terms of entrepreneurship and education, but he identifies as a weaver foremost. Larsen expanded the dimensions of handicraft in proportion to the post-war economy: he urged that qualities of handicraft could be integrated to produce high-quality mass production and for the preservation and appropriation of global techniques and traditions. He demonstrated this by buying small batches of hand-spun fibre and integrating that non-standardized material into power-loom weavings. He has worked the loom, designing patterns for upholstery, furnishing fabrics and housewares, and also established an eponymous international firm, minding the front office, supervising mill production and keeping a dexterous finger on every other location where textiles are valued. If in the 1950s he wove shaggy wool men's ties and one-of-a-kind textiles, Larsen was soon quick to perceive the many venues where his work could grow with the scale of commissions of modern architecture. While designing household linens, he also was a curator who pioneered exhibitions that redefined the 'Art Fabric', such as 'Wall Hangings' at MOMA, New York, in 1969. As noted earlier, he was the design director and U.S. Commissioner of the American pavilion in the thirteenth Milan Triennale in 1963, where Karen Karnes's work was placed prominently. He also authored numerous books, such as *The Dyer's Art* (1976), in which he savoured anonymous silk ikat cloth made in rural districts of Thailand. His affection for the variegated types of handicraft in cloth production is immense; his professional involvements were multifaceted. By 1970, when Jack Lenor Larsen, Inc. designed and produced 600 yards of lush machine-embroidered Mylar curtains for the Phoenix Opera House, his scope of ambition had transformed beyond the capability of any soloist working alone – he had developed a highly skilled firm and yet also remained a vocal and leading champion of small-scale handicraft across the globe. It might seem contradictory that he was the nation's most visible advocate for the handloom while being a designer of towels for department stores and upholstery for airlines as well as luxurious casements for premier modern corporate office buildings. One could walk into the Sears skyscraper in Chicago and see his cathedral-scaled wall hangings, engineered for acoustical improvement, and then drive into a high-end department store like Neiman Marcus and buy his linens. Larsen's magic carpet ride is not easy to reduce to a one-dimensional theme.

Newspapers such as the *Daily News* and *New York Times* as well as *House and Garden* noted the 'house that Jack built' in Long Island's East Hampton in the 1960s: Larsen's weekend getaway was photographed and lauded. Based on Bantu houses, he called it Round House. It was a theatrical stage on which all his roles, as weaver and social networker, patron and artist, gardener and curator, could coalesce. The circular structure opened to the outdoors on all sides. Inside was an exotic lair. In the 1980s he constructed a more palatial successor next door that resembles a Japanese temple – the exotic was naturalized into an American home even as the stage was also a showcase to demonstrate his skill as a tastemaker and connoisseur. Gardens were avidly cultivated. Each effort transported his body elsewhere and assembled alternative aesthetic dimensions from outside the United States as tactile pleasures. His work was accessible by virtue of its being photographed and published, but he always operated a luxury boutique business. His commitment to fabric production took on the dimensions of a biblical mission and full-on physical immersion. In a

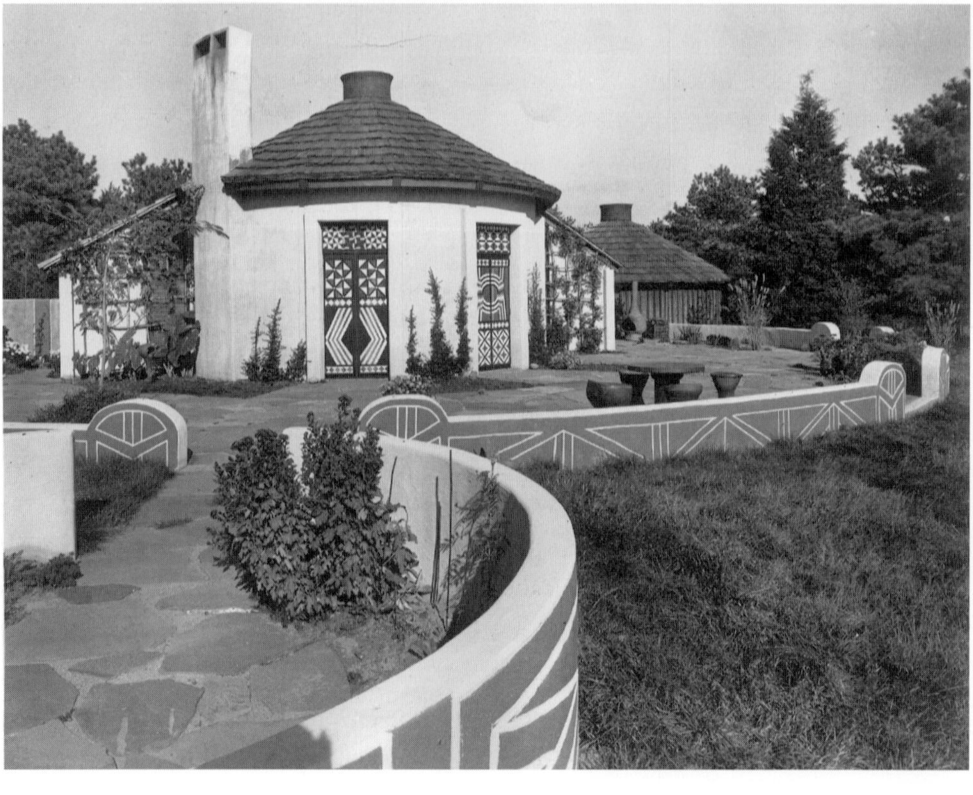

sense, he built a version of the fantastical houses that every child imagines, such as the palaces of Babar or Kublai Khan, Narnia or Harry Potter.

Larsen constructed homes and identities as well as weaving. His textiles and houses were one and the same – inventively fashioned stage props. His declaration that one of his favourite types of fabrics is a reversible double-weave speaks to his commitment to dramatic transformation, animation and suspense. His life reveals that craft is not easily pinned to fixed coordinates, much the same way that a close look at Nampeyo, Brancusi and Karnes reveals their processes dynamically engaging numerous influences, opportunities and constraints. Photographs of Larsen suggest his ubiquity and metamorphic capability to occupy a dozen niches in the craft world. He can be regarded as a sleeveless weaver working out under the sun on a deck beside the Maine coast, as a black-tied curator at MOMA, as a design consultant with Russel Wright and as an entrepreneur beside an Afghan nomad. He has been a name in lights on storefronts internationally and become at least two types of brands, a consultancy and a wholesaler, as the Larsen Design Studio and Jack Lenor Larsen, Inc.

Jack Lenor Larsen's Round House, photo published in the *Daily News*, 9 January 1967. Larsen designed his country retreat as linked rondavels (African roundhouses) with Congolese-inspired shutters and a terrace wall etched with patterns. The interior living room had 'a Moroccan divan covered with a Besarabian rug, Mexican and African accessories, a Zebra skin rug and natural mohair draperies made in Swaziland'. On the terrace is a table surrounded by four seats by Karen Karnes, and above these is one of her chiminea, also probably inspired by Mexico.

The ideal of the pastoral, a bucolic greenway that cuts through culture's marble floors and highly polished surfaces, has been essential to Larsen. Like Frank Lloyd Wright, whose home Taliesin East in Iowa County, Wisconsin, Larsen supplied with 200 yards of upholstery, the weaver has articulated the organic as his prime motivation, but he has also rolled with trends over five decades of production. The importance of commoditized rustic charm increased over the twentieth century with the spread of industrialization. Larsen recognized these currents and directed his travel accordingly. In his early work from the 1950s he incorporated randomly spaced warp and weft and combined diverse weights of fibres – contrasts such as slubby linen and goat hair to get nubs and diaphanous effects – to produce uneven orthogonal lines intentionally; these added dynamic character to the fabric. He incorporated subtle effects of colour gradation derived from Thai ikat weaving into his power-loomed upholstery. In the late 1960s and early '70s, he printed large floral patterns, moving from geometric abstraction to sophisticated stylized illustration, and eventually expanded his house wares to include rattan furniture and tableware.

Too often we diagnose a binary opposition in craft in which some types of production fall into an acceptable idealization of the rustic and the opposite sort veers into deception or self-deception. Instead of polarizing handicraft into such moralistic fields, let us remember that affectations of unrefined bucolic beauty have transpired in Eastern as well as Western cultures. When Larsen produced Chan Chan, named in homage to the ancient Chimú city on the coast of Peru, he sent bolts of cotton fabric woven in Switzerland to Kenya, where Lisa Wilcox organized local dyers to fold-dye the fabric. The dye application was a choreographed dance, a process of lines of people moving to drum beats. This cultural production zigzagged across continents, resulting in a novel aesthetic hybrid. The rhythmic grid of folds and the stains document what Larsen calls the fabric's 'thirst'. The pattern conveys a sense of time unfolding itself.

If some poets believe poetry atrophies when it strays from music, Larsen's work suggests that textiles need to stay close to human bodies: keep the weave close to the dance. Those who have woven and synchronized their feet, shuttle and beater, know that the process can be like drumming, a bodily rhythm that becomes its own drumbeat. Larsen's energy and athleticism – and the entanglement of his identity with fabric – are hinted at in a 1963 photograph that shows him weaving en plein air, bending over a loom. The weaver stands as if at a capstan on a ship's deck, aligned with the vertical pines of rocky Deer Isle, Maine, against the watery horizon. Two other figures and two other looms sit on the steps, passengers or witnesses who might not have had Larsen's ambition or network to dream on his scale. It is hard to imagine that by that point in time Larsen, captured in morning light wearing shorts and a tank top, was managing an extraordinarily complex business spread across dozens of countries and yet also teaching summer sessions on the handloom at an artisans' community, the Haystack Mountain School. The campus of shingled, low-profiled studios designed by Edward Larrabee Barnes was both a retreat and a seedbed. If Larsen was enjoying a reprieve from meetings on Park Avenue and visiting mills, he was also busy inventing and growing.

As he plies his shuttle independently on the deck in Maine, Larsen counts out new patterns and tests diverse combinations of yarns with a mind to translate them into power-loom production at the Bolan family's mill in New Jersey. In 1952, during one of the first of his thirteen summers at Haystack, Larsen's experimental handloom work directly evolved into a commission for the J. Irwin Miller House in Columbus, Indiana.

Revisiting Larsen's Miller House commission reveals his ingenuity and process of translating small-scale freehand experimentation into high-end hundred-yard textiles in which he could deploy his penchant for variegated fibres and random repeats. The architect of the chic villa, Eero Saarinen, had also attended Cranbrook Academy, where his father, Eliel, had been president. Cranbrook's ethos of valuing craftsmanship on all scales and in numerous materials shaped Larsen's breadth of vision, as it had previous graduates. The collaboration on the Miller House was one of the most ambitious of its kind, as Alexander Girard choreographed the interior decoration and Dan Kiley orchestrated lush classical plantings. Girard used Eames furniture made by Herman Miller and, exercising his opulent eye as a colourist, brought in Larsen for upholstery and casement cloths.

To contrast two of Larsen's several contributions to Miller House, Jason, a window casement, and Remoulade, an upholstery fabric, both began as hand weaves and then were adapted for the power loom. Jason is a subdued grid of cool geometry while Remoulade added a flamboyant and ostentatious eruption of colour to the conversation pit, where pillows matched winter and summer palettes. Jason germinated in his appreciation for Maine's landscape. Both can be considered architectonic, largely because they reverse the predictable relationship of weft and warp. Initially, Larsen had oriented Jason horizontally and was seeking 'to work out a quiet rhythm of random stria [sic] that would reflect the woods and the sea'. The beige colours of goat hair and linen shimmer quietly on close inspection because of the addition of flecks of metallic thread. The diaphanous weave is interrupted by seemingly random hefty gimp. Reorienting the stripes vertically, Larsen added a rhythm of twisted supplementary warps. If transparency was one priority, Larsen's taste for 'buckled wefts and wavy warps' lent body to the curtain. Fine goat hair was not commonly used in casement cloth. But it was not an untested ingredient, only an idiosyncratic choice – goat hair was used to stiffen the lapels of men's suits in the garment industry. Larsen's application of the economical fibre to window casements is indicative of his ability to think laterally across traditions. 'I was trying to imitate birch bark,' says Larsen of Jason, which warmed Saarinen's choice of cold white marble on the walls and floor: the dining room could be closed off and become intimate with Larsen's Jason. Today, the diaphanous veil demarcates Larsen's own bedroom on Long Island. Remoulade, with its hotter chromatic flair, was a plaid that came in three colourways mixing silk, Lurex, cotton, wool and jute, evoking the polyvocality one would want in

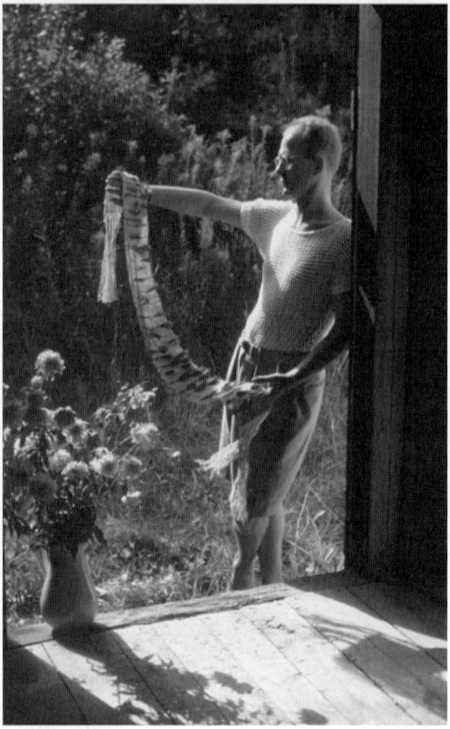

Jack Lenor Larsen posing in August 1955 at the Haystack Mountain School of Crafts, Montville, Maine, with what resembles a prototype of Jason. The composition implies weaving springs from the power of nature.

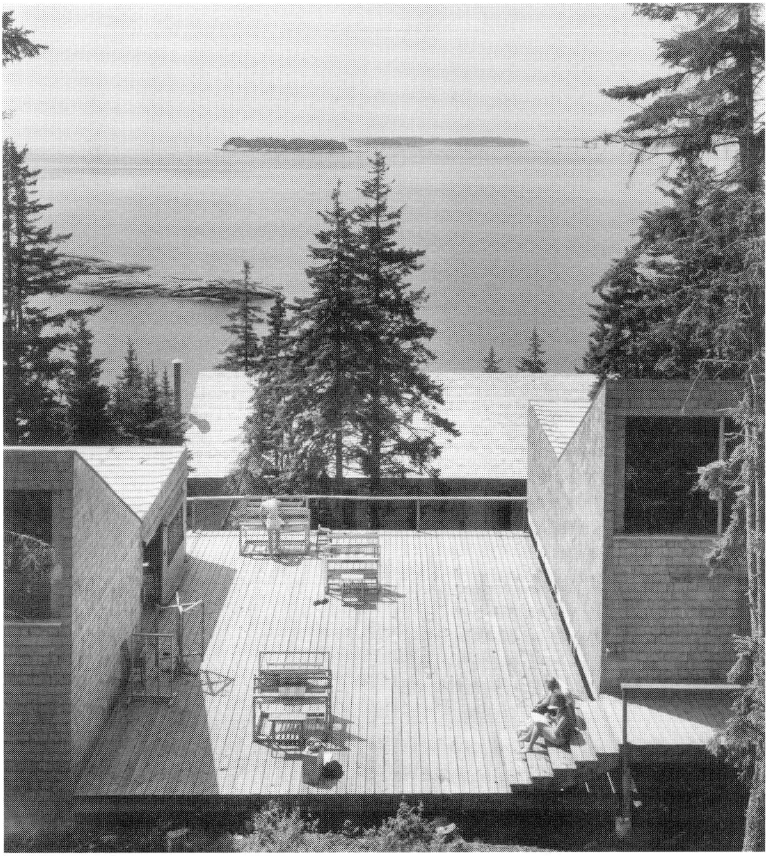

View of Larsen and others at Haystack Mountain School of Crafts, Deer Isle, Maine, 1963. Larsen taught for thirteen summers, in direct contact with the loom, while also journeying across the world to cultivate relationships with workshops in Thailand and Swaziland. He fused the cosmopolitan and rustic: 'I admire those who work in a straight line born in themselves, I am an eclectic . . . I admire many styles, most of them not courtly, stodgy or elaborate. Best of all, I respond to the work of tribal artisans.'

a conversation pit. These high-end luxurious weaves were custom-made to enrich Saarinen's cool geometry in specific complimentary moments.

Jason and Remoulade went through several iterations on the floor loom before they were spun in a mill, but neither were ever made at the fast pace of conventional power looms. Larsen's ramping up of tools from the hand to automation confounds most expectations of craft. Remoulade is an explosion of colourful silks whereas Jason is mellow, a beige plain-weave. Remoulade has a breadth of ingredients: natural (undyed) wool, cotton, linen, silk, jute, rayon, nylon and metallic yarns. From hand to power loom, the warp changed orientation, transforming from a hanging into upholstery. Larsen needed three warp beams and a number of weighted spools hanging off the back of the loom to negotiate the variegated tensions of this diversity in types of weft. If the architecture maintains a modernist stylistic sensibility based on the grid, the textiles are closer to the range of the Millers' social spaces and art collections – Larsen's craft and Girard's colourful interiors have a breadth of human emotion without becoming contrived.

Larsen speaks glowingly of the beauty of ikat, *plangi* and batik, methods of patterning and colouring that he saw in textiles from such places as Thailand, Japan and Indonesia; he rarely praises his own yardage to the same degree. He interpreted these ancient techniques as contemporary tools to anchor the twentieth-century mind and keep open proverbial windows-on-the-world:

> the ambiguities of contemporary lifestyle could be offset by these examples of an essential order. One parameter is that we sustain, through patronage, the highest level of handicraft still available in remote parts of the world. Second is that we create our own interlacings.

And Larsen has fulfilled these ambitions and pledges. If he had only written books, or only imported foreign goods, or only completed his major commissions his career would be noteworthy. That he has done all of these tasks means that Rossbach's comparison to William Morris was apt. Larsen ought to be known in every art school and taught as an exemplar on the basis of his generosity to artists, too: Dale Chihuly credits Larsen with his career's turn towards glass. Acclaimed by the ceramic artist Nan McKinnell as 'the boy that did everything' when he rescued the design of an exhibition of her pottery and textiles at New York City's

America House in the late 1950s, he has always maintained connections to craft organizations and museums as well as individuals. Larsen's patronage of Karen Karnes was noted in Chapter One – she made custom sinks, a fireplace, seating and tiles for his Bantu hut. His pantry today is still filled with her tableware.

Making and appreciating are intertwined in Larsen's mind, another reason he can be regarded as an exemplary figure. In one of his books, Larsen stands on a mountain high above Banff, Alberta, admiring the way a tree growing in the absence of soil has sent its root system to clutch yards of the hard rocky landscape in hundreds of tendrils. He sees the knotted tangle of growth as a rudimentary exercise in knotting and senses that he is near the transcendent modular unit of all fibres, textiles and baskets. Larsen introduces this bucolic ideal and although it hints at an adoration of 'the simple life' that haunts craft, he himself is much too smart to suppose that he is 'getting back in touch with nature' or 'attuned to natural materials'. He is explaining the complexity of weaving and trying to foster common-sense affection for this uncommon power of a material structure.

Another casement cloth that particularly embodies the contradictions of Larsen – his admiration of both nature's roots and industrial looms, African huts and skyscrapers – is Interplay, a warp knit that appears to be coarse straw or raffia at first glance. Designed for a competition to diffuse light and reduce glare in the twenty-storey-high windows of a Philadelphia bank, Larsen's breakthrough was to use polyvinylidene chloride, a fibre made by Dow Chemical Company and marketed as Rovana that is part of the Saran family of polymers. The rigid fibre is flame-resistant, washable and can be heat-set into a pleated form. He did not receive the commission, but his competitor produced a curtain that needed to be sporadically trimmed with shears over time as it sagged under its own weight and impeded the doors directly below. His production of the knitted fabric endured for three decades, and he marketed the lacey pattern as a part of his 1963 African Collection. Made in colourways that resembled the beige range of natural fibres, a black version of Interplay absorbed the most direct sunlight. Larsen clothed modern office buildings, inspired in equal degrees by his appreciation for ancient diverse cultural traditions and recent innovations in plastics, achieving a remarkable synthesis.

Jack Lenor Larsen, Inc., Interplay, 1960–86, warp-knit Rovana (saran monofilament). As a counterpoint to the austere offices inside glass corporate towers, Larsen wove casement cloth to screen the sun and add texture in novel DuPont fibres. Depending on the context, Interplay could lend antiquarian or rustic notes to a room. It came in white and beige tones, too. Heat-set after it was knit, the casement would not sag over time.

Look in the MOMA's collection closely and you will find that Larsen generously donated more than a dozen weavings by the Bauhausler Gunta Stölzl, so he must be accounted for as a preservationist as much as an artisan and designer. He developed his initial aesthetic in emulation of Dorothy Wright Liebes (1897–1972), whose San Francisco studio he had once visited in pursuit of a position. Although Liebes rejected Larsen as an employee, when he eventually opened a firm in New York City he used his full name for his company as she had used hers – a sign of his respect for her business acumen and pioneering role balancing handicraft and automation. Jack Lenor Larsen, Inc. expanded upon Liebes's colour range – 'Chinatown' chromatic effects, in her words – and also her 'hunky weave' with exaggerated textures that integrated a variety of spun yarns and other materials, such as bamboo, metal components and synthetics.

Larsen's incredible breadth and shifting scale suggests craft can be applicable to all types of solo and collaborative endeavours. His own firm could range stylistically from a bright yellow Scandinavian Neoclassicism to nocturnal velvets suited to an altogether more informal space. *Material Wealth*, one of many books authored by Larsen, is subtitled *Living with Luxurious Fabrics*, an apt description of the price point of most of his firm's exclusive textile production. Yet his work has been in public spaces and within reach of everyday life. Having collaborated with Alexander Girard on the extremely luxurious Miller House, he would do so again a few years later when they sought to replace the standard industry 'plain plane' with a complete overhaul of Braniff Airlines, using pinks, oranges and brilliant

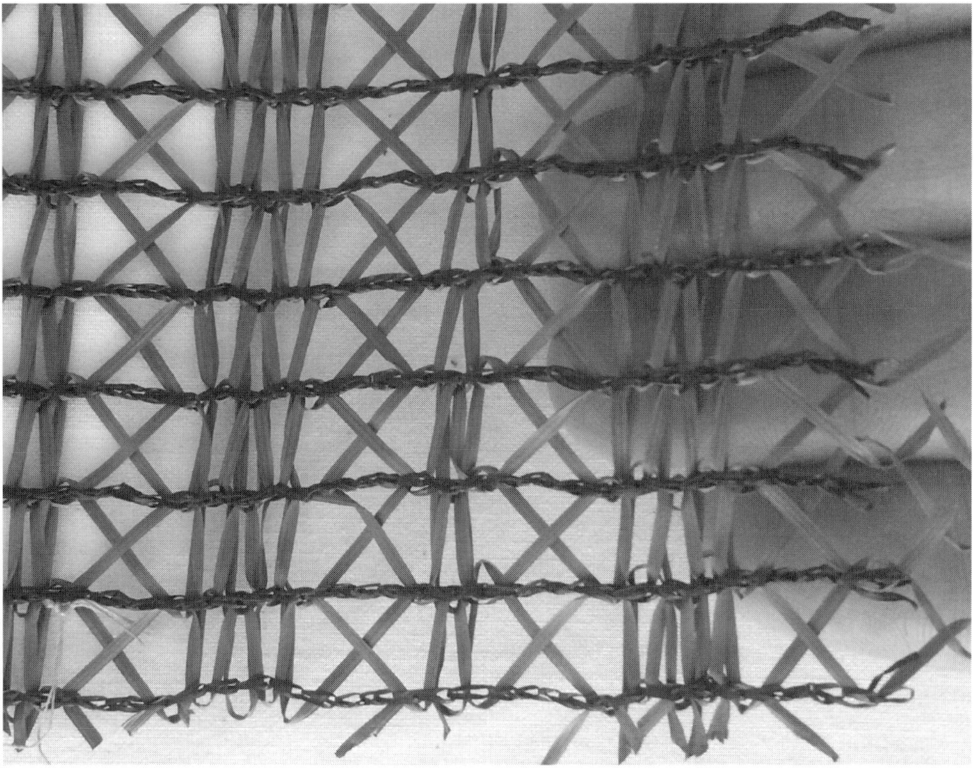

blues to enliven aeroplane carpets, upholstery and curtains – as well as playing cards, Emilio Pucci stewardess uniforms, tickets and lounges.

His bath towels, affordable luxuries, are intriguing to evaluate as comforting devices and an artistic endeavour – and as mass production informed by handicraft. The downy, deep-pile terrycloth towel is one of the wonders of mechanized power looms; it is a luxury that became democratized in post-war America and integral to beach and athletic culture. The bath towel was among the most novel twentieth-century developments in textile comfort, a furnishing dependent on the rise of powerful dryers becoming standard appliances. As such, the towel, while hardly as dignified as his greatest achievements and commissions for cultural institutions, might be representative of this era of American affluence and of Larsen's particular skill set as a craftsman.

Terry cloth has two warps, one or more for the ground and one for the pile looping. The texture is mechanically constant and yet far from machine-like in our tactile associations. The weave's superior utility is noteworthy; it is almost magically absorbent. In his Manhattan studio, Larsen's team of weavers made terrycloth samples to test the colours and patterns; the product was purely handicraft before it was sent down to J. P. Stevens, one of the largest American textile manufacturers of the time, to be woven on a power loom. Among Europeans, terrycloth is described as Turkish (to distinguish it from a waffle or flat weave) – and this might very well be its place of origin. Strangely, we have come to take towels for granted as plush, colourful and body-sized. The luxury and technical mystery of looped pile has become naturalized. But the ways that we use towels, generally in intimate, private spaces, suggests that they are for hedonistic pleasure and less often for storytelling or communicating our tribal identities to other beachgoers or to guests who wander into our bathrooms.

Running your hand over Architecture, a towel in Stevens's 1966 Fine Arts Collection, you notice the variety in the pile. Larsen's design also gives the eye a feast, a landscape to read. The rooftops seem to be Roman, an interpretation of the baroque imaginary engravings of Giovanni Battista Piranesi or the twentieth-century fantasias of Piero Fornasetti. Domes, windows in staccato, columned porticos and even an arabesque portal can be touched as well as seen. 'The bas-relief derives from voided velvet techniques,' explains Larsen. The towel has visually sumptuous colours that took advantage of then recent innovations at Fieldcrest, a rival firm that had hired as consultant Everett Brown Associates, a noted authority on dye chemistry. The tawny yellow version of Architecture, with its two shaded warps, evokes the effects of sunset on travertine and marble, unlike the other colourway in darker red and navy blue. Larsen, eager to

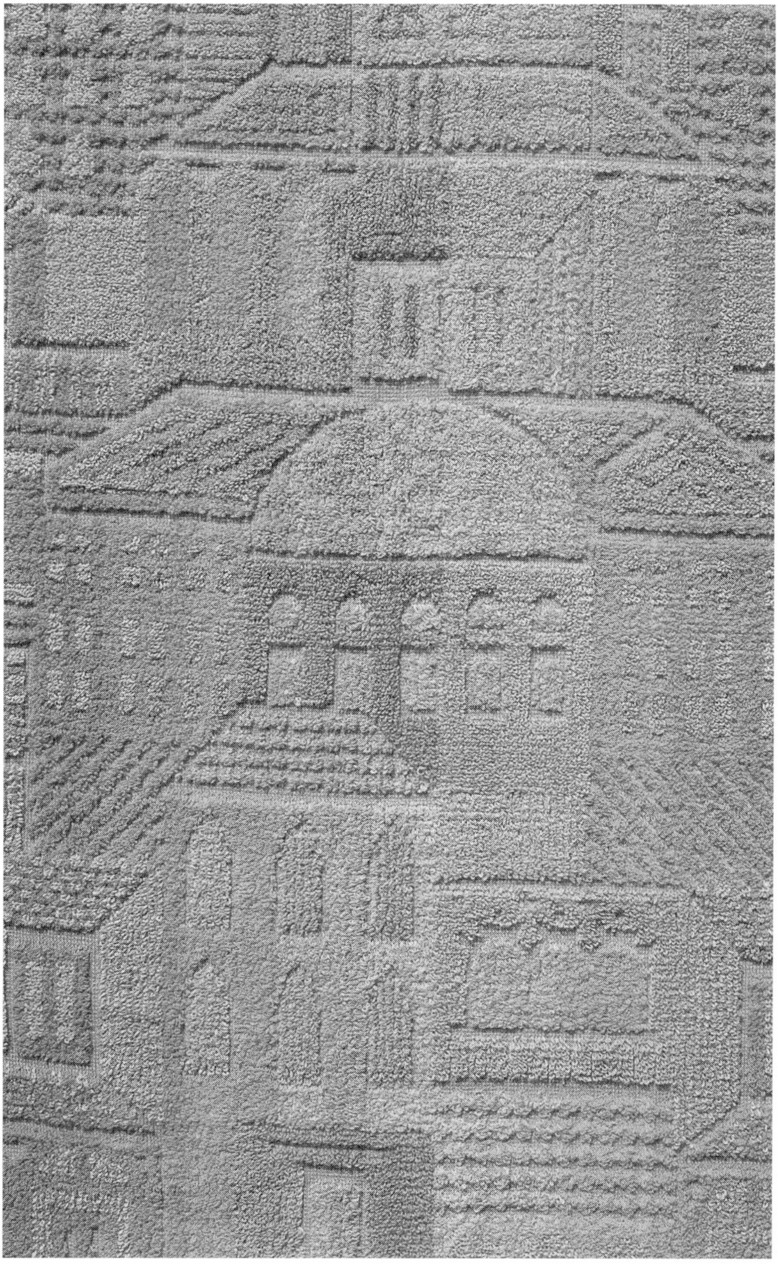

Jack Lenor Larsen, Inc., Architecture, cotton towel in jacquard weave, *c.* 1965, manufactured by J. P. Stevens for their Fine Arts Collection. Larsen might have contributed the most regal and complicated jacquard woven terrycloth bath towels to the modern bathroom, the sole space in the contemporary interior that tends to be more heavily furnished with textiles than it ever was historically. He transformed the towel by weaving a landscape into it and sculpting rooftops and windows in the pile itself, satisfying both our eyes and fingers and turning ordinary mass production into an extraordinary sensory experience.

try his own variation on Dorothea Liebes's 'Chinatown colors', had sent jars of chutney to help his corporate collaborators appreciate the beauty of his plans. Larsen recalls that his towel collection was the first to exploit the jacquard technique with representational images – and if many other fancy towels followed suit with complex floral patterns, few aimed to tell stories. Larsen aggrandized a towel to depict fantastical time travel. His integration of numerous ideas afloat in the trade was certainly a weaver's delight, impossible to conceive on the drafting table or in the managerial arena. To go back two generations earlier, towels had been plain white in his youth. Today, most coloured towels are batch dyed. Stevens's – and Larsen's – Fine Arts Towel Collection was a confluence of corporate indulgence and individual creativity. If the product was the result of machinery, wizardry and many hands, it is also clearly a monument in the history of towel production, were such a narrative to exist.

If Larsen's Architecture transports users to the Eternal City, Rome, on a spectacularly bright Grand Tour, his other forays into mass-produced terrycloth in the 1980s for Martex cultivated American myths in mute tones. One series of umber patterns, called Terra Nova, was inspired by Native American geometric designs, while the grey and white Recollections included representational illustrations of classic American saltbox cottages – a stereotypical modest New England dwelling with a central chimney, one window and one door. The orderly and tidy repetition in the row of houses resembles a plantation. Yet there is a tactile surprise lying in the towel: when it is flipped over, the colours reverse and the roofs go white, seemingly snow-capped. Terra Nova was woven out of unwashed cotton, as Larsen pursued slightly irregular textures; a minor problem was the inherent oils in the untreated fibre. His friend Stanley Marcus, the brilliant steward of Neiman Marcus, called Larsen to praise his invention of a waterproof towel – in jest: Terra Nova needed to be laundered before it could be a practical towel.

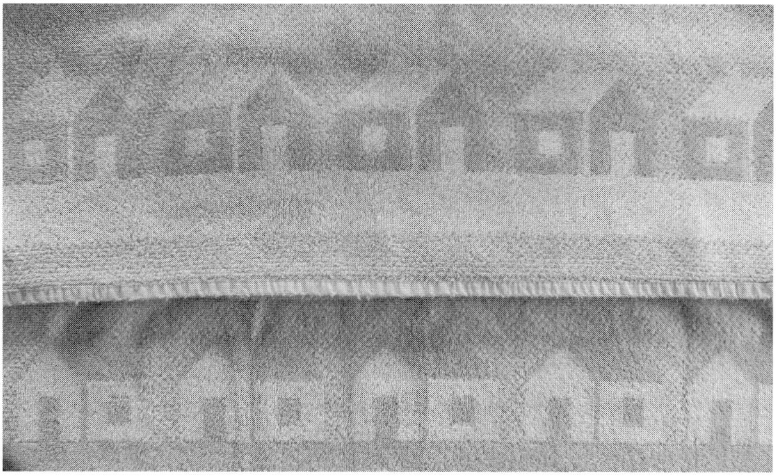

Jack Lenor Larsen, Inc., Recollections (saltbox houses), cotton towel in jacquard weave, 1988, manufactured by Martex. 'Of all fabric structures, double cloths are my favorites. I enjoy the visual pun,' Larsen states, describing his most sumptuous uses of Thai silks but also perhaps the humour of this nostalgic image, which could be flipped seasonally to match the weather.

Whereas Larsen's other works are featured in museums as exemplars of art, craft and design – most notably the Museum of Fine Arts, Montreal, and the University of Minnesota's Goldstein Museum of Design – these towels are a type of object that is perhaps too banal and even a bit indecorous, as it indexes physically intimate use. Towels, like toilets, are generally too undignified to put in museums. Made by machines and many hands, the condition of production of the Fine Arts Towel Collection can be lamented as de facto drudgery, but can we consider mindlessly repetitive labour a recently invented human experience? In reality, the most beautiful Flemish tapestries, Ghiordes prayer rugs and Peruvian manta required months of brutally repetitive work, from the dyeing to weaving and finishing. The cosy bath towel affording comfort to one's naked, wet body might sit enigmatically in regards to the category of 'craft', but the Fine Arts Towel Collection can hold a specific claim on the honorific title. It certainly is easier not to make a towel beautiful, or a ceiling flat for that matter, but perhaps the towel does make us more sensually alert and even warmer if it contains a bit of Roman light, just as a smooth white ceiling cools a weary mind and soothes it to sleep.

Craft is a human act of devising and improvising and yet it is also about returning to fundamental acts of refining our resources into a more imaginative world. One without the other is weak: to engage in invention without drawing on material traditions and social associations is to add more trivial production to an already crowded world; to mindlessly repeat historical conventions and maintain ancient guild-like rules is to force craft into heritage, usually under the auspices of nationalism or some other parochial identity. Larsen's Architecture towel is remarkable as an affordable magic carpet that departs from the clinical feel of the modern bathroom. It could be said to encourage travel and cultural tourism, taking mere factory production and breathing ancient techniques and soulful art into the machinery. Larsen's power loom dances close to the human body. A public sensualist, Larsen is such a private man that it seems unbecoming to praise one of his most ephemeral works of art, a towel destined to fade in sun and laundering. That his many houses were profiled and photographed extensively, and that each was a stage set through which New York City's elite artists passed, matches this duality whereby we gain intimacy with Larsen's taste but little access to his lived life. He plied his loom and tended his gardens barefoot, living mostly in society pages or off-camera. His invention of domestic regal splendour remains beguiling and seductive, as he makes craft a focal point of each room, a texture on every layer. Still to this day, his private house operates as a museum, living archive and harbour – a 'stately pleasure dome' in a bland world. Jack Lenor Larsen is a debonair globetrotter to whom all the world belongs.

ALICE'S 'EYES' THROUGH THE LOOKING GLASS

Cross two sticks and bind them with fibre. You might see this as a religious symbol, a cross, or delineation of the cardinal directions, especially if you look at the wood as the primary form. This bound device has been a fundamental product of handicraft in numerous cultures for thousands of years – used in recent times as body adornment among the Bantu of Angola and the Pilagá of Argentina and preserved in ancient Peruvian archaeological sites, too. In these crosses the wooden substructure is often concealed entirely by wrapped thread – which then becomes the primary visual form.

Perhaps you, too, made versions of these bound crosses as a kindergarten activity. Such interlacings of acrylic yarn and wooden tongue depressors crept into North American primary school education in the 1960s, largely emulating the *ojos de Dios*, or 'God's eyes', made by the Huichol, or Wixáritari as they call themselves, of western Mexico. The Wixáritari marked transformative events like the birth of a child with the radial-patterned form. They wove and made 'God's eyes' (*tsikuri*) and miniature votive chairs (*uweni*) out in the elements as a form of ritual prayer. In the hands of twentieth-century art educators, wrapping colourful yarn around two sticks was a good, therapeutic fine motor exercise; inadvertently, these resulted in countless Christmas tree ornaments. In kindergarten classrooms they retain their role as apotropaic devices: hanging inside large plate-glass windows, they aim to lower the avian mortality rate by warding off birds.

Alice Kagawa Parrott made and sold thousands of *ojos de Dios* – small, delicate and vibrant forms, sometimes two or three on the same branch, using hand-spun wools and dyes of her own. The radial patterns of wound cloth are not complex, but her selection of potent colours and coarse, genuine wool distinguish Parrott's 'eyes' from modern ones made out of acrylic. Tourists to Santa Fe visited the Parrott shop and bought her 'God's eyes' – perhaps more than any other single type of product. They were coveting a piece of the Southwest to take home, but were they also bringing a talisman into their own home as a memory of another, distant

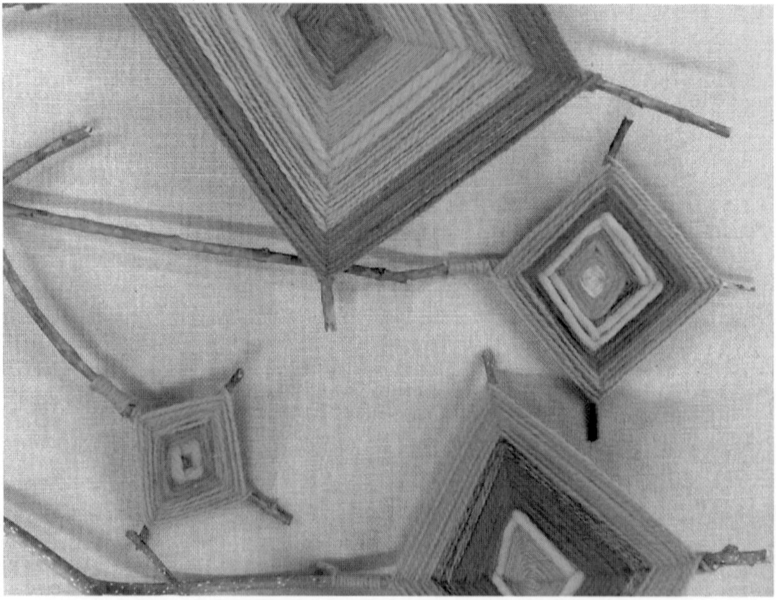

Alice Kagawa Parrott, God's eyes, undated, wool on twigs. Versions of these bound crosses hang in kindergarten windows and Parrott made them out of wools that she handspun and dyed, to sell in her Santa Fe store. The God's eye, largely emulating the *ojos de Dios* made by the Huichol, or Wixáritari, is a near-universal form that has remained a mainstay in American primary school education since the 1960s.

crossroads, the old adobe workshop where Parrott laboured at 'the right unhurried pace'?

In 1960, when Parrott wrote a profile of her own work for the New York City-based periodical *Craft Horizons*, she identified tourists as her core constituency and began her article with their primary question for her: 'Which tribe are you from?' Their suspicion of her ethnicity endured, Parrott wrote, even after she demurred and informed them of her Hawaiian-Japanese ancestry. This perception of Parrott as exotic needs to be handled with care and historical understanding; in her article and in her weavings, she self-consciously cultivated a relational role with Navajo tradition and honoured indigenous weaving as a lineage that nurtured her, perhaps even liberated her from academic confines and modern industrialized conventions of production. Contemporary critics might see Parrott's *ojos de Dios* as an instance of cultural appropriation, but to regard her as bearing an imperial or colonial attitude towards the Navajo or any other tribal cultures is to judge her too swiftly and by contemporary standards. Moreover, Parrott was probably aware that the form of the *ojos de Dios* was near-universal, having been found on every continent and in several ancient archaeological sites. If the appreciation of indigenous handicraft had inspired late nineteenth-century Anglo-Americans to 'play Indian' in dress-up costume, that sort of fantasy was not Parrott's intention. Humbly, Parrott walked in the footsteps of ancient weavers, with the intention to honour them, but also keenly aware that she was an outsider as a Japanese American. What better way to prove herself American than to be pan-indigenous and pan-American? A God's eye was a declaration of alterity that seemed to state, 'If you see me as Indian, I will weave myself Indian.'

Alice Kagawa Parrott's *ojos de Dios* moved away from 'the Cranbrook style', which she characterized as advocating 'a kind of place mat neatness'. The aesthetic seems to have been inhibiting. Would Cranbrook have

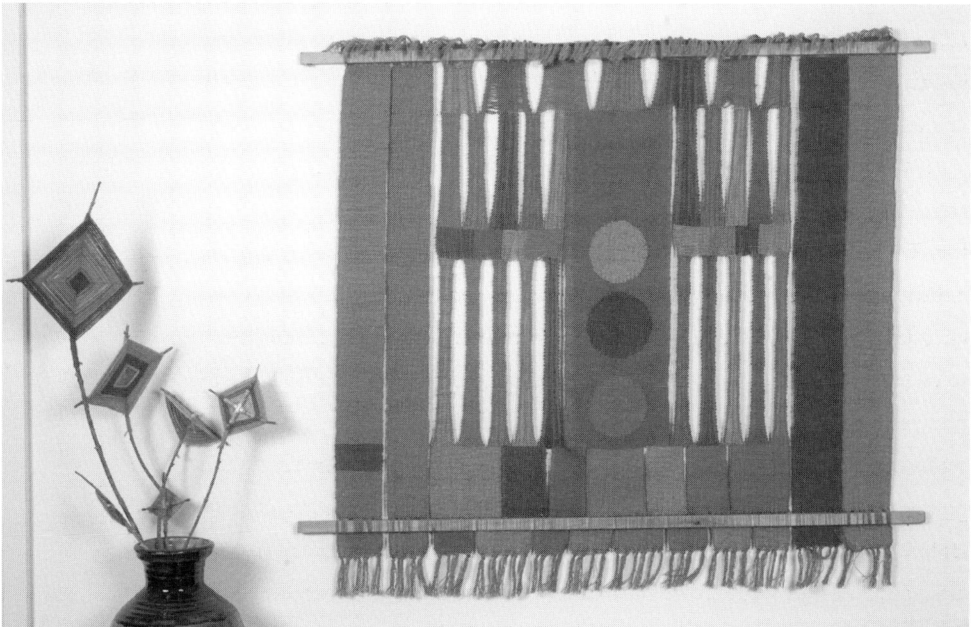

Alice Kagawa Parrott, *Orange Gate Form* with God's eyes, *c.* 1969. Selling mostly useful pillows and clothing, Parrott also wove a limited number of works intended purely for contemplative viewing.

considered her sentimental diamond-eyes not serious enough, too geared to tourists and fashion? To complicate the issue of selectively adapting ethnic resources, Parrott also made versions of her Swedish-Finnish teachers' *rya*, thick-piled knotted rugs, so she cannot be seen as rejecting Cranbrook entirely. She built onto it. Her peer at Cranbrook Toshiko Takaezu was another Hawaiian who was *nisei*, a child of Japanese immigrants, and Takaezu also made *rya*, even though she was much better known as a ceramic artist. Takaezu also saw herself as culturally related to Japan and travelled there for the first time in 1955. Alice Kagawa Parrott was proud to cook up an eclectic mixture of cultural associations and traditions. In addition to selling her *ojos de Dios* individually, she made them in ensembles to match her hangings and accompany them, almost as shoots that sprung out from the wall, bringing her colours and rhythms into a room, almost as if she were designing a layered hedge or yard. Ancient bindings of string once operated as systems of visual communication. Fibres, just string and knots, have been potent communication systems. In Parrott's hands, fibre was primarily a physical marker: her *ojos de Dios* made the idea of 'home' a portable woollen floral bouquet.

An ardent gardener, Parrott set her *ojos de Dios* in vases. They have a satisfying tactile presence at close range. Viewed from afar, beside a wall hanging, six of these bright, diamond-patterned twigs dance and sparkle like living things. Using twigs and hand-spun yarn, handicraft assumes an elemental structure and yet maintains complexity. As she made journeys to Mexico, South America and India, Parrott increasingly felt free to add new techniques and colourways to her repertoire. Her borrowing and re-enactment of a historical tradition in the God's eye provided her with metaphorical ties to a broad world. If her *ojos de Dios* slip between authentic tribal artefact, contemporary decor and the woeful category of tourist knick-knack, it deserves to be regarded as a potentially meaningful textile. Anything that is intensely comforting and a homing device is not without function. It also fitted her schedule. She once voiced her regret to her friend Takaezu that she could no longer work in clay, noting that weaving was more practical and sympathetic to parenting as she could drop her shuttle and return a few hours later to pick up precisely where she had left off without the wool changing or drying out as clay was prone to do. Parrott's domestic responsibilities and role as a mother were immensely time-consuming, and the *ojos de Dios* were small projects that could progress while onions simmered or children ate a meal.

Parrott's artistic contributions have not been fully catalogued or documented yet. Although she was prolific, making large tapestries for commissioned installations in civic buildings in Hawaii and exhibiting regularly, her family is only slowly beginning to organize her estate. She has not benefited from a major retrospective exhibition and has received little attention from art historians. She and her husband Allen Parrott, who left his job as an assistant curator at the Santa Fe Museum of International Folk Art to work alongside her, have passed through the world leaving only a few scattered artefacts for us to find and enjoy. Their focus was day-to-day life. Their ambitions were more tied to their family than a larger stage or market. However, they were not insular, and their home remained a vibrant destination where entertainment and dining were memorable experiences. Friends and former classmates from Cranbrook often visited. The Parrotts' social circle included summer residents like Sue and Robert Turner, who lived in Alfred, New York, where he taught ceramics. The woodworker Sam Maloof and his wife Freda bought Parrott's pillows to complete his furniture and the Maloofs also wore her woollen shirts and vests, as did the Turners. The sculptor Isamu Noguchi and painter Agnes Martin both wore Japanese jackets called hanten made by Parrott. When Noguchi came to visit his sister in the Southwest, Parrott was proud that he came to her home for solace and rest and that he thought Parrott's cooking superior to his sister's.

Because Parrott was an avid gardener, we can think of her artistic oeuvre as having seasonal rhythms. Her humility and philosophy prevented her from thinking of her legacy as a monument. For many visitors, such as fellow weaver and Cranbrook alumnus Ted Hallman and his partner Michael Barnett, Parrott's garden was an enchanted and hallowed annual destination. The Parrotts' verdant enclosure was a central axis of social life in Santa Fe. They dined and entertained there, and Cranbrook artist-in-residence and then director Gerhardt Knodel remembered Parrott fêting students around her table, too. Like Toshiko Takaezu, she found horticulture not simply a chore or a leisure activity but an essential engagement of time, mental energy and affection with place: Takaezu believed students needed to handle soil and nurture plants in order to develop responsive craftsmanship.

For Parrott, craft was a lifestyle as well as a livelihood. After 1970, she travelled less to exhibitions and exhibited less in art museums and galleries; her store was successful and grew threefold over the decades. The *ojos de Dios* she made and brought to her sister in Hawaii is a delicate and broken fragment of a large and full life – and even if these bits of work disappear over time, succumbing to dust and decay, they are worth memorializing, like Larsen's equally ephemeral towel, as markers of a specific time and place and as textiles which conjured global vistas and intimacy – albeit in commonplace houses and common ways.

Jack Lenor Larsen and Alice Kagawa Parrott are incomparable but are worth contrasting to flesh out divergent pathways in craft. If there is only one Larsen and a thousand or more Parrotts in the United States who toiled in semi-obscurity far from the spotlight of magazines and museum exhibitions, these figures represent the fact that there is no singular path in weaving. Her life is a more representative tale of craft in the second half of the twentieth century; today tens of thousands of practitioners of craft operate small workshops in regional areas as amateurs, hobbyists and professionals. If Larsen aimed to be a city dweller, Parrott was committed to the idea of regionalism, even if she was international in her interests and travel. If his textiles tended towards the luxurious and refined, hers affected peasant-like rawness. Craft has often diverged between the palace and the cottage, the aristocrat and the labourer. Yet the degree of artifice and their shared education at Cranbrook underscore the healthiness in regarding craft as diverse, multi-temporal and of infinite variety. The school championed the process of weaving as a tool for finding one's way. Today, schools of art, design and architecture are struggling to be grounded in their locations and responsive to their surrounding communities, but a road map to develop cultural diversity in such a sheltered precinct remains elusive. And for individuals, fear of cultural appropriation might inhibit the process of self-invention.

PLACE AND PATTERN AS PERSON

Parrott and Larsen are examples of reinvention in cosmopolitan craft and are peculiarly American in their respective journeys. Their coming of age in an era of affluence, continual economic growth and increased personal freedoms might seem too good to be true as we look back from an economically more precarious twenty-first century. But their independence and ability to chart a path outside the academy and art gallery into everyday life is what marks them as invaluable sources of inspiration today. They wove outside institutional channels. Their audacity to venture beyond national cultural boundaries and traditions is worth contrasting to contemporary fears of perpetuating cultural appropriation. They boldly ventured beyond insular notions of culture, even if they might have at times indelicately broken conventions.

Sheila Hicks is another weaver who eloquently articulates that thread has no pure identity, no authentic essence. In Bernard Monsigny's film *Hicks: Tissages Métissés* (1987), she explains, 'We can begin with the pure material in its natural form, virgin material . . . we can begin with less pure material, one that has a history, even a very dense story. We can recycle something . . . A textile has a memory.' As the film's title suggests, Hicks self-consciously conceives of her weavings as hybrid; she wants her work to expose the pathos of humanity. For instance, her massive installation of nurses' uniforms in the 1970s was purposeful recycling. 'By expressing the interconnectedness of disparate elements . . . I structure a small world of elegant incongruity.' Like Parrott and Larsen, who tap multiple cultural resources, Hicks sought to endow power-loomed upholstery for Knoll with an 'Andean hand-woven quality' and also, in a most modern manner, 'playful mistakes'. She, too, wove for an aeroplane, the Concorde. What Hicks articulates about textiles goes for Larsen and Parrott, too: no textile is perceptibly local. Together, this work makes the most of an American aesthetic that roams and ranges freely across the globe – and might indicate the weaver's natural compulsion to connect fibres together, to give us warmth.

Sheila Hicks's *Chronology* is a Venn diagram with intervals that cannot be breached and an autobiographical explanation of her polyglot weavings. Larsen and Parrott similarly engaged craft as a theatrical process of self-invention. Both journeyed far from their birthplaces and assiduously cultivated radically distinct domestic havens. Larsen invented a new home every few years, and each one became a tableau on which to reveal new interests and showcase his eye and social network. His Bantu-esque hut, Round House, and Manhattan lofts were stages on which to spotlight his taste and audacity as an aesthete. Larsen and Parrott were both photographed working in their homes. Larsen was always a bachelor and usually photographed professionally. Parrott was caught in family snapshots in her role as a mother, school trip chaperone, hostess and small shop owner. Today, Larsen's cultural centre on Long Island, the

Sheila Hicks, *Chronology*, undated, ink on paper, 14 × 11 in. (35.5 × 28 cm). Instead of a linear timeline of her life, a standard cliché for conceptualizing artistic progress, Hicks sketches out her passage through places and work opportunities. The list of places and dates begins with a few circular gestures and then is a patchwork that seems open to additional stitches, with each country or city name standing for a much larger body of work.

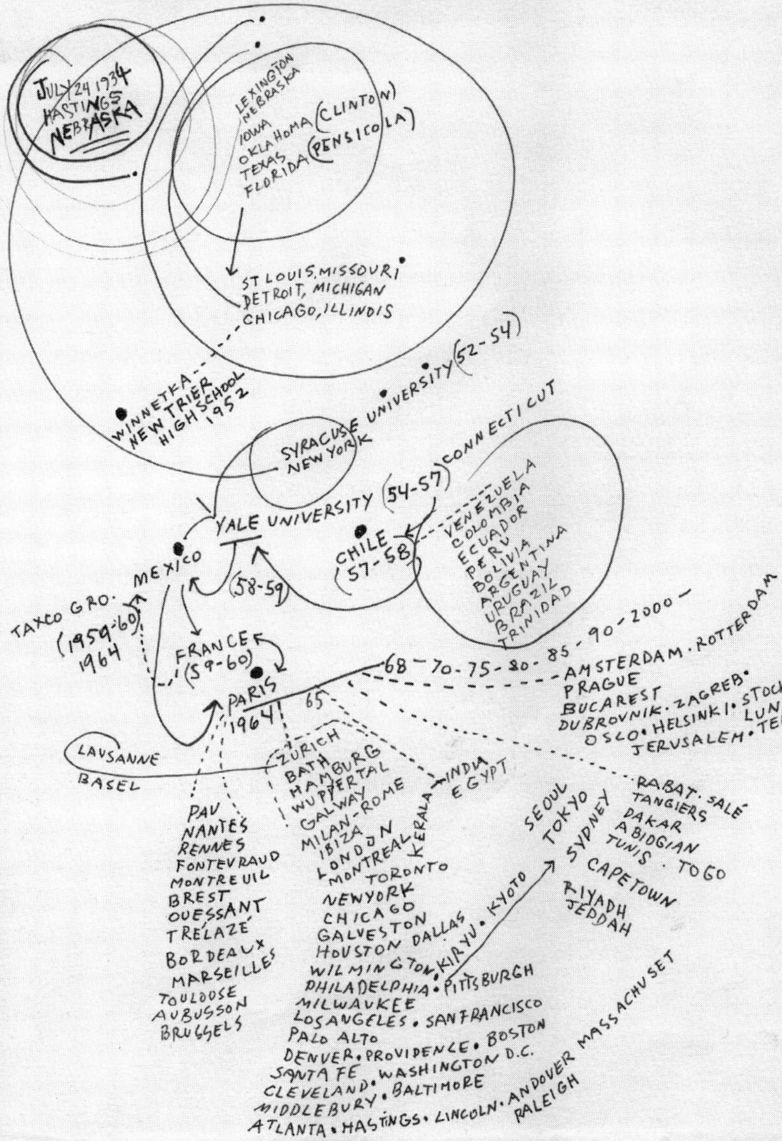
JULY 24 1934
HASTINGS
NEBRASKA
LEXINGTON NEBRASKA
IOWA
OKLAHOMA (CLINTON)
TEXAS
FLORIDA (PENSICOLA)
ST LOUIS, MISSOURI
DETROIT, MICHIGAN
CHICAGO, ILLINOIS
WINNETKA
NEW TRIER
HIGH SCHOOL
1952
SYRACUSE UNIVERSITY (52-54)
SYRACUSE NEW YORK
CONNECTICUT
YALE UNIVERSITY (54-57)
CHILE (57-58)
VENEZUELA
COLOMBIA
ECUADOR
PERU
BOLIVIA
ARGENTINA
URUGUAY
BRAZIL
TRINIDAD
(58-59)
MEXICO
TAXCO GRO.
(1959-60)
1964
FRANCE (59-60)
PARIS
1964
65
68 - 70 - 75 - 80 - 85 - 90 - 2000 -
AMSTERDAM. ROTTERDAM
PRAGUE
BUCAREST
DUBROVNIK. ZAGREB.
OSLO. HELSINKI. STOCKHOLM
LUND
JERUSALEM. TELAVIV
LAUSANNE
BASEL
PAU
NANTES
RENNES
FONTEVRAUD
MONTREUIL
BREST
OUESSANT
TRELAZE
BORDEAUX
MARSEILLES
TOULOOSE
AUBUSSON
BRUSSELS
ZURICH
BATH
HAMBURG
WUPPERTAL
GALWAY
MILAN-ROME
IBIZA
LONDON
MONTREAL
TORONTO
NEWYORK
CHICAGO
GALVESTON
HOUSTON DALLAS
WILMINGTON. KIRYU. KYOTO
PHILADELPHIA. PITTSBURGH
MILWAUKEE
LOSANGELES. SANFRANCISCO
PALO ALTO
DENVER. PROVIDENCE. BOSTON
SANTA FE
CLEVELAND. WASHINGTON D.C.
MIDDLEBURY. BALTIMORE
ATLANTA. HASTINGS. LINCOLN. ANDOVER MASSACHUSET
RALEIGH
KERALA
INDIA
EGYPT
SEOUL
TOKYO
SYDNEY
RIYADH
JEDDAH
RABAT. SALE
TANGIERS
DAKAR
ABIDGIAN
TUNIS . TOGO
CAPETOWN

LongHouse Reserve, is within orbit of mostly moneyed New Yorkers, a place for celebrity spotting, and the acreage features large art installations by the likes of Yoko Ono and Dale Chihuly among stately hedges and cultivated plantings. Indeed, it is where Chihuly's first environmental installation, cacti-like forms, bloomed. LongHouse is poised to endure as a monument that will foster Larsen's legacy of interlacing contemporary and older notions of handicraft, art and design. Most of all, it is a harbour for the senses, where Larsen's stage can be shared by others.

In our era when identity politics burns brightly as a consuming issue and motivation for artistic production, Larsen and Parrott deserve consideration for their ways of inventing new dramatis personae outside census boxes and other preconceived institutional categories. They did not come of age during twenty-first-century notions of self-exposure – we are wrong if we want their identities to more overtly match the possibilities we consider real or 'authentic'. Their work preceded our era when identity politics brings ethnicity or sexual orientation or religious affiliation to the fore. These weavers' inventions of a persona saw artifice as the essential component of their craft.

Patterns become modes of physical connection and textiles bridges – not data but actual fibres. Numerical data may represent pattern, but implies weaving is an intellectual abstraction and not a tangible metaphor, which is much more seductive. Instead of categorizing types of craft according to style, taste or perceived authenticity, we can touch actual lives in the patterns of actual fibres, such as in Parrott's *ojos de Dios* and Larsen's towels. In these, craft is both a noun and a verb. 'Pattern is both a noun and a verb,' writes the mathematician Ian Stewart, 'but as a verb it is an active way of seeing the world, a process by which to take in and make coherent the random and often chaotic information the world has to offer.' There is no 'truth to materials' in pattern or distinctions between hand and machined. Instead of a rigid ideal, Diderot asked us, 'What more beautiful, more delicate, more singular projection is there than that of a pattern?' With hope, after looking closely at the work of Larsen and Parrott, Hicks and Rossbach, among others, we commune with authentic responses to pattern's pressures and possibilities. There is no distinction between 'natural' and 'unnatural' pattern, and no pattern is inauthentic. Weaving is comprised of numbers, intervals and interference – we only travel farther in this world if we keep a grasp on our filaments and fibres and nurture our awareness of these indispensable arts. Textiles are a key to staying comfortable, but they are the fundamental tools upon which our self-invention depends as humans. Each of us has the choice to hunt for readymade costumes or aspire to the radiant inventiveness of a Hicks or Larsen. What will be the next pattern and textile that transports us? If we keep weaving we will discover our next identity, our next invented homeland.

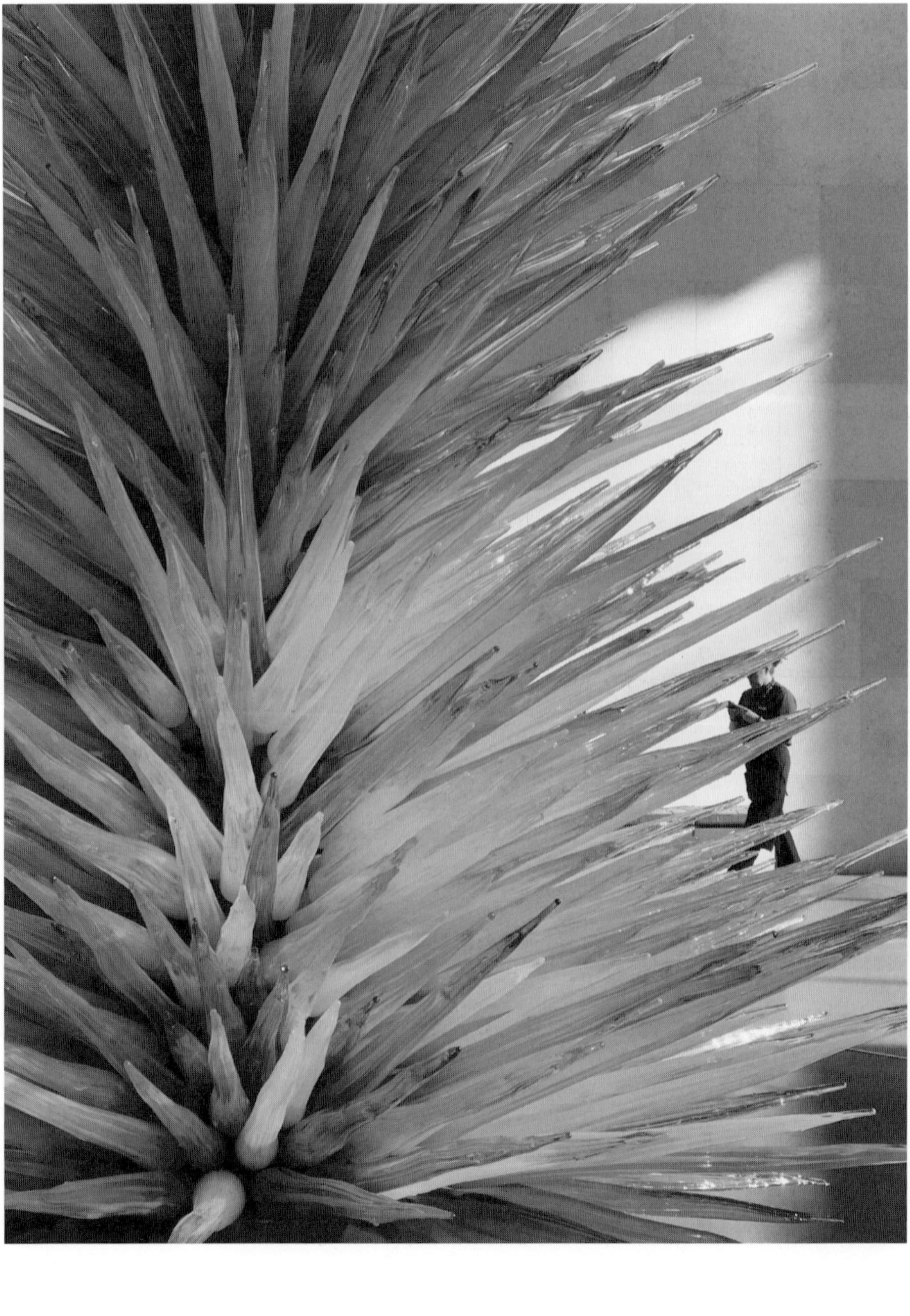

FIVE

TIME IN GLASSCRAFT

Large glass sculpture can appear airborne, yet making it is a craft requiring an immense technological infrastructure of resources – a furnace, annealing ovens, a team of artisans, and a profusion of fuel, fuel and yet more fuel. One must imagine the vast tributary of preparatory labour dedicated to amassing charcoal, cleaning sand and grinding shells at early forges and smelting facilities. Such a smoky, sweaty, multi-headed, multi-handed organization lies unseen, offstage, behind the towering installations by Dale Chihuly that have given glass visibility and magisterial status in art museums in recent years.

Dale Chihuly, *Lime Green Icicle Tower*, 2011, blown glass and steel, Museum of Fine Arts, Boston. Chihuly's visibility in the USA is comparable to the della Robbias in Renaissance Florence, and just as their work arose to suit a novel architectural style, his work is tied to the contemporary plate glass atrium. To describe Chihuly's sculpture as 'craft' or 'studio craft' only obscures his work and distracts us from larger questions about the meaning and style of the glass.

These are the paradoxes of glass, which has arguably never been a 'handicraft' made solo – it has always been industrial manufacture in the best and most accurate manner. Glass is born of teamwork, a grasp of chemistry – or at the very least a functioning sense of alchemy – and ample resources. Glasscraft has always been rooted to a dedicated manufacturing space, the furnace. It is the antithesis of a nomadic textile made without a loom, like felt, or a basket woven freehand as quickly as a branch can be snapped off a shrub. A necklace of cobalt glass beads dating back to the sixteenth-century Age of Exploration of the New World and Africa should be savoured as high-performance enchanting technology, not as a trinket. The expansion of Venetian and Dutch glass factories was a strategic necessity: beads were tools to procure land or the semblance of alliances. The high-tech pea-sized export promised to confer immediate status and membership to a club, much like a contemporary celebrity wristwatch. Glass can fool an educated consumer into mistaking the artificial as natural: a scarab entombed with king Tutankhamun in 1323 BCE was recently identified as a chunk of silicon dioxide from the Libyan desert formed by a fiery meteorite 26 million years ago. The capability to be transparent, reflective and incandescent makes for optical games that misplace our tactile knowledge; this chapter seeks to reconnect glass to material and social networks.

Contemporary glasscraft is especially seductive because of the sense that the floral luminosity within is eternal. Students have confided to me that they first mistook Chihuly's *Lime Green Icicle Tower* in the Boston Museum of Fine Arts (MFA) for a tropical plant. Glass has the semblance of an immaculate conception – often there are no visible signs of human hands and the colours seem impervious to time. Egyptian or Venetian techniques might be evoked, but aside from the archaeological record we prefer glass to show no age, carry no unwanted history. The eminent cultural critic Walter Benjamin lamented that glass eradicated human traces. This born-untouched quality aligns with our expectation for commodities to appear 'new' – a compulsion related to our ever-accelerating pace of consumption and progressive obsolescence, as well as the aesthetic celebration of autonomy and originality. The values of laboratory and museum glass coalesce here, too, into the overwhelmingly popular idea of glass standing alone, apart from social interaction and above the fray of use. The museum vitrine, although usually made of acrylic, epitomizes this falsehood of transparency by implying the commodities within it have fixed values when they do not.

This final chapter reintegrates such sparkling artefacts into the labour of the glasshouse as well as our uses of the material as a mediating layer on our phone cameras and electronic devices. Contemporary craft is more shaped by glass than by any other material. Glass screens streaming video inform the word 'craft' today more tangibly than verbal definitions or static images. Despite being emblematic of modernity and the artificial – such as the contemporary skyscraper, a sterile laboratory beaker, a light bulb or a touch-screen on a communications device – glass is also a primary conduit to nature through expansive windows, diaphanous buildings, telephoto cameras and immersive liquid crystal displays.

Chihuly's work is usually read, if not as nature itself, then as a metaphor for or abstraction of sublime forms in nature. The visibility and large scale of his environmental installations, especially in garden settings such as LongHouse Reserve in East Hampton, New York, where Jack Lenor Larsen was an early patron, certainly encourages such associations. So where to contextualize Chihuly's massive installations? Glasscraft is rarely part of the canonical history of art; the history of architecture incorporates the engineering and orchestration of glass more adroitly. Can we read his work as a product of both individual genius and a firm or workshop? Only recently have curators like Gerald Ward punctured the myth of the invention of 'studio glass' as an assertion of American exceptionalism and individualism by situating its emergence as a convergence of four forces. What was necessary for the florescence? Ward acknowledges that factory skills and industrial and corporate patronage have been overlooked and undervalued in relation to academic artistic freedom of inquiry and counter-cultural self-determination. Without the large factories like Corning, Libbey and Pittsburgh Plate Glass, there could not have been heroic figures such as Harvey Littleton or Dominick Labino, considered the 'fathers' of the studio glass movement, or their students, like Chihuly. Our optical relationships far exceed our studied assessment of glass, and it is time to reconcile these disparate experiences with an understanding of its social and historical contexts.

The seismic role of glass in Western civilization is intoxicating – lenses and glass laboratory equipment shaped the emergence of modern science in numerous ways, and basic tools like eyeglasses expanded individual working performance as much as the light bulb contributed to transforming factories into continuous operations. Our understanding of the constituent parts of glass in relation to molecular chemistry is very recent – and due to the magnifying properties of glass itself. Yet of all the crafts, the leap between a hot-shop where a handful of workers manipulate glass and the largest, most up-to-date factories, where 36-foot-long sheets are laminated into insulated, hermetically sealed units, is daunting. The finest works of architectural glass are surely the work of collated craft: for complex variegated facades, often, human-sized graphite moulds, sculptural in their own right, have been milled to shape the substance. Beyond our predilection for taking self-portraits in these contemporary caverns of light, what is the relationship of the individual to such collaborative monuments? What temporal connections might we perceive between Chihuly's material explorations and these much more 'high-tech' adaptations of glass?

Hourglass and shadow. Glass made timekeeping a portable hand-held accessory. Hourglasses first became industrial design during the Renaissance and then slipped back into the category of craft by the 20th century: their manual pleasure remains unchanged.

GLASS WITHIN REACH: THE HOURGLASS AND THE LIGHT BULB

Glass is mostly silica; melted sand. Ever since inventing ways of blowing it molten with a pipe about two thousand years ago, humans have made the material levitate into the air and spin into curvaceous forms. The beauty of blown glass is that it acknowledges and also defies gravity. A liquid that performs as a solid, glass can maintain a droop without ever falling, swirl with waves of colour that never dissipate, and be sealed – forming a vacuum – but still permit light to pass through unobstructed. Consider two commonplace and yet remarkably significant little objects,

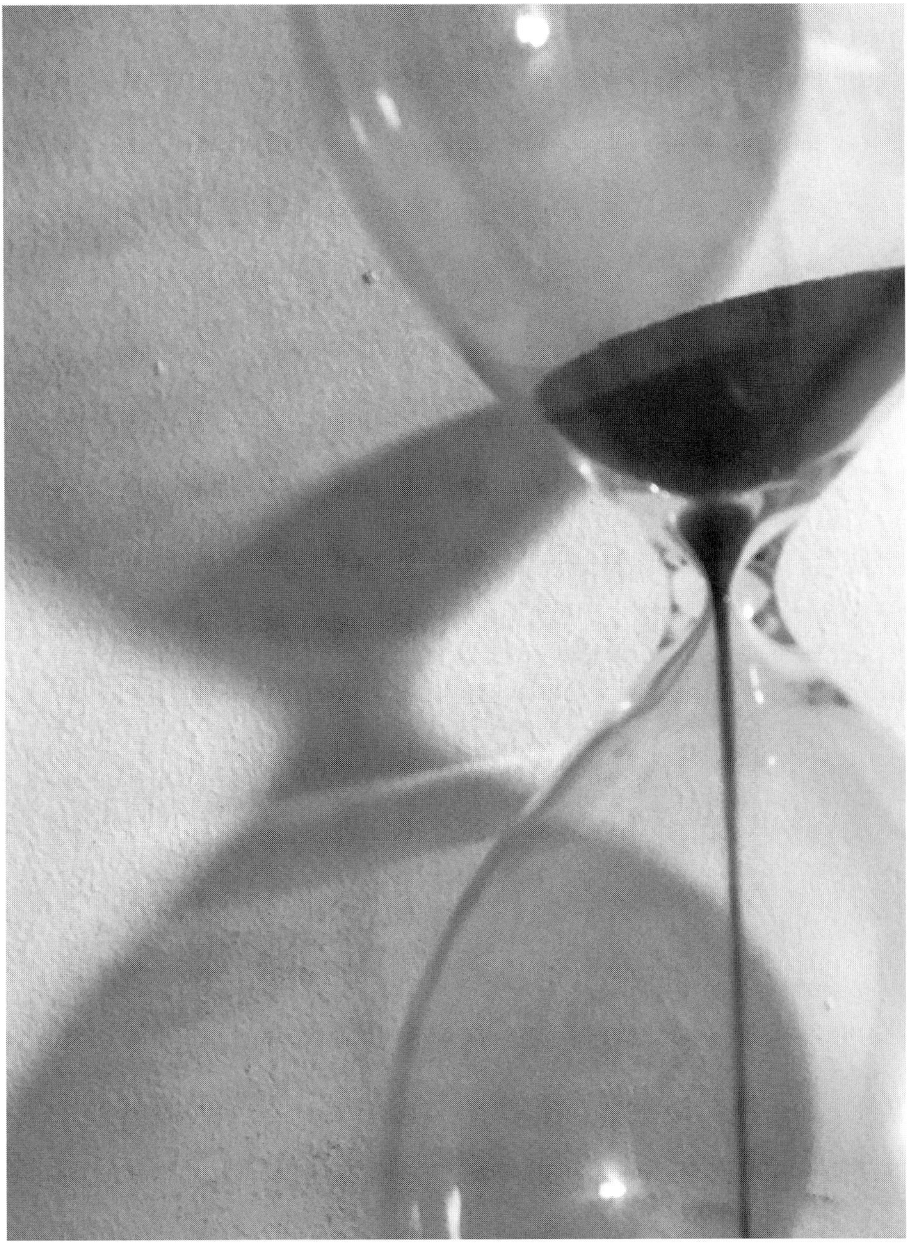

the hourglass and the pear-shaped incandescent light bulb. One seems ancient – from a world when manual dexterity mattered – and the other emblematic of modernity. Both sport anthropomorphic curves that suggest human scale and agency. The contrast between them pulls into relief the strangeness of measuring the industrial qualities of glasscraft.

The hourglass, a device in which granules drop from a higher to a lower chamber through a slender regulating passage, is also called a sand clock. Our interest lies in its transparency; numerous earlier tools measured time by the passage of sand or water from one unit of measure to another. The precise date of the instrument's invention is a mystery, but as early as the fourteenth century, recipes for the preparation of marble dust for use in an hourglass were committed to paper (angular grains of sand are less reliable particles). Pendular clocks do not work at sea, but hourglasses track time in any weather and through starless nights. The simplicity of the hourglass form is elegant, but the modern seamless tube is of recent invention. Before the eighteenth century, the two glass chambers were separate units that a cabinet-maker or jeweller bound at the narrows by wax, rope or metalwork. An artisan other than a glassblower made the hourglass into a functioning tool, but transparency was essential to its function: the Venetian discovery of clear *cristallo* made an hourglass mesmerizing. Now obsolete, the hourglass remains a timekeeper in children's games and in kitchens. Although it no longer qualifies as 'technology', the device is deployed in motion graphics as an icon during the frustrating delays inherent in modern communication networks. When waiting for a computerized bank teller to authorize a cash withdrawal, we watch pixels drip in a schematic hourglass, a technologically retrogressive image that sends a confusing message about the way we perceive or value time.

Glass made timekeeping a portable hand-held accessory. Sets of sandglasses broke an hour into four fifteen-minute increments. By the fourteenth century, numerous texts mention them and significant visual records exist, as well – see Ambrogio Lorenzetti's *Allegory of Good and Bad Government* (1338) and Albrecht Dürer's *Saint Jerome in His Study* (1514) – which parallel the expansion of Italian merchants into global trade. When Columbus set sail hoping to stumble upon India, the manufacture of glass was already proceeding at such a fast clip that Venetian and Florentine merchants were taking orders by the thousand for eyeglasses from merchants in the Middle East, who specified the quantities of spectacle and the types of frame, the more select being of bone or bogwood, according to historian Vincent Ilard. Venetian glassmakers considered 'Levant soda ash' superior to Egyptian and were fairly dependent on the trade of raw materials as well as finished goods. The earliest hourglasses in museums date back to these years when Venetian 'crystal' glass was the world's envy.

The hourglass is wonderfully recyclable, as the apparatus can operate in a mine or a kindergarten class – unlike a sundial or a candle. It is a rarity, a clock that still seems to exemplify craft. In contrast, batteries and electronics meting out strictly standardized beats hardly seem worthy of respect. Today's cheap, store-bought plastic sandglass is obviously not artisanal but still preserves the elegance of transparency and lightness. It is an archetype of human ingenuity and yet also an incremental step towards the mechanization of Western civilization.

Hourglasses could be said to have become industrial design during the Renaissance and then slipped back into the category of craft by the twentieth century, but the pleasure we find in them, like their use as a visual metaphor for time passing, retains potency. We move through the present moment while looking ahead and behind us through funnels, imagining a greater number of possible futures and pasts the further we squint from our tenuous perch. If an hourglass seems prosaic, pause to admire its mechanical ingenuity. It is a resilient emblem of rationality and empiricism. Its fall in status parallels the descent of the adjective 'mechanical' from esteemed virtue to mere drudgery.

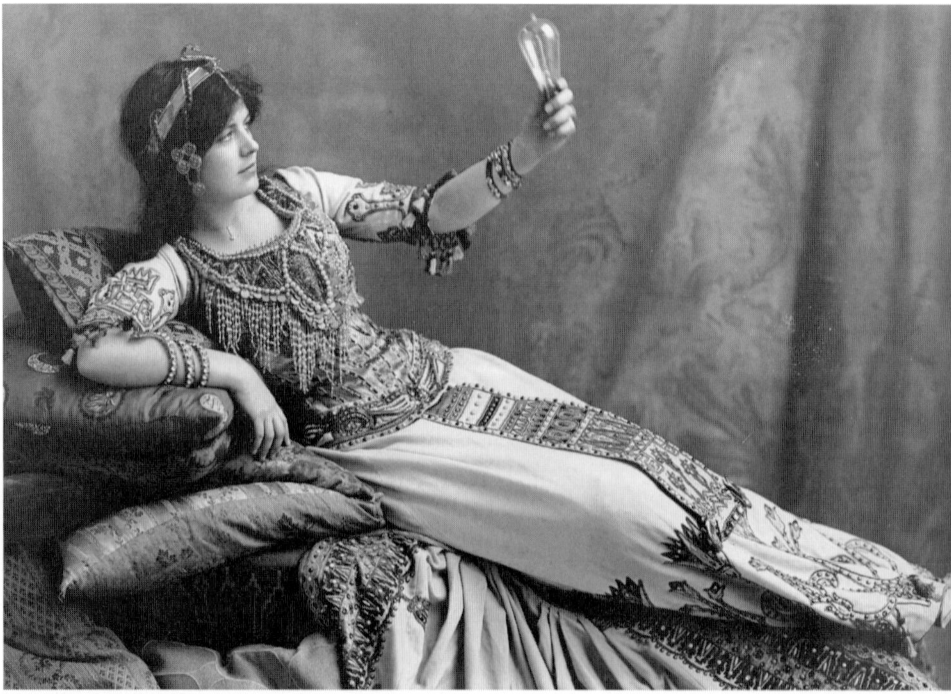

General Electric advertising photograph, undated. Do we still fetishize technology, and glass in particular, and think of it detached from its conditions of production? In about 1900 an odalisque, then commonly used to sell cigarettes, held up an incandescent light bulb to convey the promise of such magical equipment to give pleasure.

Although today's light bulbs are made by mechanically injecting air into molten glass, they have a tactile charm that defies their throwaway status and, like hourglasses, their scale alone suggests human agency. Even when the filament inside has burned out, the bulb pleases our grip as an egg does. The surface is reflective and smooth; the form light and strong. It has endured long past what should have been its expiration date: it defies logic by symbolizing human invention and progress when it should be a sign of progressive obsolescence and inefficiency (only 2–5 per cent of the energy that such light bulbs consume is channelled into light, as most of the energy radiates as heat). Resembling the first stage of an inflated balloon, the simplest light bulb is pear-shaped: this 'A-type' is still the basic form it was in 1910, when pairs of skilled gaffers and assistants would blow two bulbs per minute.

In 1915, in a single factory in the United States, artisans produced more than 30 million individually blown light bulbs. Between 1875 and 1915, the number of glassblowers employed in human history reached its zenith with the onset of electricity. Edison created a greater need for glassblowers than ever before. Astonishingly, there is little distinction between a bulb made in 1910 by an artisan and one made by the automated ribbon machine around 1930. Visual similarity between the products of manual and automatic labour are not what we expect, but such is the way of industrial craft, which aims at modular compatibility and therefore is self-effacing rather than self-expressive.

For its first four decades, the incandescent light bulb was an artisanal product – it sold for 17 cents in 1910. Production was mechanized in the 1920s, at the hands of a glassblower. William Woods's insight was to harness the plasticity and behaviour of a molten droplet. When hot glass continuously ran over a perforated ribbon of metal, gravity helped standardized droplets. His innovation came through first-hand observation. The Corning Ribbon Machine, patented in 1927 by Woods and the engineer David Gray, produced two thousand light bulbs per minute in 1926 – the product of craft knowledge as much as corporate research. Woods and Gray improved an 1890s machine made by another glassblower, Michael Owens, who had first apprenticed to work on glass production in 1869 at the age of ten for Hobbs, Brockunier & Company in Wheeling, West Virginia. Owens and Woods live on in patent records more than histories of craft, art or design, but their genius materialized in the glasshouse, not on a drafting table.

Bottles and their volumes had long been standardized and tediously made in the thousands; mechanization reduced labour costs. If the twenty-first century sees the bottle machine as 'deskilling' craft, the twentieth regarded it as a tool to humanize an industry in which life expectancies were as grim as in coal mining. In the 1890s, Owens took out several patents, one for 'an apparatus for blowing glass . . . mechanically, what has heretofore been done manually'. His ten-armed bottle machine patent of 1903 aimed for automation: 'to gather the glass, shape it into the desired blank, and blow it to form without the intervention of any labour whatever'. The manual insertion of filaments into these bulbs still required fine fingers for decades to come. Because the human cost of historical glasscraft is no longer visible, we can romanticize ancient production and vilify more recent industrialization – despite being the beneficiaries of both.

Lamentations about the demise of skill in manufacturing tend to isolate individual glassblowers as heroic. Bert Haanstra's documentary *Glas* (1958) paints this sort of picture of humans pitted against automation. First, a montage isolates individual, mostly middle-aged, gaffers with eyes squinting as they pull gathers of molten glass from a furnace. Then, Haanstra shows the groping insensitivity of automated robotic hands unable to recognize a broken-necked bottle. Many more are smashed in rapid-fire succession: the moral is that manufacturing turns into a site of mass destruction when stewardship is ceded to robots. The denunciation of mechanization and praise for artisans is not subtle, and in the end the film accelerates to a frenzied pace as only a motion picture can, foreshadowing other fast-frame denunciations of industrial production such as Godfrey Reggio's *Koyaanisqatsi* (1982).

In the aftermath of the destruction of the Second World War, the use of the word 'craft' spiked in publications in England, America and Continental Europe. Haanstra's film can be seen as part of that concern with preserving cultural heritage. The pressing question was how to define the loss of manual trades in relation to techniques of automation. *Glas* is misleading in isolating the blower as a solitary worker facing off against the furnace, instead of a member of a team of four or five. Assistants, in the nineteenth century often children, always surrounded the lead artisan, who sat in the chair, the gaffer's bench flanked by rails on which the blowpipe rolled. Watch any prominent glass artist demonstrating their skills at the Corning Museum of Glass or at Pilchuck, a school dedicated to glass established in rural Washington state by Chihuly in 1971, or any other school and you will see teamwork: blowing and rolling the blowpipe are distinct but synchronized individual tasks. When critics (especially students) lament Chihuly's success because he doesn't 'make it himself', they overlook his skilled choreography.

General Electric photograph, undated. The romance of blowing glass has rarely been associated with the assembly line installation of filaments and a vacuum seal, and the work was gendered.

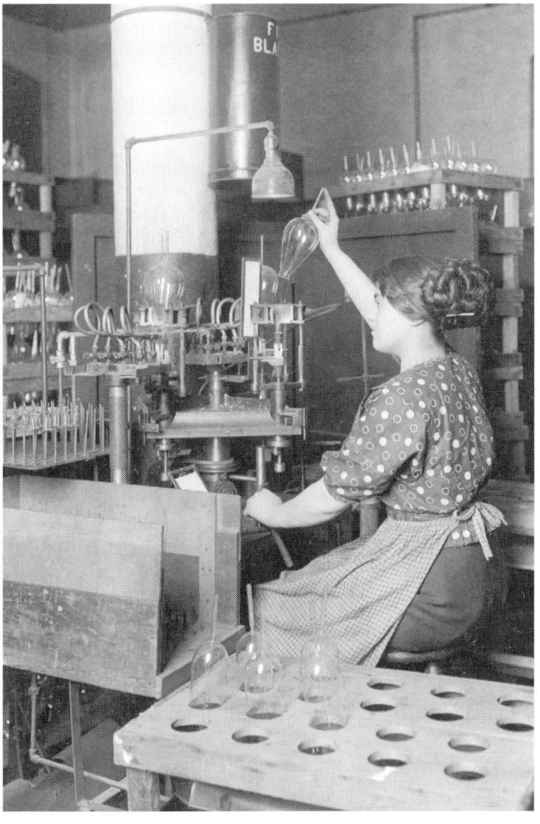

There has never been a glasshouse worked by a solitary artisan. Teamwork has rarely been as overtly acknowledged as in the 1920s at Orrefors, Sweden, where the highly skilled blower Knut Bergqvist sometimes signed his name alongside that of the designers Simon Gate and Edward Hald. And between distinct eras of production, skills are incomparable. Can the maker of crown glass, who seized a gather, blew a bowl and spun it outward to make window panes in 1750, be said to be more or less skilful than the maker of cylinder glass of 1830, who walked a plank and twirled an elongated molten tube, only to pass it on to another artisan specialized in slicing it open and annealing it? It is best to shy away from such judgements.

In 2014, a student pursuing an advanced art degree in studio glass, Riikka Haapasaari, videotaped a performance that it is worth contrasting to *Glas* because hers is a less moralistic celebration of craft. In *Glassblowing Without Glass*, Haapasaari filmed three expert Tuscan glassblowers, Giancarlo Prosperi, Sanseverino Franco and Sergio Serra, walking through the sequence of production at the Museo del Vetro in Empoli, Tuscany, in 2013. The footage is a strangely mournful affirmation that skill is immaterial. It is almost but not quite a documentary: the three artisans go through the physical motions of glass-blowing without the molten liquid. Rolling their hands in the air, they turn and blow into an invisible blowpipe. In contrast to the artisans in *Glas*, who were lit dramatically by the furnace, Haapasaari's perspective is deadpan, even mock-heroic. Her humans look sceptical and keenly aware of their displacement. Without material context, craft resembles a ritual gesture without an articulate meaning. Haapasaari's empathy and respect for the non-transferable skill of glassblowers is encouraging. Too often, we take for granted the humans who make things. We forget that self-expression in glass is a totally new concept: the division of labour historically separated designers and makers. Many students in art schools share Haapasaari's emotions of sincerity and cynicism today and are equally unsure where craft training leads. Her video is a poignant attempt to reconcile contemporary individualism with factory manufacturing.

The great majority of museum-quality glass is factory production; a few little figurines were made in factories by gaffers using up their pots – so-called 'end-of-day' glass, when the artisans indulged themselves. The whimsical creations that came into being were usually fairly predictable curios and trinkets. Some after-market productions became 'folk art', such as glass rolling pins with inscriptions, but for the most part glass requires an infrastructure that is fundamentally at odds with our modern concept of the individual artist, let alone the 'outsider'.

We can hardly understand the ancient production of glass in Egypt and Syria as 'handicraft'. Marbles and beads have always been made in the thousands, not by the handful. The glasshouse has always been a factory workshop relying on a substantial base of unskilled labour. Ancient glass factories made goods for aristocrats and priests, bottles and bowls that were often coloured to approximate the appearance of chalcedony and rare stones. The Romans were the first to produce glass on an industrial scale, building factories that could make approximately sixty thousand perfume bottles a year. The twentieth-century discovery of an ancient 9-ton slab of glass in a cave outside Haifa, Israel, attests to the volatility involved in controlling the chemistry and furnaces. This prolific factory was unable to make a holding vat and its ceramic furnace failed. The cooled block had once been an immense pot of hot glass that went afoul. Glassmaking has never been efficient or ecological.

FRAMES OF REFERENCE

We started examining glass by admiring Dale Chihuly's green tower of glass spikes, but neglected to mention the larger cavernous vitreous box that allows the 42-foot-high gem to sparkle. The new wing of the Boston MFA, by Norman Foster & Partners, completed in 2010, provides a soaring atrium with light pouring in on all sides, where Chihuly's work has minimal visual competition. This contemporary extension to a Beaux-Arts temple, a rectilinear, insulated glass unit, aspires to be a 'jewel box', in the words of Foster & Partners. Architectural glass has matured over the last seventy years, several generations after steel and concrete, the other essential modern building materials: these spectacular spaces are a standard attention-seeking strategy to make businesses (museums included) appear contemporary. Reconciling these diverse material applications that dwarf individual human hands and bodies is instructive: glass is associated with the future even if its history stretches way back.

In the atrium of the MFA, the steel that is visible is slender, a grid and neutral foil for the green spike. This environment is anathema to the shadows in Isabella Stewart Gardner's museum nearby, where ancient stained glass windows from Europe were deemed suitable for illuminating Whistler and Sargent paintings in 1920. The difference in presentation is not merely aesthetic: glass in each case facilitates a parenthetical temporal boundary: the Gardner historical escapism, the MFA contemporaneity. Transparency implies immediacy, whereas dim caverns with chromatic glass disconnect us from the specific season or hour of the day. These vitreous spaces, both theatrical spectacles, seem polarized between the sacred and profane.

The story of modern architecture's addiction to transparency as a temporal condition is often traced back to the first World's Fair, the Great Exhibition which was held in London in 1851, and the immense temporary shed built to hold it that was nicknamed the Crystal Palace because its glass roof and walls were breathtaking. In the centre of that massive interior, the largest enclosed space at that time, a fountain by Osler, a Birmingham manufacturer, was admired both for its craftsmanship of clear crystal and as a spectacle that commingled the natural and artificial. Waterworks were titillating novelties. This 1851 fountain is a significant historical precedent for Chihuly's aim to awe. A few years earlier, Edgar Allan Poe's short story imagined finding a bottle on a beach containing a message from the future: this first World's Fair used glass as a framework within which to imagine the conjoining of pasts and futures in the present. The reinvention of stained glass in Victorian England around the same time prompted specimens of modern versions of the Gothic art to be exhibited at the fair as well. The Crystal Palace scrambled consumer crazes and fads, the spectacle of commerce and religious art with scientific and mechanical demonstrations; in the MFA's atrium, all of these strains vie to varying degrees.

One of England's largest firms, which provided the overhead panes to erect the Crystal Palace, Chance Brothers, produced lighthouse lenses, stained glass windows, tubes for thermometers and other scientific and industrial uses, microscope slides, and lampshades and window panes of many different types. As Raphael Samuel has pointed out, technological mechanization irrevocably automated labour in some sectors such as textile production but not in the processing of glass, which remained dependent on skilled tradesmen until 1895. Samuel pointed out that the Crystal Palace was regarded as an emblem of the machine age because it took a mere six months to erect, but that artisans at Chance's had blown the cylinder glass to roof it with nearly a million square feet of panes, each of which glaziers set in place manually. Making these hundreds of thousands of panes was an astonishing achievement in terms of production speed. The steam engine did not kill craft, Samuel argued; it drove handicraft to breakneck speed. Industrialization made craftsmen more in demand than ever before. And layered in reflections, vitreous commodities were placed in front of mirrors, behind glass.

While the need for artisanal labour at the furnaces did not falter, a glassblower from 1830 and one from 1860 might have been perplexed at the rapidity of change in techniques and by which were considered state-of-the-art and which traditional. In the 1830s, crown glass production, in which the size of panes was limited to what could be cut from a disc twirled concentrically at the end of a rod, was superseded by cylinder glass, in which large cylinders were blown and then sliced open. Gradually, the manufacture of rolled plate glass, in which the liquid was poured onto an iron table, grew more competitive as grinding was mechanized. By the 1860s, Chance Brothers used a four-storey room in their seven-storey building to pull increasingly large panes of sheet glass but also still made plate and cylinder glass: change was incremental and unceasing technologies – or should we say crafts – overlapped. Still today, glass production methods gain new tricks every 25 years; photovoltaic windows with electrochromatic colour-shifting capacities might yet camouflage our future cityscapes, but these seem destined to come from the desks of engineers.

The reinvention of stained glass in the last half of the nineteenth century might appear to be the antithesis of the Crystal Palace; it was indelibly connected to historical ornament, didactic imagery and saturated with colour. But the surge in overall glass production only increased the numbers of manufactories and the range of production of firms like Chance Brothers; and growth in stained glass became possible only with industrialization. The use of the Siemens regenerative furnace, which made workflow continuous, influenced churches as much as shop windows. Thomas Hoving, the director of New York's Metropolitan Museum of Art in the late 1970s, once quipped that there was more stained glass in all the lobbies of pre-war Manhattan apartment buildings than was ever made in medieval Europe. In hindsight, the abundance of stained glass windows in churches, public buildings, banks and homes was especially strange in the United States, where the material was never made until steamships and trains were on hand to transport it. If the stained glass revival in Northern Europe was recuperation and romantic celebration of history, it was wholesale invention in the USA.

The jagged, seemingly jewel-encrusted windows made in Boston and New York by the painters John La Farge and Louis Comfort Tiffany in the 1880s exemplify artistic innovation more than tradition on two counts: the lack of a pre-existing model and their purposeful inclusion in windows of fragmented chunks, which had never before been pursued intentionally as elements of design. La Farge and Tiffany, initially colleagues and surely inspired by Émile Gallé's vocabulary of textured and coloured glass, personally selected imperfections and began to fold sheets and treat them dimensionally. Their rippled and layered method of assemblage came to be called 'opalescent glass'. Whereas traditionally, details had been daubed with a brush, they puddled glass, literally folding it like fabric. Some compositions resemble lapidary settings of gems, while others preserve a sense of the liquid or molten state – the glass is not a flat plane, defying our basic expectation of a window. The opalescent aesthetic of La Farge and Tiffany – long seen as an attempt to identify a calmer, gentler, utopian moment in the face of ever-increasing industrialization – can also be read as purposefully mitigating the cold light of transparent plate glass, and as beginning the poetic blurring of 'natural' and 'artificial' glass exploited so skilfully by Chihuly.

The tactile and chromatic breadth of nineteenth-century factory glass intended to bejewel homes, from mantelpieces to table settings, is also noteworthy for this slippage between artifice and cultural associations. Colour-fades and other techniques – gold and silver lustring, gold chloride colour shifts, cameo cutting, acid etching – required and sustained a breathtaking diversity of artisanal skills. Some, such as 'peachblow', emulated Asian precedent. The names that the Mt Washington Company of New Bedford, Massachusetts, gave to its products suggested grand themes that were pretentiously self-conscious of art history as well as eclectic: Albertine, Royal Flemish, Crown Milano and Napoli were some of the brands evoking aristocratic European finery. Sicilian Glass, patented on 28 May 1878, was a lustrous black amber body flecked with bits of gold and bright colour, marketed as containing a volcanic material. By rolling a sticky gob of molten glass on the marver of the glasshouse, a clean, flat, fire-proof work surface made of graphite, steel or brass, the gaffer could knead or twist colourful fragments into a black body. The heated shards fused into the body of the blown glass and, similar to a delicate marbling, resulted in smudges of colour and metallic blooms. The molten effect was named as an evocation of volcanic Mt Etna: modern talismans recreated the past as well as natural wonders.

If the metaphor of a colourful crystalline future figured heroically in the Glass Pavilion (1914) of Bruno Taut, by the 1920s a prejudice against colour in architecture was strong and influential: European modernists such as Le Corbusier, Walter Gropius and Mies van der Rohe advocated the use of standardized, clearly transparent factory windows, and Frank Lloyd Wright, who had revelled in stained glass, abandoned it, too. As noted in Chapter Two, the graphic designer Beatrice Warde, an American who worked in London, lectured on the 'The Crystal Goblet' as an allegory for clear type and texts where the typographer's hand was invisible, and published her argument in 1932. This idea sounds simple enough, but Warde excoriated historical ornament as much, if not more, than she praised the quality of transparency:

> The book typographer has the job of erecting a window between the reader inside the room and that landscape which is the author's words. He may put up a stained-glass window of marvellous beauty, but a failure as a window; that is, he may use some rich superb type like text gothic that is something to be looked at, not through. Or he may work in what I call transparent or invisible typography.

Warde demonstrates snobbery in her dismissal of wanton self-expression and the application of colour: 'There are a thousand mannerisms in typography that are as impudent and arbitrary as putting port in tumblers of red or green glass!' Reeling from the doctrinal nature of such a text, we can recognize that Warde offered a lesson in canonical modernist aesthetics in her suppression of colour, ornamental style, historical allusions and tactile pleasure. Warde would surely not have approved of the gilt ruby glass service that Osler's made for Queen Victoria in 1856. Would she also have disapproved of Aino Aalto's mute-coloured and ripple-ringed pressed-glass tumblers of 1932? Deciding which sort is impudent and which is cultivated is deeply subjective. By the time Warde wrote, colour was increasingly seen as deceptive and regarded with class-bound condescension. Self-righteous views that materials should not masquerade as one another had been part of Victorian aesthetic arguments, but seems especially strange in the elimination of colour from glass. Much decorative and cunning glasscraft was unable to fit the idealization of Warde's 'crystal goblet' free of historicist ornament. If most participants in today's contemporary world of glasscraft would theoretically agree with Warde in disapproving of recursions into historical style (Art Nouveau or Art Deco, for instance), examples of colourful and illustrative recollections of history abound, from Judith Schaechter's gothic parables to Dan Dailey's attenuated caricatures. Popular pleasure in coloured and reflective vitreous curves is ubiquitous in sunglasses, where prismatic colours and iridescence can seem bizarrely reminiscent of nineteenth-century glass forms. Overall, alternatives to transparent glass have slowly been peeled away from public spaces and the domestic interior – which does not mean we should believe in the neutrality of invisible architecture or typography.

Laminated safety glass (developed by warmongers who believed they could survive the First World War unscathed) and insulated glass with argon gas vacuum-sealed within still represent futurist space and time, while coloured or textured glass struggles to go beyond an idiosyncratic presence in architecture. However, styles in futuristic glass have rarely lasted very long. When glass towers, an architectural dream of 1920s modernists, finally moved into practice after the Second World War, the material was still imprecisely manufactured. Plate glass was the material of choice for architects until the 1950s and for ambitious post-war skyscrapers such as the United Nations Secretariat Building (1947–52) and Lever House (1950–52) in New York City. The early glass curtain-wall buildings have now had their plate glass windows entirely replaced due to failure. The UN's 5,400, including the celebrated 'world's largest window' of 280 by 500 feet – a symbol of an era of transparent politics – have all been changed. Lever House's green-blue 'Solarex' glass was promised to deflect 45 per cent of the sun's heat but could not withstand more than twenty winters without the spandrels cracking. The technological solutions to the problems set by glass became pragmatic on a large scale after the invention of float glass by England's Pilkington Glass in 1957 – sheets made on a bed of molten tin that needed no grinding or polishing.

An ever-expanding range of engineering solutions continues to pursue the dream of transparent and dematerialized buildings. Novel structural glass facades now have a forty-year history dating back to Norman Foster's Willis Faber & Dumas building. Hanging on cable nets, suspended in point-fixed glazing systems, glass sheets are tempered to withstand terrorist bomb blasts or vandals' scratches, to dance like textiles and bounce like rubber in silicon or epoxy sealant. To reconsider Foster & Partners' Boston addition in this light, their preliminary schematic plans resemble axonometric drawings more than architecture: a rectangular shed snuggles beside the classical facade with its columns and pediment. This is how glass is often perceived: as an architectural enclosure that is weightless and in need of little to no structural support. An even more celebrated use of a transparent envelope, here to display glass artefacts, is the Toledo Museum of Art's Glass Pavilion (2006) by SANAA, the firm headed by Kazuyo Sejima and Ryue Nishizawa, in which the interior is a sea of reflections and re-reflections, as floor-to-ceiling curved, laminated translucent walls divide the single-storey space. Inside SANAA's pavilion, a hot-shop demonstrates hands-on techniques in glass, but it remains intellectually challenging to appreciate the architecture in relation to the manipulation of materials, largely because of the super-sized scale of the bent sheets, custom-made in China. The human hand and body seem slight against these sweeping geometries.

The number of architects disposed to variety in colour and texture in glass are a minority today, largely because of the costs of customization, but several argue that glass can be a more social and complex material. James Carpenter Design Associates pursues precisely this strategy, using prisms, mirrors and lenses to bend light into a lively textured and moving presence, perhaps even a cinematic experience, on skyscrapers and private residences today. Carpenter awoke to the beauty of glass when he was a student at Rhode Island School of Design and collaborated with Chihuly. Today, his studio works as a consultant to architects, creating immersive environments and specializing in what might be described as skyscraper dermatology. He alters window fenestration into greater complexity. For example, he might turn a window on a brick wall into a periscope to supply interior occupants with fields of reflected and re-reflected information from their airspace overhead. Working in the rebuilding of Lower Manhattan, he clothed 7 World Trade Center in prisms to obscure a massive electric substation and wired these to respond to the presence of pedestrians by flickering blue. The motion-activated facade, as Carpenter sees it, provides urban signage and interactivity, but depending on one's sense of insecurity it could as easily be experienced as surveillance. Such frames of reference are contingent and keenly subjective experiences.

Against this backdrop of continuous production of flow glass and the symbolism of a transparent United Nations, the studio glass movement of the 1960s asserted the relevance of human gesture and the idea of liberating glass from conventions and constraint. Although Europeans are deferential to American artists for their role as pioneers in studio glass, Stanislav Libenský and Jaroslava Brychtová had already delved into abstraction in glass in the 1950s and exhibited regularly at world's fairs. Co-opted as a political symbol by diametrically opposed camps during the Cold War, abstraction could be a flashpoint in painting but safe in the decorative arts. In the case of these Czech artists, abstraction developed out of specialized glass schools. Originating in academies flush with post-war funding in the United States, the first glass departments developed as part of sculpture and craft programmes in the 1970s, with furnaces often adjacent to metal foundries or ceramic kilns. The American liberation ideologies of the 1960s slipped into aesthetic explanations of glass: traditional forms were to be rejected and individual expression and imagination could seemingly flourish untrammelled by institutions and corporations.

In this context, Chihuly flourished, scaling up swiftly from objects to installations as his flowing forms erupted into calligraphic gestures. He assembled dense clusters from hundreds of glass tendrils. Some carried historical allusions to Venice, others were realistic floral bouquets. The interest in colourful glass like his was also perceptible in museums and collecting: Boston's MFA exhibited and owned Tiffany Studios glass at the beginning of the twentieth century but had deaccessioned its iridescent vases by the 1970s, when Chihuly began to be appreciated. These aesthetic biorhythms can be explained as postmodern historicism and eclecticism succeeding modernist austerity and purism, but only partially, as Chihuly is regarded for his dedication to glass as a singularly potent material. The cliché of being 'a victim of one's own success' applies to Chihuly, unfortunately, as his status as a craftsman has increasingly been questioned, as if art and craft were mutually exclusive. I find myself arguing to convince my students that the craftsmanship of his work is still worthy of respect, largely because of romantic ideals about individualism.

Fast-forward to a less affluent moment in the twenty-first century, when schools are struggling to maintain glass facilities that require 24/7 maintenance and a blank cheque for fuel. If doubt about the stand-alone value of virtuosity in glassblowing is tangible in Riikka Haapasaari's *Glassblowing Without Glass*, so too is the idea of an individual working independently. Craft training that emphasizes individualism at the expense of collaboration is strangely ahistorical as well as out of touch with the marketplace. Artistic freedom is now exemplified by the idea of a laptop hooked up to 3D printing; seemingly any idea for a design can be downloaded into materialization. Where does this leave the material?

Recently, MIT Media Lab's Mediated Matter research group has developed a machine that deposits a bead of molten glass into a sculptural form (imagine a high-tech squirt gun that shoots vitreous icing at 2,100° Fahrenheit/1,165° Celsius). Neri Oxman is spearheading this novel idea, producing contorted, biomorphic vessels. If their concentric erection is similar to Karen Karnes's coiled seats, their quality of line is closer to coarse spaghetti and feels just as homogeneous. Oxman's overall shapes are reminiscent of Alvar Aalto's Savoy Vase (1939), an organic, asymmetrical form inspired by the lakes of Finland. Glass with this linear texture is not entirely new; for thousands of years humans have fused rods, *filet de verre,* into slump moulds (and contemporary artist Toots Zynsky makes such purely sculptural vessels in bursts of colour). The transparency of Oxman's vitreous explorations might be rooted in their relationship to the glass architectural building block as well as modernist ideals. She offers her parabolic, gestural forms as tentative prototypes for future architectural speculations. While theorized as socially motivated, the spectacular eye candy seems to relate more to metaphorical vessel forms, as the fantastic bricks seem impossible to stack and uninviting to touch. The technology promises freedom more than the artefacts themselves deliver it.

The desire to build without specialized knowledge in a glass is now widespread. The revival of apprenticeships conducted by Chihuly's generation seems both out of fashion and outdated. Time, it seems, is too precious to dedicate to manual technique or technical knowledge.

Celebrations of glass as a heroic solution have faltered in architectural criticism too, giving way to paranoia about surveillance. But the widespread use of transparency in rhetoric as a metaphor to theorize accessibility and connectivity with nature continues, despite being especially problematic in relation to craft. Glasscraft has historically been artifice, not close to nature. Identifying any specific quality of glass as the material's singular essential characteristic often inhibits the imagination – or seems destined to be short-lived. Glass has been a way to fake tortoiseshell or rubies and will be continually reinvented to serve needs and aspirations.

As an interface, glass is often at our fingertips for many hours of the day – on our electronic devices and appliances. Glass shapes us today more than ever before, via the paper-thin screens on phones and personal computers. Archaic vitreous wonders still tug on our minds, like an hourglass or a snow globe, but today we anticipate enchantment by looking into electronic screens. Our pocket glass is now a portal through which you might see yourself a dozen times a day unintentionally. In the 1940s, Lewis Mumford believed the mirror to be the primary force shaping the modern notion of the individual self, so today we must ask how quintupling and micro-mirroring shapes our ability to know our selves and our surroundings. Lens, satellite, fibre optic cable, screen, lens, satellite, fibre optic cable – this is the rhythm of dataflow that moves so fast we forget each step is mediated by glass. To rely on such optics more than our own eyes suggests that we value the skill of manipulating lenses more than developing individual skills of perception. But a pixel is a dangerous premise for cultural production – if it moves into production without the friction of a social and material context.

Glass makes the labour of craft look easy even when it is not. Our sensory organs operate by filling in information around selective points of absorption and we cannot accurately infill texture and spatial understanding into visuals unless we have experience. Knowing when glass is hot enough to blow or sticky enough to absorb shards cannot be accurately imagined – trial provides the information. A frictionless surface means that we have a diminished feedback loop. We are less acquainted with tipping points. At what stress will a glass window crack? A windshield? A wine glass? These might be the only remaining points of failure in glass that we know by first-hand touch; we appreciate our glass buildings as gem-like incrustations, retinally drinking in their faceted reflections. Games on an electronic device imply that things can be built without friction. Note the way people brush through information on their touch screens – even cataclysmic events like earthquakes, heinous crimes and civil wars. It makes us think we can flip through time, too, as easily.

Glass mediates our emotions at both work and leisure in other ways, too – you might even be reading this on glass. You might only know Chihuly's *Lime Green Icicle Tower* as a jpeg online. To touch our loved ones or reach out for a memory, most of us reach towards a photograph on a screen more often than a fellow human body. Instead of thinking we need to grasp a handle on a manual tool to apprehend its essence, that we need to endure the friction of engaging material, we assume that a video tutorial can open the doors of perception just as we assume a transparent facade might imply a building is more accessible.

In our snapshots of ourselves beside Chihuly's work, the insulated hermetic glass enclosure and the idea of individual artistic gesture are strangely reconciled and redistributed as social media. A parallel metaphor might be the difference between Apollo 17 astronauts in 1972 photographing the Earth for the first time from outer space and today's digitization. The astronauts miniaturized the planet into a glassy marble; today, each of us feels as if we have that marble in our pocket. A live video feed or a clear window makes it appear that what is happening elsewhere is an event transpiring at the same rate, on the same clock. But social life suggests otherwise. The door opens and the room we were admiring is discovered to be sweltering; air conditioning is transparent, too. Unless we occupy the same space, glass walls remain obstacles to social exchange and tactile knowledge. The museum is not inherently made accessible by glass; quite the contrary, it can just as often seem to lack quiet, contemplative space.

Champions of the 'Internet of things' and increased data-material connectivity sound like they are promising to embed material like fibre, ceramic and glass with limitless unpaid interns to attend to our most petty needs. But will human behaviour actually interface with materials and experience complex responsive manipulation? Do we need dichromatic windows that can shift from translucency to opacity momentarily and suddenly? Advocates for embedded artificial intelligence such as Jeremy Rifkin believe that it 'frees human beings from the market economy to pursue nonmaterial shared interests on the Collaborative Commons'; it is worth noting that glass as a tactile material does not fit into our concept of generative work or 'nonmaterial' play. In fact, material invention in glass has been the result of commercial desperation, factory conditions and market pressures, and sweating beside a furnace. Has innovation ever come from labour cut off from the actual pressures and constraints of economy or the imagined marketplace? Not for Michael Owens or William Woods. The craft of glassblowing or casting might be seen today as historical re-enactment, creative therapy or purely as art, but it is significant that a glassblower invented the machinery for light bulb automation, not an engineer. Will future innovation in glass be a nonmaterial pathway or a material one? Maybe it's not more freedom or data that people need but more engagement with unpredictable materials, as well as tangible tools.

A cracked windshield or a distorted windowpane aged to a violet cast can prompt the imagination. These are sweet moments of interference when friction, gravity and tension are productive. Infecting glass so that it grows imperfections and disabilities might be one way to cultivate devices that make us smarter, so that a glass screen grows silica warts to curtail usage and enforce digital detoxification. What forms of interference increase the chance of daydreaming, as opposed to distraction? A camera that dilates and contracts, bobbing in and out of telescopic and telephoto vision? Mondaugen's Law in Thomas Pynchon's *Gravity's Rainbow* (1973) is an argument that 'Personal density . . . is directly proportional to temporal bandwidth' and posits that the more weathered an artefact like a baseball bat or a leather saddle, the more the mind inclines back in time. 'The more you dwell in the past and future, the thicker your bandwidth . . . But the narrower your sense of Now, the more tenuous you are,' writes Pynchon. With glass the bandwidth of memory and individuality can be elusive. For instance, the White House, the presidential home, stockpiled glass panes from Chance's factory in order to make sure that the nineteenth-century texture of artisanal labour would be preserved in the course of twentieth-century restoration. A false sense of history, manicured and manipulated, does not build our human 'personal density'. Cheap imitations of Chihuly's chandeliers abound due to the mass customization of all things artisanal and online retail brokers such as Alibaba quickening the pace of global trade. Confusion reigns in aesthetics, intellectual property and artistic purpose. If an old rippled window can transform the most boring view into a meditative journey, how might contemporary production?

'How does our material world today define us as humans?' should be our primary concern, not whether we are preserving one artisanal skill or another in glass, or an aesthetic ideal or style. The medieval mind already imagined drinking glasses could alternate between clarity and opacity, responding to the presence of poison in wine, that chromatic signals could be meaningful messages as well as optical pizzazz. The Internet of things might yet result in the invention of tableware that contains holograms of prior happy and sad occasions, warnings of allergens or other medical issues – and these might not be triggered by calendars or by algorithms but by reading our blood pressure, temperature and hormone levels as well as nearby aromas. Aiming for the thickening of Mondaugen's Law, these might recycle Facebook memories into our soup spoons, but this only extends the screen of data, risking information overload. Our windshields might be able to inform us how many unmarked Native American graves or leaking gas pipes are underfoot – in the gentlest and least sensational fashion – and still only increase our distractions. In the oncoming futuristic data-immersive digiscape, materials will retain an ability to cultivate a sense of deep time. Materials etched with history, such as footprints or abandoned walls, whisper that others have preceded us. Transparent stairs might unnerve us to unwittingly believe no one else had ever used them before us – and to think only in an absolute present. So what might glass be aside from 'new' or 'fake old'?

Breaking glass, not making it, seems to be a more intuitive and transformative act. Though it seems absurd, it is probable that more people seek relaxation listening to cascades of glass shards than to the waves of the ocean on any given night – by watching a Hollywood blockbuster. Delete the sound of breaking glass and splintering debris from an action movie and there would be little excitement left in the car chases or gunfights. To sensationalize violence we exploit this material more than any other. We have little moral opposition despite knowing that *Kristallnacht*, the night when Nazis expressed their rise to power by smashing the windows of every Jewish-owned store, still defines society gone awry. Glass is a metaphor that defines some of the most nefarious aspects of institutions in Western civilization. We are a mess of contradictions: if cinematic glass shards prompt an adrenaline rush, broken mobile phone and tablet screens are strangely shame-making.

FRAGILE TIMEKEEPERS IN REACH

Do you place an emotional or psychological value on the visible movement of a clock? Does the second hand – the one that keeps ticking – soothe you some days and on others appear maddeningly inhumane, disconnecting you from a thoughtful pace? Timekeeping is rarely a neutral presence. The visualization of time is essential to our understanding of being human

– to our notion that it is either a universal mechanical measurement or more of an hourglass that we can flip manually. And glass is pivotal to expressing time.

Maarten Baas potently visualizes human subservience to and manipulation of time in his Analog Digital Clock (2009), an app that undermines the 'smartness' of the phone or device on which it is played. The miniaturized twelve-hour film shows the manual management of a seven-segment digital clock by live actors. The screen is actually a red glass window that Baas filmed. People behind the window alternately covered and revealed segments as each minute passed, and the film stock was then edited to synchronize with time. The app is a functional clock and part video art, but certainly all about the trials of perceiving and enduring time.

Debuted at the 2009 Salone del Mobile in Milan, Baas's work points out our current sense of temporal and technological dislocation. He advertised his app amid the upscale fair of costly goods by taping up a photocopy – and listing the price as if he were selling it in a cheap American dollar-store. Time, one of the most complex abstractions, becomes accessible and tangible in Baas's clock. By hustling his work on the streets of Milan for 99 cents, he renders it a part of a throwaway culture, democratically accessible and cheap. But his clock also suggests a tender commentary on planned obsolescence, even if he is complicit with the strategy of capitalist retail. His suggestion of 'direct sales', a mode popularized by American companies such as Tupperware and Avon cosmetics, speaks to our desire for direct contact with craftsmanship, even if he makes this seem absurd. Baas plays with an enduring metaphor: time is imbricated in our concepts of useful labour and mechanical perfection. And his clock is seemingly just a red-delineated seven-segment timekeeper, until one sees the small inconsistencies. Curiously, this stylized segmental display is regarded as more futuristic than a dot-matrix projection of numbers, despite being patented by F. W. Wood in 1910. In Hollywood drama, every countdown to the explosion of a fiendish incendiary device involves a seven-segment display. An old language remains somehow symbolic of the future.

In another of Baas's works, a video exploring timekeeping, a bird's-eye view looks down on street sweepers pushing neat lines of debris that depict the hour and minute hands of a clock, so that useful labour is made useless, except for its ability to keep moving time forward. The app disperses these questions to a broader community, sharing Baas's commentary on measuring productivity and the use of clocks as a tool of social control, as well as our use of mobile phones in lieu of a wristwatch. The app is a craft specific to today and is a medium that might be obsolete by the twenty-second century. Baas identifies and materializes the issue of continual obsolescence and shows that it haunts both technology and craft. If the Analog Digital Clock is also a video we watch of glass on glass, and reliant on transparency, keep in mind that Baas is subverting the very idea that time is predictable. He is reinventing a way to be a clockmaker in an era when artisans no longer serve that role. In Baas's hands, glass is a layer behind which we hide the human hand to suggest a slippage between abstraction and mechanization. And glass is red.

If not by looking at a clock, many of us gauge time's passage in a mirror, by looking in one daily, if not hourly, in miniature on our devices.

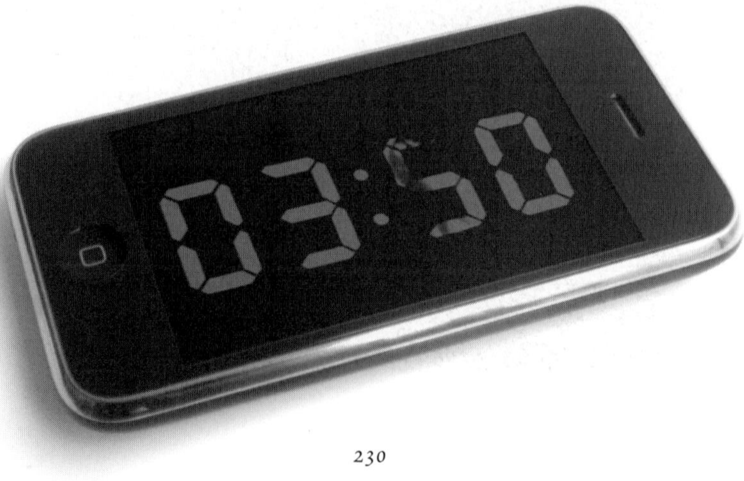

Maarten Baas, Analog Digital Clock, iPhone app, 2009. The app subverts the 'smartness' of the device on which it is seen, as the miniaturized film records the manual management of a seven-segment digital clock by live actors. It returns time to being a movement that we watch and regard as a personal possession.

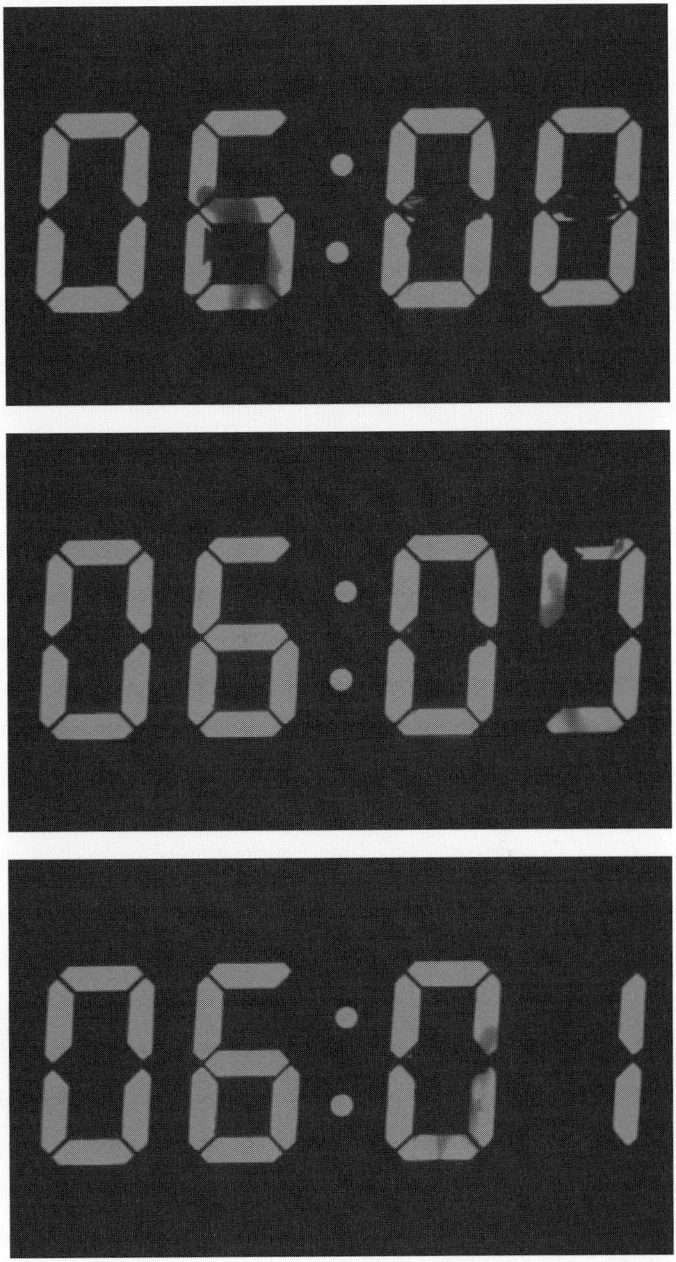

Maarten Baas, Analog Digital Clock app, sequences at 06:00 to 06:01 on iPhone, 2009. The screen is actually a red glass window that Baas filmed as people behind it alternately painted and wiped it down as each minute passed; the footage was edited to be accurately synchronized.

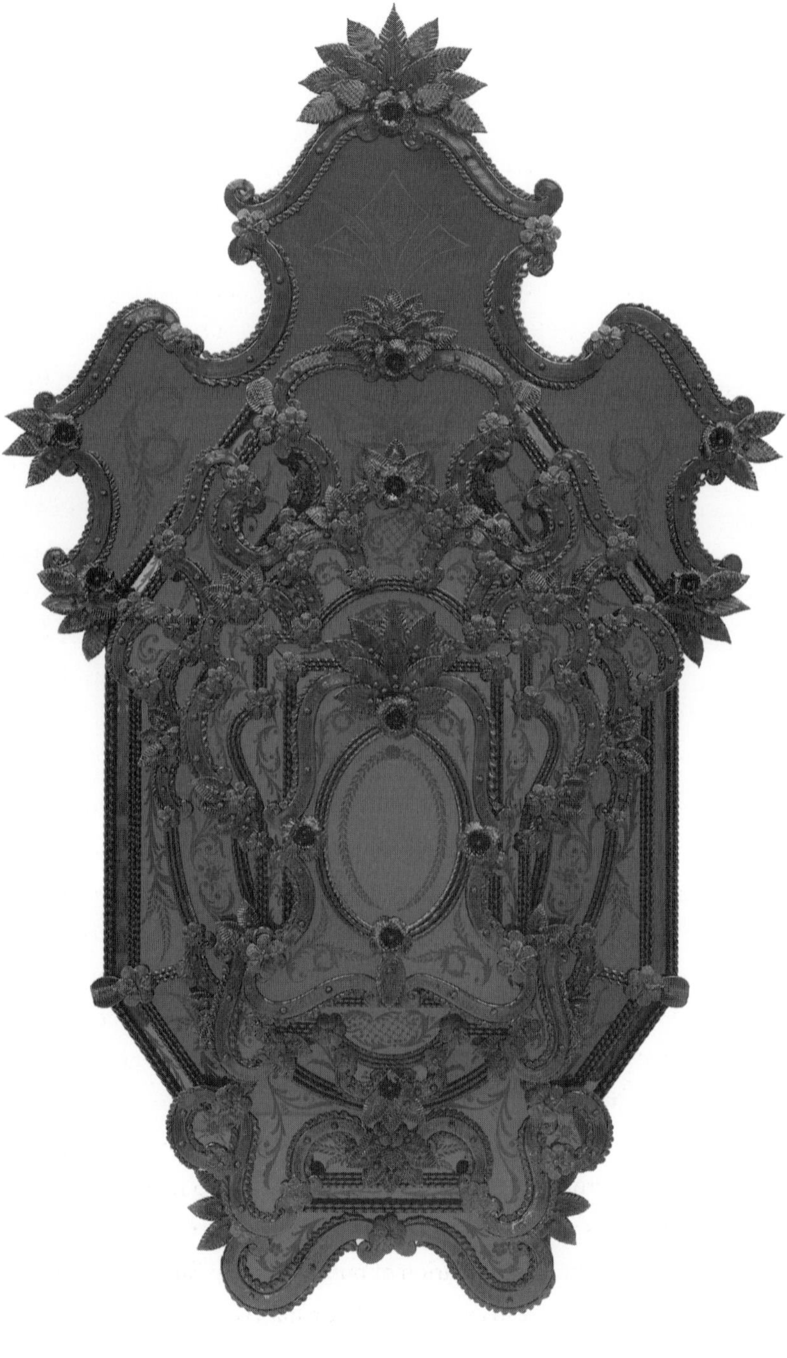

Fred Wilson's *Iago's Mirror* (2009) is a stately, regal artefact that from afar one might not recognize at all as a mirror – it is a glistening black, seemingly winged form that beckons because of its intricate border and illegible surface. Named after the Shakespearean villain who ignobly manipulates and tragically ruins the life of Othello, its blackness is essential to its narrative content: the soldier, Iago, looks into a mirror and sees only the blackness of his own soul's manipulations. He also sees Othello as black, only a 'Moor'. Using the living heritage of Murano glasscrafters to build a set of five tiered Baroque frames, Wilson drew on traditional skill sets as well as his desire to upset a conventional vernacular Venetian object (Wilson's first exposure to glasscraft was at Chihuly's Pilchuck Glass School). There is no silver in Wilson's mirror, no heightened reflection of light and no suggestion of optical transparency. If Venetian *cristallo* was celebrated for transparency, Wilson reverses such criteria. Like another celebrated Renaissance Venetian export, lace, Wilson's device is about framing power, manipulating silhouettes. As a layering of mirrors upon mirrors, *Iago's Mirror* reinforces our experience that the obstruction of vision is both the central phenomenon and the meaning of the work. Wilson gives glass a novel identity as a visually unyielding material. This mirror does not show the self, as Lewis Mumford assumed.

Fred Wilson, *Iago's Mirror*, 2009, Murano glass and wood, 80 × 48¾ × 10½ in. (203 × 124 × 26.5 cm). Wilson began working with glass after a residency at Dale Chihuly's Pilchuck Glass School, Stanwood, Washington, in 2001, making black glass teardrops. If Chihuly expanded upon his mentor Jack Lenor Larsen's success at ornamenting modern architecture with light and colour, Wilson uses glass to make introspective decorative objects that question our perception of humans and power relationships and the ways traditional objects perpetuate myth or hinder our capability for insight.

As in 'Mining the Museum' (1992), Wilson's pioneering exhibition at the Maryland Historical Society, where his use of domestic furnishings delved into racial politics and the wilful subversion and perversion of both function and social relations, *Iago's Mirror* redirects a decorative object into antisocial sculpture. Opacity turns into a spiritually and emotionally charged state of being. Frothy and spiked, the overall shape of Wilson's non-mirror resembles armorials and military pins, threatening things. He cultivates an implicit tension between the mirror as a framing device and as a deceitful manipulation of public identity. Successively smaller frames nesting one within another are like a matryoshka doll and like the multiple personae that each of us uses selectively. Wilson's mirror denies visitors their intimate reflection and purposefully confounds the viewer's experience. By extension, he thwarts our relation to the museum. If 'Mining the Museum' questioned the use of vitrines to manipulate power relations in our society by presenting them as falsely neutral, Wilson does the same with the material of black glass in *Iago's Mirror*. He turns the object into something that cannot be satisfactorily photographed and frustrates our narcissism. Fred Wilson's glasscraft revokes the ideology of transparency by suggesting that it is neither a neutral condition nor a necessarily equally empowering quality. Glass is deprived of its usual retinal seductions and turned into something else, an artefact recording antisocial behaviour.

Shari Mendelson's bottles exemplify another contemporary homage to ancient glass. Her re-enactments of ancient Assyrian, Babylonian and Sassanian bottle forms are made from a contemporary material, plastic waste. Mendelson turns the pentagonal nubs that serve as feet on soda bottles and transforms them into rosettes. Ancient partially moulded and blown vessels are suggested, both in their form and fragile, distressed surfaces. In Mendelson's work, our collective carbon footprints become a shimmering ornamental turn. Her bottles refute the idea of originality and self-expression: the forms pay tribute to ancient survivors and obsolete forms. They suggest that 'copying Old Masters' is a worthwhile craft. They do not proclaim any inventive originality or power in self-expression.

Historically, we discuss bottles as anthropomorphic things: we drink with our lips from their lips, stand them on their own feet when we need to get up and go, and grab them from their waist, shoulder or neck as we might a lover or dance partner. Mendelson's forms are bottles with no lips; they are all feet – plastic bottle bases. And the necks of these bottles ask that we do not touch them. They are not misanthropic, but they are speaking to our ruinous consumption of bottled liquids, most of which are unhealthy beverages. One cannot see Mendelson's work without associating her forms

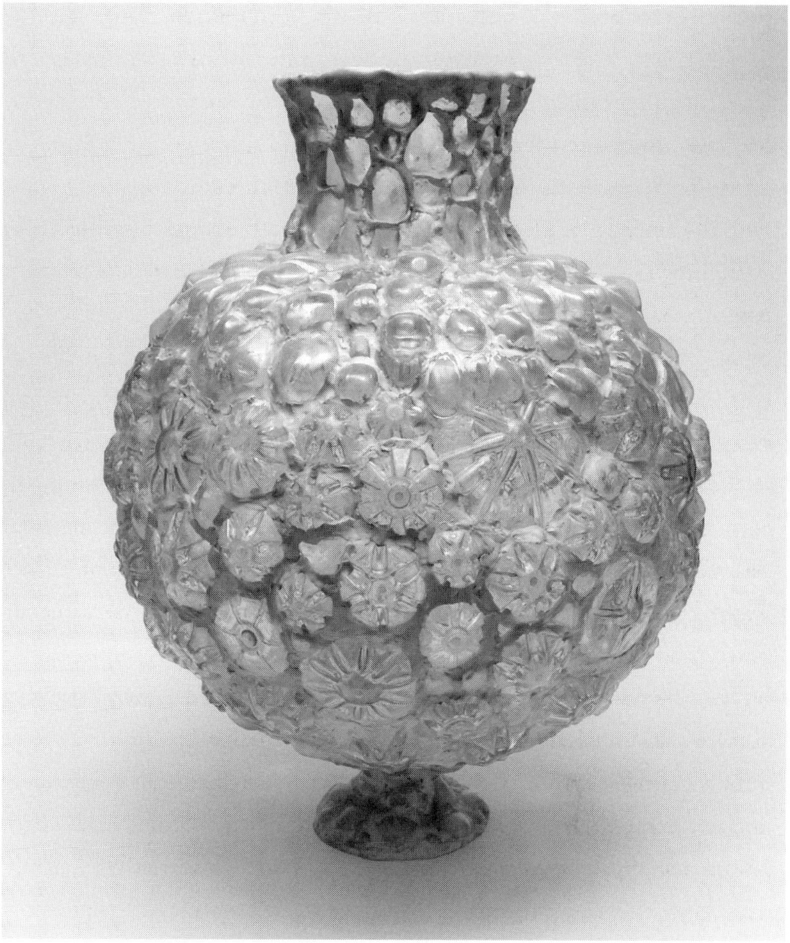

Shari Mendelson, *Round Blue/Green Vessel*, 2015, plastic bottle pieces, hot glue, resin, acrylic polymer, paint, 23½ × 18 × 18 in. (60 × 45 × 45 cm). What appears to be archaeological glass fogged by salts and weathering is in fact the everyday plastic bottle: the rosettes we are familiar with on ancient vessels are vacuum-moulded penta-pedal feet that balance the carbonated bottle of Sprite or Coca-Cola. Temporal awareness waxes and wanes, flowing from the enduring form to details such as the universal recycling symbol and printed expiration dates to an awareness of the visible and invisible toxicities of our dalliance with plastic.

with the Great Pacific Garbage Patch and the crackle of our own detritus underfoot, even as we march through a city breathless with anticipation to arrive at a beloved museum's treasury of ancient, brittle flasks.

These three objects – Baas's app, Wilson's mirror and Mendelson's bottle – suggest ways we can value the fragility of the material as a metaphor and use glasscraft to heighten our awareness of our quotidian life. They are versions of commonplace things in every home, on one level, and yet each reverses expectation. The range of content is dissimilar – the app teases out the complexity and absurdities of both technology and time, the mirror hints at Western culture's use of commodities to shape human identity and the catastrophe of race and skin colour when reified into systems of identification, and the bottle tugs the mind to think about civilization's collapse and preservation in relation to ecocide and the use of fossil fuels. Glasscraft is central to each and yet each is irreverent, perhaps heretical, in regard to material purity and the shibboleths of craft. They are also melancholic, evincing respect for the past and ancient habits of everyday life. Yet they challenge idealizations of the past or future and argue for action today. They do not solely entertain the idea of artistic originality or of the 'brand new' – past and present and future are all in play. These bits of craft are not intended as models to follow or emulate. The three philosophically enriched artefacts tap into the ways that craft lingers in our banal possessions, like the light bulb and hourglass, and the potency of first-hand tactility.

Glass pervades the signature possessions of modern comfort and middle-class consumption that each reader might have at hand: a cheap tumbler, a pair of reading glasses or sunglasses, a light bulb overhead, a mirror on the wall and a portable smart device. Such objects map where we are, what is worth bothering to make, and how profitable it is for makers to think about unmaking. Any widely used object is a cipher worth revisiting to discuss the strange state of social relations – and the agency of objects and materiality. If previous civilizations mistook gold for nobility or saw the written word as insolubly meaningful, such banal things as the iPhone app, the mirror and the bottle show that we take glass for granted. These examples of glasscraft disrupt our expectations about transparency and reflectivity – in short, the very idea that glass might have any singular essence or allegorical function as a material. Wilson's mirror, Mendelson's bottle and Baas's clock give us a critical awareness of material, which is the essence of craft: by empathizing with the social meanings of glass, not proclaiming eternal truths, they identify contemporary meaningful metaphors. These suggestions gesture at ways that individual agency can meld with glasscraft, even though these examples also confirm that it is difficult to distinguish 'studio' production from small-scale manufacturing.

DIY AND DELUXE TIMEKEEPING

Most craftspeople today go about work focusing on production more than reception, largely because they don't hear the direct voice (or pinch) of needs or of patronage. Operating in a studio setting, aims can drift to seeing artefacts in isolation, such as an enriched showstopper, a luxury object that might only serve as a pretty paperweight (or nicely contrasting blotch of blue against a beige interior). It is nigh impossible to create an enduring object without latching on to the metaphorical value and social meaning of a material, a function or a social context. The recent invention of luxury hourglasses filled with millions of nanoballs coated in yellow gold exemplify the tendency towards conspicuous consumption. Designed by Marc Newson and retailed by Ikepod, a Swiss boutique brand, such hourglasses sell for tens of thousands of dollars. Such exquisitely fashioned knick-knacks will always be a part of craft; costly goods are essential to demonstrating status. Turning away from that, search the Internet for instructions on how to make a DIY hourglass and you can find one that converts two burned-out incandescent light bulbs into a sand clock.

Between the how-to activity and the virtuosic artefact on which no effort has been spared is a gulf in which those who love craft must journey, savouring both extremes at times, if possible. Watching streamed videos of both increases one's empathy, to a point. An hourglass remains a fantastic demonstration that time is precious and can be an enchanting technology. The glut of instructional videos on YouTube showing how to build an hourglass suggests that enormous numbers of people have a sense of purpose in the manual rediscovery of an ancient technology – disregarding the invective we hurl against 'reinventing the wheel' as a waste of time. These videos pleasantly disrupt assumptions about the value of skill in making and the control of knowledge by institutions. Often the assumption is that craft is attainable through a dedicated apprenticeship: ten thousand hours is what Richard Sennett approximates as the base minimum commitment. The woodworker David Pye disagreed: 'Two minutes experience teach an eager man more than two weeks teach an indifferent one,' he wisely wrote, paving the way for us to recognize the passionately wrought lash-up by the amateur who wills form into meaning and meaning into form as well as the seasoned virtuoso.

We do not need one stringent definition of the time it takes to learn a craft or one fixed ideal of expertise. There is reason to believe that more crafts will develop as humans build ever-larger things like satellites and large telescopes or attempt to fix natural and human-made disasters, so quantification is pointless. As Raphael Samuel wrote about 'the rise of a whole number of new industrial crafts,' 'Nineteenth-century capitalism created many more skills than it destroyed, though they were different in kind from those of the all-round craftsmen, and subject to a wholly new level of exploitation.' The discarding and creation of entire bodies of craft knowledge has been constant over the course of human history.

The temporal span of any type of craft knowledge is not mine to quantify; many have tried to weed out the obsolete from the useful, the pretty from the garish and the noble from the degenerate. Look to other authors and dictionaries and encyclopaedias for aesthetic and moral judgements. The question of how to discern genuine education from mere training should be a more pressing issue. It is invaluable to reckon with the unevenness of experience and to reflect on the disparate conditions of production and the subjective nature of craft. Craft will still most likely remain an individual understanding, a term describing a phenomenon that occurs between humans and materials involving tooling and technology, even as the movements of the seasons and the sunrises and sunsets suggest that the joys and achievements of the phenomenon happen in collective experiences. To recall Ed Rossbach's instinctual turn to basketry as a manner of self-preservation and meditation, craft 'might be a sort of clock, not a measuring device, but something devised by man to enforce an awareness, a savoring, of time through its arbitrary division into rhythmic units'. Go make the metaphorical hourglass you think we need. Such craft is a worthy pursuit, if, as you work, you look around and carefully count which hourglasses matter and are meaningful as collective metaphors.

To claim 'the time for craft is now' is to contradict the great majority of essays that see craft as a historical phase or earlier golden age. But this is imperative for the craftsperson to believe in order to connect to current ideas, tools and social pressures. To relate to one's era is on the one hand to live dependent on sunshine and oxygen. And yet to be truly in the present is to be mindful of potential futures and pasts. Trees live in a very shallow present. Wood, clays, metals, textiles and glass gain the texture of time through craft. Humans reveal the rings and grain: artisans show that a timber spans three generations and can imbue ceramics with the memory of geological formations. Working a material, humans can impregnate stuff like glass with a sense of time, either passively or actively and intentionally. If St Augustine declared that he knew what time was until someone asked him, the same might be said of craft: we grasp it as a coherent and clear-eyed commitment to action when we are moored in the present moment. It is time to cease describing craft fatalistically as belonging to the past or in opposition to the future.

CONCLUSION

MNEMOSYNTHESIS

Craft cannot be regarded as a method of manufacture held over from some romantically imagined pre-industrial epoch, a time and space of free individuals at work outside capitalism and corporations. It is more useful and pragmatic to begin to think of it as a contemporary banal object in an as yet unmapped backstreet informal economy, like an unattributed plastic toy made by the hundreds in a workshop in Karachi. Such a trinket operates like a time machine, knitting together highly localized habits and forms from the past into the present and projecting these into future play. Craft continues to thrive in nooks and crannies which we must seek out.

As we have seen, it is often teams of specialized skills organized into action that produce the most enduring, meaningful craftworks, such as quilts, ships, pianos and other complex musical instruments. Even for each plastic toy that sells for less than a penny there was a mould maker. To treasure the plastic toy, or a bamboo fish trap or a kite, or the old wood screw I have admired since my childhood, is to counter the corrosive aesthetic ideals of the colonial imperialist mindset and the gadget-crazed present. I know others might find it bizarre that the old wood screw prompts my speculation and imagination with as much vigour and validity as a Brancusi sculpture in an established museum. My admiration might not be transferable to the reader through words alone and my sense of sharing this pleasure with Brancusi might be insufficiently proven. The storytelling might be attributed to that old criterion of art history – taste.

In this book I have looked closely at the limited number of workshops of the world that I have visited; I hope and expect to see further afield still in order to incorporate more. I have not travelled as far as my protagonists and have not roamed far from my birthplace, not under the pressure of defining my own cultural identity, as was demanded of Isamu Noguchi and Alice Kagawa Parrott. I hope I have shown how the present is thick with numerous ways of working that can always be traced back into the past and yet are suggestive of looking afield, to straying from canonical histories. I am grateful that I have fondled the brittle and unbearably fragile plastic Karachi toy as a gift from the art historian Iftikhar Dadi; both he and it expand my repertoire and empathy and impulse to continue to encompass new workmanship and craft unabated. If that toy is from his home, I hope we all will search for similarly overlooked commonplace craft.

We still have both factory craft and individual isolated craft, and we are 'beyond' neither. And workmanship defies time; time does not define craft. Touring a piano factory, I have seen eight sets of hands wrestle a sheaf of maple planks into a mould, and realized that this was the minimum number required to clamp the wood into the cloud-like curve of a grand piano. Other instruments also require several steps in their manufacture, and in the piano the freehand shaping of a soundboard or notching of a bridge still courts risk, still sets one set of hands against a sharp edge with little margin for error. Steve Meltzer, the lead carver at Steinway & Sons, creates numerous designs from their catalogue, now over a century old, and he loves his work, still weighing his chisels in his hands with pleasure. He might render a rococo shell in relief while never feeling it is peculiar to his culture or his taste. His work travels from Queens, New York, across the world to wherever patrons value the manufactory's

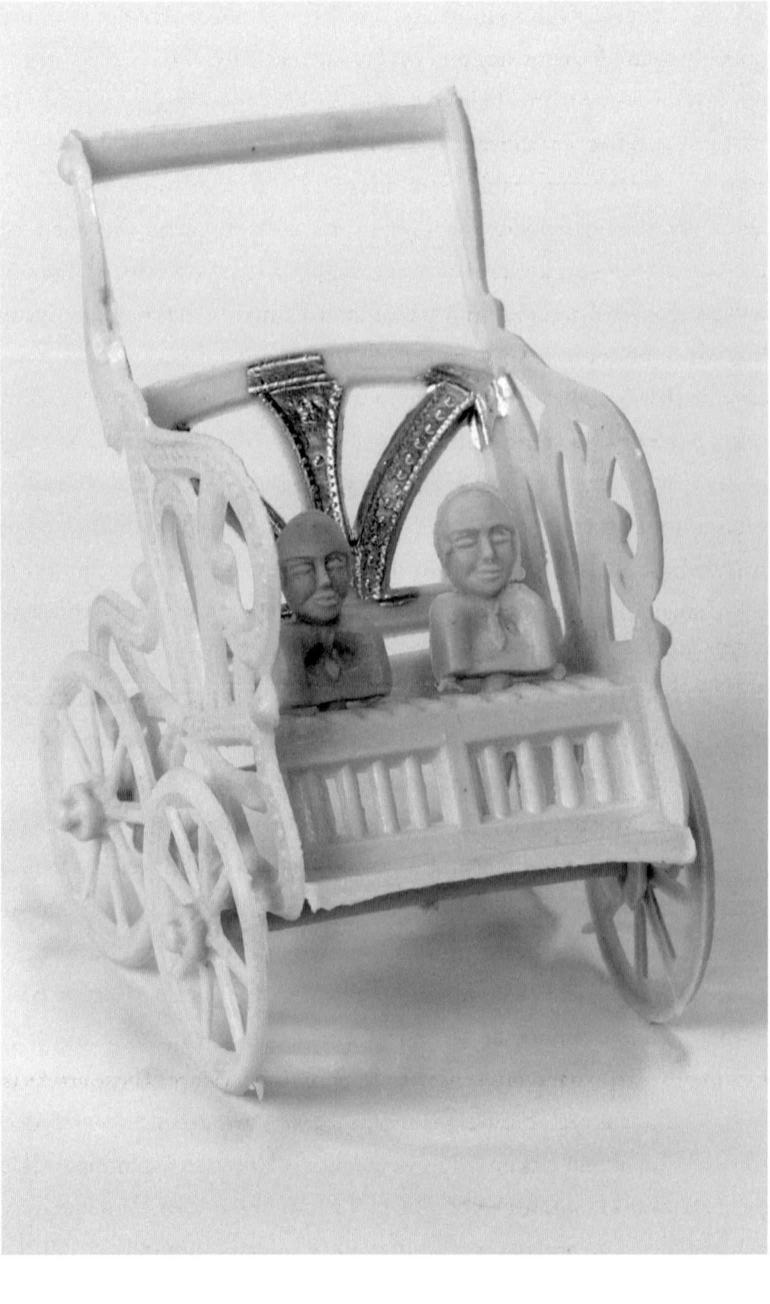

Plastic toy, manufactured Lahore or Karachi, Pakistan, *c*. 1990s, unattributed. Plastic rarely figures in histories of handicraft, yet now that it has a long history (especially if precedents like gutta-percha and *papier-mâché* are considered) it is time to welcome it to effect a discussion of broader global issues and the larger economic contexts of manufacturing. If craft is solely the history of human ingenuity and imagination, these toys still should gain admission to the dialogue.

collated craftsmanship, to Russian oligarchs and the United Arab Emirates' recently minted aristocracy, and his labour meets those clients' tastes. He also carves the occasional piece of wood himself on his own, and his portrait of a woodworker conveys his sense of humour as well as his passionate admiration of workmanship. Steve is not a factory worker you can generalize about or pigeonhole. He is not alienated by following directions or filling orders. He is aware that a Steinway piano is larger than his work will be, that he is part of a grand tradition that may or may not keep going but which he is proud to be a part of in the present moment. *Fuck-it* is a carving that is like a weekend howl, a release to please his whim (and not a self-portrait). Care and deliberation tame the cuss, denaturing any suggestions of anger. The work of carving seems to be conducted as a way to negotiate the world's problems but not to solve any specific issue. The carver merely lettersets a narrative into the grain; Meltzer suggests the words will change and be different next time but the work will go on, he will stick to his chisels.

In contrast, the temporal mechanics of a basket transubstantiate vegetal terroir and numerical pattern, literally binding together landscape, labour and one or more other functions – aesthetics, pleasure, status or some more utilitarian action like winnowing – into one tangible baton to pass from generation to generation as a tool. Let us call this fusion mnemosynthesis, after the Greek Titan Mnemosyne who personifies memory and the ideal of synthesis, cumulative learning. We used to have many temporal ligaments like craft in our lives. Today, we are lucky if we have a single precious pot to hand off to the next generation, or to mend, or to kiss in order to expand our sense of a temporal experience. Those artefacts that do make us feel that we are enveloped in a vitality that goes beyond the measure of our eyes or clocks we might declare 'mnemosynthetic'. This portmanteau elaborates the cliché of 'making memories' – for memory production is integral to the manufacture of material goods. Ursula K. Le

Steve Meltzer, Baroque-style relief carving, 2010, Honduran mahogany, 10 × 20 in. (25.5 × 51 cm). One component of a large panel that Steve has been working on for several years, this relief shows his manual expertise and ability to meet the needs of Steinway & Sons. Like Kevin Millward and many others, Meltzer's interest in carving is not necessarily about self-expression.

Guin supposed 'story is our only boat for sailing the river of time', but so is well-spent meaningful labour, even banal maintenance like the scraping and patching of the hull of an actual wooden boat. To concur with Le Guin, no virtuosic craftsperson is ever medium-specific for they weave time, too, in play as an element of their compositions. And some give us access to those encapsulated hours.

Materials like wood, clay, metal, fibre and glass have no understanding of time: it is humans who count rings and wrinkles and value something that spans three generations. Metaphorically, mnemosynthesis might carry us through a geological formation to integrate material and human dexterities and bodies. Nampeyo's and Karnes's clay and Brancusi's hewn timbers are things that tug at my emotions and conscience. Meaningful craft is like a constellation carrying old rays of light – conversations with people now dead, previous encounters and sensations – and illuminates the present moment by informing it with previous experiences. Material synapses can connect us, therefore are worth imagining into existence. Mnemosynthesis is a human growth pattern as chemically potent as photosynthesis – self-aware craft grows that consciousness.

Steve Meltzer, *Fuck-it*, relief carving, 1984, Honduran mahogany, 10 × 20 in. (25.5 × 51 cm). That an artisan would carve wood as a full-time occupation in a manufactory and then come home to pursue his own creative ideas with the chisel seems improbable, yet that is exactly what Meltzer does.

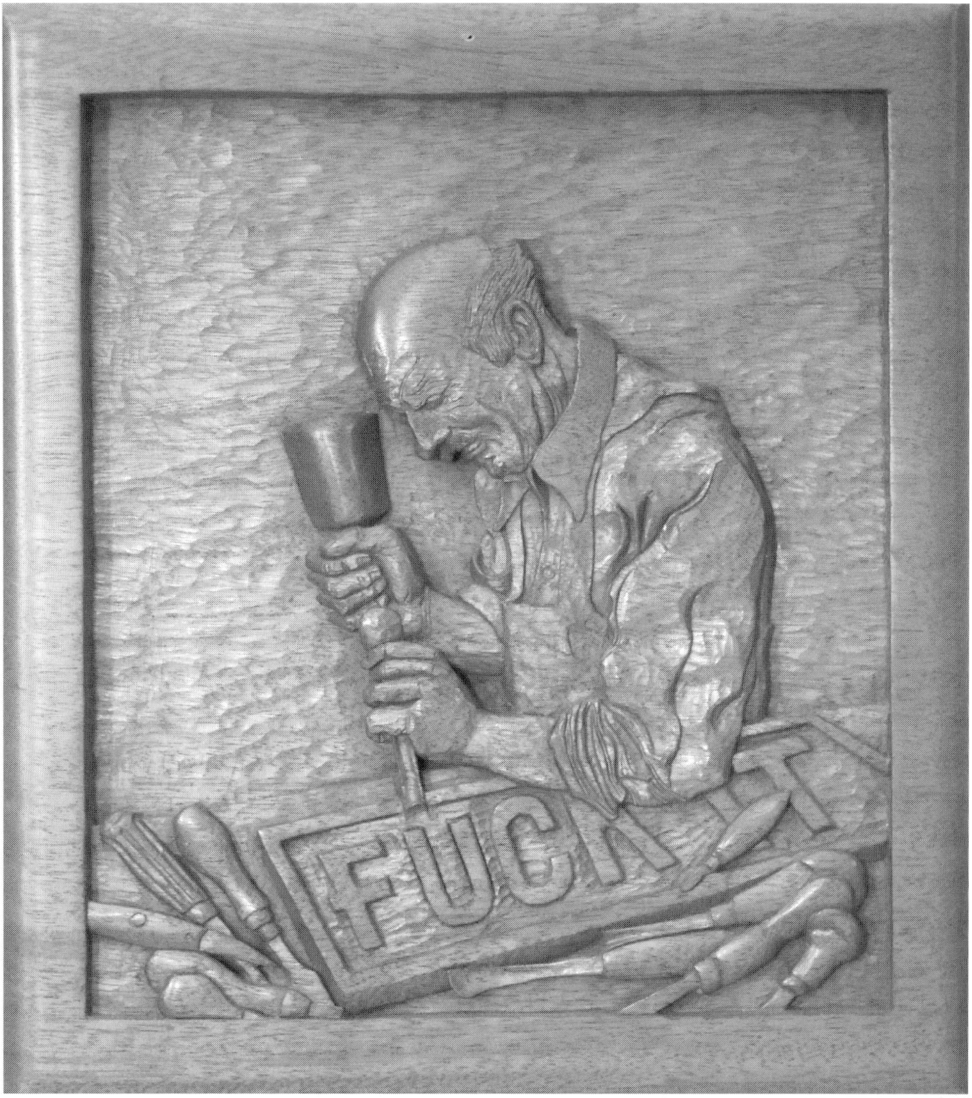

As I admire a make-do before me, a glass with six metal staples holding together a crack that languidly spirals around the goblet's bowl, Virginia Woolf's image of memory personified as a seamstress comes to mind, and the potency of mnemosynthesis to engage other labour seems worthwhile and desirable. This method of repair, almost hidden to my finger, as I can barely feel it, is now a lost skill. Like bricklaying, it is never again to be practised as a valued task on a large scale in the economy in which I live. However, the mended crystal goblet retains a compelling texture and trace of human presence, evidence that self-expression might be second-fiddle to utility or even to the memory of human use. This glass invokes the idea that civilization stretches beyond the present moment. 'The actual is like a moist handshake, damp with nervousness or the body's heat,' wrote the poet Delmore Schwartz, and it is this transmigration of anxious and emotional humanity that the mended glass evokes, leaving us less insulated and isolated as humans.

Human-made or repaired things – intimate possessions or architecture, clothing or vehicles, stuff of any type – are necessary ways in which to extend our reach and pass on human sentience. Like a mobile phone or book, a basket or bowl has meaning only if it promises to convey sustenance, to connect us. This book's idiosyncratic journey across one hundred years, from Nampeyo and Brancusi to Fred Wilson, Shari Mendelson and Maarten Baas, should feel like wading into a long now, a choppy and temporally uneven moment in which 1900 and 2000 are equally a part of tomorrow. Wilson, Mendelson and Baas create pathways that actualize a sense of identity and homeland, both for me and for themselves, as did Alice Kagawa Parrott and Jack Lenor Larsen. I hope to have illustrated the ways that materials can be intermeshed with human intentions and aspirations. Meaningful craft propels forwards like an old tool suitable to new uses: the instrument surprises fresh generations of hands and bodies with its old applications. We are

Repaired glass 'make-do', *c.* 1890, glass with metal staples. Glass was also once repaired, much the same way as ceramics, with a drill and a sure hand, and probably given to children or servants for use. A highly visible spiral crack runs around nearly the full circumference of this glass but the crack is almost imperceptible to the finger, aside from the six staples.

lucky to catch sight of these rippling currents, to touch these batons of workmanship as they pass.

Craft can transform us, giving us new identities and agency for re-invention. Merely possessing craft can also give owners the sensation that they can access others' identities vicariously. Craft transforms materials (such as clay, metal, wood or glass) and the act of weaving or welding can integrate the sinews of a willow shrub into a part of our heightened consciousness. Craft can anchor us to a sense of place, literally stitching our lives into environs. Craft materializes time, making it our inalienable human possession. To be human is to be a mnemosynthesist, to cultivate the environment with vital and useful memories. Recursive action is a fundamental component of consciousness, and in its own way craft is as essential as language.

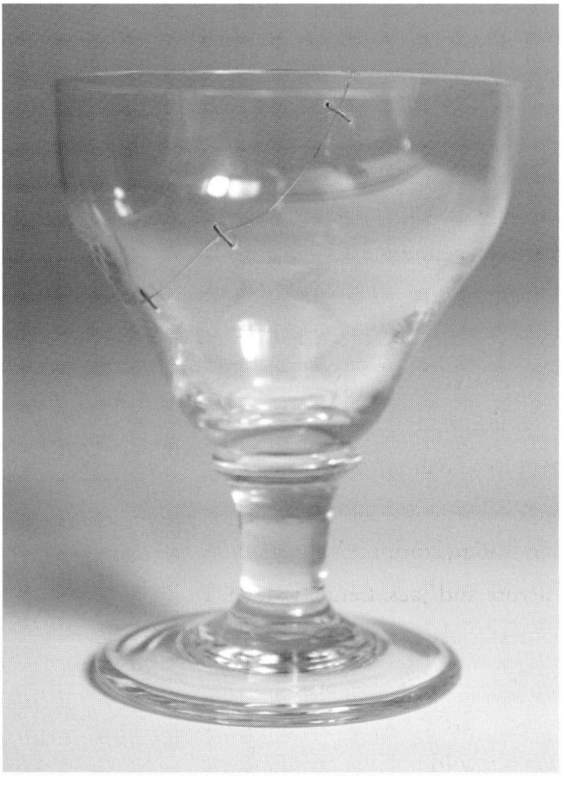

Mnemosynthesis might be seen by some as a term that fosters cultural appropriation, an enduring issue in the politics of artmaking in Western civilization and an aspect peculiarly internalized to craft. I hope that the neologism is not used in this way but instead as a criterion to evaluate the ways that working with tools can be regarded as a form of humanist research. Shouldn't the anthropologist studying basketry test the pliancy of rattan? Shouldn't the art historian studying frames have a feel for the distinction between one that is carved of wood and one cast in plaster? Mindful re-enactment fuels historical reflection and ideally does not veer towards insensitive neo-colonial appropriation of ritual objects or ornament. Moreover, it is painful that we have yet to develop a terminology more nuanced than 'appropriation', for artistic production is often a search for alternative parentage or a recuperation of lost ancestry for which there is no universal criterion of authenticity. If cultural appropriation is a search for a homeland, as it is in the work of Parrott and Larsen and many others, then we must recognize that time travel is often predicated on a journey to the past to fix or find father and mother figures, to reweave or construct anew a sense of family history.

And let us briefly return to an issue mentioned in the Introduction, the enigma of situating craft in the triangulation between computers, paintings and photographs – that 'Bermuda Triangle' in craft criticism. I have suggested that often a craft *is* technology. Most production of contemporary craft that I have surveyed uses advanced computing technology as a part of its toolkit. Kevin Millward throws pots to the specifications that Portmeirion's designers delineated in digital files. Connie Chapus at the CUTCO cutlery company works with her hands, alongside robotic production. Obsolescence is imposed upon the narrative of craft more than being intrinsic to it: we degrade human culture when we decree a basket-maker or basket to be obsolete. Painting is a larger thorny issue as it remains the perennial yardstick of cultural activity. If the power structures of museums, art history and art schools are still patriarchal, then work that is done in them can be considered stuck inside the 'paintriarchy': those white-walled spaces are made for looking and not touching. Painting remains the index with which to judge art sales. Oil on canvas originated in its use for religious devotion and there it remains: find an art controversy and it is generally an iconoclasm. Because paintings float on the Internet as a museum without walls, they tend to suggest an operation outside material contexts: the very idea of a space removed from human touch presents us with a loophole outside an ecological continuum. Chapter One began with photography to explore how we misunderstand craft through photographic images, as wonderful as they are as windows to look through back into the past. Photography of craft tends to build biographical portraits. This triangle of digital technology and the genres of painting and photography is a place that allows little room for the admiration of the physicality of a wood screw, seat or towel to develop. Craft is not ontologically different from photography or painting, but is not nourished by being cross-referenced to these activities.

Calling for a 'craft commons' as this book does might sound silly when modern ideals in communications are the inversion of slow learning, material engagement and communion. The glass screens of our devices rarely hurt us the way a willow branch, a knife or an annealing oven can. If craft does not compute – if it fails to pass through contemporary messaging systems and networks – then we should accept that craft might be a working model, but it does not model a system. It can have no unvaried theory and can only offer specific actions and habits – some tools, others traditions – to contrast against theories.

While electronic communication is rippling across the world, the power of craft is residential and residual. Like memory, craft operates at a slower rhythm, generally speaking, and is certainly not about instant connectivity. Finally, craft has a dialogic mode of messaging: there is no sense of 'wireless' transmission or of the unidirectional messaging we are accustomed to in email or texting. Our memories bubble up but we cannot disinter them from fusion, or bottle them or hand them off, hard as we try.

Whereas we think of data as seamless, mnemosynthesis might begin at a signal such as the lip of a cup or the handle of a door, contingent upon sensitive and responsive muscular systems as well as temperature and sociability. We can be insensitive to those scripts. Binary code might simplify language by reducing it to 0s and 1s, and such a system suggests that information has a consistency; data is particulate. But craft is a tactile language that does not have a routinized molecular composition. Ash wood riven a week ago and ash split today might be the same in terms of constitution but not in terms of behavioural dynamics. Feeling how soft glass or plastic metal can become is a sensitization, a form of research that merits inclusion in our education even if we cannot verbalize this in precise terms.

Celebrating the reverberation of touch is contrary to our use of telecommunications or satellite signals. Yet the resistance intrinsic to heavy tools might be more essential to remaining human than forays into open-ended creativity. Through the friction of tooling we gain sensitivity. By stating these ways that craft does not fit our expectations of the sort of coherent system of communication as we think of it today, my aim is not to claim it as pre-digital or opposed to digital tools. Mnemosynthesis argues that a basket is a non-verbal language worth sustaining as we move into the future. Certainly Noguchi's touristic photograph of a half-dozen baskets in Indonesia seems to co-opt these wonders into a Euclidean universe of primary geometric forms. His photograph suggests that these are forms capable of building new worlds as well: this is mnemosynthesis. We have long argued that art comes from previous art; this book argues that the material mess and workmanship of the world is a wider swathe of pleasure and tactile engagement that deserves as much consideration. Flowers become all the more potent when we try our hand at horticulture.

To turn craft into a story that includes design, decorative arts and a few select pieces of fine art does not undermine it – rather, this aims for accuracy. Mnemosynthesis does not follow purist laws such as being 'made by hand' or 'unique' or inherently 'personal'. If we take a restrictive path, as many people do when they assess only electronic goods as 'technology', we risk losing civilization itself. Baskets can be mind-blowingly complex technologies, too. Craft mirrors humanity's willingness to enthusiastically

Isamu Noguchi, photograph from his Bollingen Fellowship travels, Indonesia, *c.* 1949–56. The admiration and close examination of vernacular modes of workmanship will surely motivate future generations of artistic production as well as touristic engagement with other cultures – and we would do well to build regard for the power of basketry.

engage constraints of time, need, strength, balance, surface, size and price. Craft does not obey laws; material constraints and human needs are beautiful pressures enough (to borrow from Charles and Ray Eames).

Our future self-transformations and mnemosyntheses will come through working with more diverse materials, and whatever sentience we infuse into things will be 'true' and 'authentic' despite being concocted from plastics or other engineered materials. Take hold of what you can and work it: brew your own craft consciousness by taking stock of how complex human production has been and how each complicated moment is its own specific opportunity, each pressure issuing a call for peculiarly resonant materials and tooling. A broad craft consciousness that begins with the tools and issues at hand reveals that we need to recover how we have worked together in the past, not merely as individuals. Our future depends on our learning collaborative crafts that flow with, not against, our environment as conditions change and as we do, too.

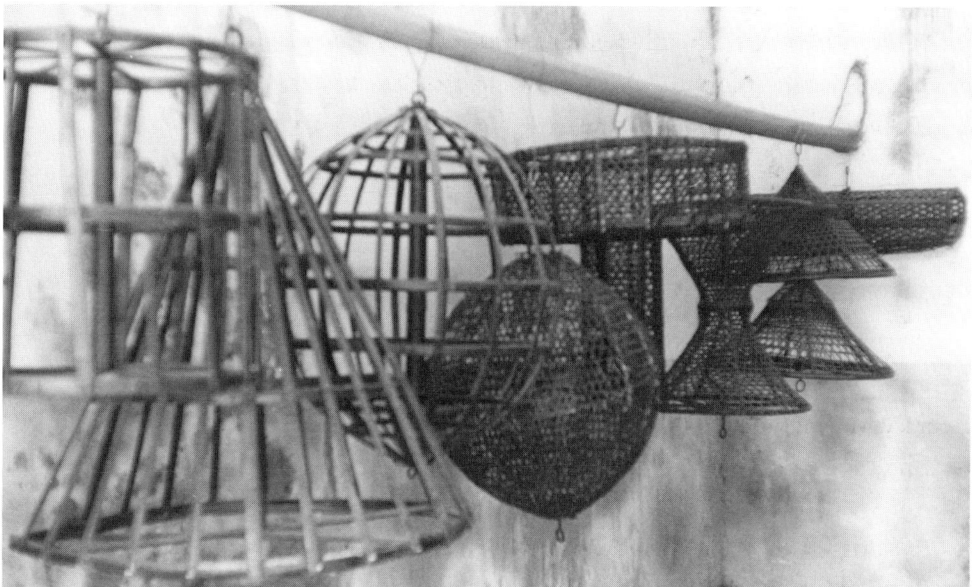

FURTHER READING

GENERAL

Adamson, Glenn, *The Invention of Craft* (London, 2013)
—, *Thinking Through Craft* (London, 2007)
Alfoldy, Sandra, *NeoCraft: Modernity and the Crafts* (Halifax, NS, 2007)
Auther, Elissa, *String, Felt, and the Hierarchy of Art and Craft in American Art, 1960–1980* (Minneapolis, MN, 2009)
Boris, Eileen, 'Crafts Shop or Sweat Shop? The Uses and Abuses of Craftsmanship in Twentieth Century America', *Journal of Design History*, II/2–3 (1989), pp. 175–92
Bryan-Wilson, Julia, *Art Workers: Radical Practice in the Vietnam War Era* (Berkeley, CA, 2009)
Charny, Daniel, *The Power of Making*, exh. cat., Victoria & Albert Museum, London (2011)
Dormer, Peter, *The Culture of Craft* (Manchester, 1997)
Greenhalgh, Paul, *The Persistence of Craft* (London, 2003)
Harrod, Tanya, *The Real Thing: Essays on Making in the Modern World* (London, 2015)
Jönsson, Love, ed., *Craft in Dialogue* (Stockholm, 2005)
Kardon, Janet, and Rosemarie Haag Bletter, eds, *Craft in the Machine Age, 1920–1945*, exh. cat., American Craft Museum, New York (1996)
Kirkham, Pat, *Women Designers in the USA, 1900–2000*, exh. cat., Bard Graduate Center, New York (New Haven, CT, 2000)
Kubler, George, *The Shape of Time: Remarks on the History of Things* (New Haven, CT, 1964)
Murray, Kevin, *Craft Unbound: Make the Common Precious* (Melbourne, 2005)
Sennett, Richard, *The Craftsman* (New Haven, CT, 2008)
Smith, T'ai Lin, *Bauhaus Weaving Theory: From Feminine Craft to Mode of Design* (Minneapolis, MN, 2014)
Sorkin, Jenni, *Live Form: Women, Ceramics and Community* (Chicago, IL, 2016)
Sutton, Gloria, *The Experience Machine* (Cambridge, MA, 2015)
Veiteberg, Jorunn, *Craft in Transition* (Bergen, 2005)

CHAPTER ONE

Appadurai, Arjun, *The Social Life of Things* (Cambridge, 1986)
Berlo, Janet, *The Early Years of Native American Art History* (Vancouver, 1992)
Burton, Scott, 'My Brancusi', in *Artist's Choice*, exh. cat., Museum of Modern Art, New York (1989)
Chave, Anna, *Constantin Brancusi: Shifting the Bases of Art* (New Haven, CT, 1993)
Díaz, Eva, *The Experimenters: Chance and Design at Black Mountain College* (Chicago, IL, 2015)
Fane, Diana, *Converging Cultures* (New York, 1996)
Geist, Sydney, *Brancusi* (New York, 1983)
Kirkham, Pat, *Charles and Ray Eames: Designers of the Twentieth Century* (Cambridge, MA, 1995)
Kramer, Barbara, *Nampeyo and Her Pottery* (Albuquerque, NM, 1996)
Morris, Robert, 'Aligned with Nazca', *Artforum*, 14 (October 1975), pp. 28–37
Parker, Rozsika, and Griselda Pollock, *Old Mistresses: Women, Art and Ideology* (London, 1981)
Phillips, Ruth, and Christopher Steiner, eds, *Unpacking Culture: Art and Commodity in Colonial and Postcolonial Worlds* (Berkeley, MA, 1999)
Pye, David, *The Nature and Art of Workmanship* (Cambridge, 1968)
Rybczynski, Witold, *Taming the Tiger: The Struggle to Control Technology* (Cambridge, 1985)
Shapiro, Mark, *A Chosen Path: The Ceramic Art of Karen Karnes* (Chapel Hill, NC, 2010)

CHAPTER TWO

Barron, James, *Piano: The Making of a Steinway Concert Grand* (New York, 2006)
Cooke, Edward S., *Making Furniture in Preindustrial America* (Baltimore, MD, 1996)
Samuel, Raphael, *Miners, Quarrymen, and Saltworkers* (London, 1977)
Shales, Ezra, 'Appreciating the Hands that Manufacture: Factory Craftsmanship at Kohler Co.', in *Arts/Industry: Collaboration and Revelation* (Sheboygan, WI, 2014), pp. 69–84
—, 'Corporate Craft: Constructing the Empire State Building', *Journal of Modern Craft*, IV/2 (2011), pp. 119–45
—, 'A "Little Journey" to Empathize with (and Complicate) the Factory', *Design and Culture*, IV/2 (2012), pp. 215–20
—, 'The Politics of "Ordinary Manufacture" and the Perils of Self-serve Craft', in *Nation Building: Craft and Contemporary American Culture*, ed. Nicholas Bell (Washington, DC, 2015), pp. 204–21
—, 'Where What's Done Comes Undone (Is a Museum)', in Ceramics in the Expanded Field, Westminster University online research forum, at www.ceramics-in-the-expanded-field.com, 26 May 2015

CHAPTER THREE

Baxandall, Michael, *Patterns of Intention* (New Haven, CT, 1985)
Bell, Nicholas, *A Measure of the Earth: The Cole-Ware Collection of American Baskets*, exh. cat., Renwick Gallery, Washington, DC (2003)
Cohodas, Marvin, *Basket Weavers for the California Curio Trade* (Tucson, AZ, 1997)
Collingwood, Peter, *The Maker's Hand* (London, 1998)
Cort, Louise, *A Basketmaker in Rural Japan*, exh. cat., Smithsonian Institute, Washington, DC (1994)
Ellmore, William, *The Cultivation of Osiers and Willows* (London, 1919)
Gordon, James E., *The Science of Structures and Materials* (New York, 1988)
Halper, Vick, *John McQueen: The Language of Containment*, exh. cat., Renwick Gallery, Washington, DC (1991)
Hutchinson, Elizabeth, *The Indian Craze* (Durham, NC, 2009)
Ingold, Tim, *Lines* (New York, 2007)
—, *Making* (New York, 2013)
—, *The Perception of the Environment* (New York, 2000)
Okey, Thomas, *A Basketful of Memories* (London, 1930)
Robertson, Henry, *Life on the Upper Thames* (London, 1875)
Rossbach, Ed, *Baskets as Textile Art* (New York, 1973)
—, *The Nature of Basketry* (Atglen, PA, 1986)
Siebert, Stephen, *The Nature and Culture of Rattan* (Honolulu, HI, 2012)
Smith, Cyril Stanley, *A History of Metallography* (Cambridge, MA, 1986)
—, *A Search for Structure* (Cambridge, MA, 1992)
Valoma, Deborah, *Scrape the Willow Until It Sings* (Berkeley, CA, 2013)
Wayland Barber, Elizabeth, *Women's Work, The First 20,000 Years: Women, Cloth, and Society in Early Times* (New York, 1994)
Wilk, Christopher, *Marcel Breuer: Furniture and Interiors* (New York, 1981)

CHAPTER FOUR

Auther, Elissa, *String, Felt, and the Hierarchy of Art and Craft in American Art* (Minneapolis, MN, 2009)
Grady, C. Jill, and Melissa Powell, *Huichol Art and Culture: Balancing the World*, exh. cat., Museum of Indian Arts and Culture, Santa Fe, NM (2010)
Judson Clark, Robert, ed., *Design in America: The Cranbrook Vision, 1925–1950*, exh. cat., Metropolitan Museum of Art, New York (1983)
Larsen, Jack Lenor, *A Weaver's Memoir* (New York, 1998)
—, and Betty Freudenheim, *Interlacing: The Elemental Fabric* (Tokyo, 1986)
Livingstone, Joan, and John Ploof, eds, *The Object of Labor: Art, Cloth, and Cultural Production* (Cambridge, MA, 2007)

Mayer Thurman, Christa C., *Claire Zeisler*, exh. cat., Chicago Art Institute, Chicago, IL (1979)

—, *Textiles in the Art Institute of Chicago* (Chicago, IL, 1992)

Peck, Amelia, and Amy Elizabeth Bogansky, *Interwoven Globe: The Worldwide Textile Trade, 1500–1800*, exh. cat., Metropolitan Museum of Art, New York (New Haven, CT, 2013)

CHAPTER FIVE

Armstrong, Isobel, *Victorian Glassworlds* (Oxford, 2008)

Edgerton, David, *Shock of the Old: Technology and Global History Since 1900* (Oxford, 2007)

Ellis, William S., *Glass: From the First Mirror to Fiber Optics, The Story of the Substance that Changed the World* (New York, 1998)

Fiero, Annette, *The Glass State* (Cambridge, MA, 2006)

Ilardi, Vincent, *Renaissance Vision from Spectacles to Telescopes* (Philadelphia, PA, 2007)

Jardine, Lisa, *Worldly Goods* (New York, 1996)

LeBourhis, Eric, *Glass: Mechanics and Technology* (Weinheim, 2014)

Macfarlane, Alan, and Gerry Martin, *Glass: A World History* (Chicago, IL, 2002)

Rifkin, Jeremy, *The End of Work* (New York, 1995)

Samuel, Raphael, 'Workshop of the World: Steam Power and Hand Technology in Mid-Victorian Britain', *History Workshop*, III (1977), pp. 6–72

Ward, Gerald, *Chihuly: Through the Looking Glass*, exh. cat., Museum of Fine Arts, Boston, MA (2011)

ACKNOWLEDGEMENTS

My intention with this book is to produce a bit of felt by boiling down fifteen years of conversations and critiques with inquisitive students at the Massachusetts College of Art and Design, Alfred University, the Bard Graduate Center and Parsons School of Design. Ideally, what once sounded in our seminars like woolly relativism will now read as a convincing bit of pragmatism, and maybe even feel like something worth keeping in pocket. In the spirit of George Kubler's *Shape of Time*, to which I subjected the students on my graduate seminars between 2004 and 2012, I cannot and do not lay claim to originality in these arguments, and I thank my students for foraging with me through interpretations as we tested texts against objects and actions. If there is a perk to teaching more than two hundred students a year, then it is the peculiar sensation of assaying an idea's elasticity and composition with thousands of hands in a bit of a scramble. I am grateful to have been permitted to continually revise my conclusions while standing beside objects that curators and collectors generously shared, or in manufacturing facilities that welcomed us. Stints teaching at Nova Scotia College of Art and Design and the Kunsthøgskolen i Bergen surely expanded my horizon, as did my acceptance of many generous invitations to be a guest lecturer at dozens of other schools and museums. I remain appreciative of my students/teachers/colleagues for all your questions, interjections and disagreements; these give 'curriculum' its actual currency and vitality.

Several in the circuit of craft conferences contributed their thoughts and ideas and I thank them for their generosity and *sotto-voce* advice given in the course of officious academic circuses, email banter and bar-side chats. I thank Glenn Adamson above all for encouraging me to write this and for his belief that my scattershot opinions amount to a voice – and for urging me to take this opportunity to rig up a soapbox of my own. Many other influential voices resound in my bibliography and memory, too: Sandra Alfoldy, Elissa Auther, Nicholas Bell, Julia Bryan-Wilson, Garth Clark, Edward Cooke, Iftikhar Dadi, Paul Greenhalgh, Tanya Harrod, Tim Ingold, Love Jönsson, Juliet Kinchin, Ethan Lasser, Jennifer Geigel Mikulay, Kevin Murray, Amelia Peck, David Raizman, Linda Sandino, Richard Sennett, Mark Shapiro, Lowery

Stokes Sims, T'ai Lin Smith, Jenni Sorkin, Gloria Sutton, Deborah Valoma, Jorunn Veiteberg, Jessica Hemmings, Doug Clouse, Lydia Matthews, Matt Hebert, Alexa Griffith Winton, Lois Russell, Fabio J. Fernández, Sten Madsen, Gerald Ward and Emily Zilber. Their publications punctuated the decade over which *The Shape of Craft* took form; perhaps I'm already nostalgic and feeling that conversation is 'over'. Then there is my fellow traveller, Neil Brownsword, who has shared it all – his home and manufactories, his friends and his work – since we met in 2006. Many others directly informed my pleasure of craft through verbal and material exchange: Elisabeth Agro, Magdalene Odundo, Michael Prokopow, Richard Slee, Tom Joyce, William Daley, Paul Stirton, Namita Gupta Wiggers, Ulysses G. Dietz, Matthew Partington, Robert Pfannebecker, Helena Kåberg, Paul Kagawa, Jonathan Clancy, Lee Talbot, Mònica Gaspar, John Stuart Gordon, David Higginbotham, Diana Fane, Steve Siebert, Stephen Knott, Cat Rossi and Mike Press, to list a sampling. Several conversations began at generous cultural brokerages like the Center for Craft, Creativity and Design. Yet more gratitude is due to myriad mentors – a list too long to set to type (and one that I am supposed to dispense with as I'm told that I'm now 'grown up'). I regret that several are now deceased correspondents-at-large who will never be able to murmur uncooperative 'tut-tuts' or point out errors of comprehension and interpretation that are mine alone; the living need not feel responsible for taking similar actions on their behalf, no matter how warranted my blunders. I do thank Lee Talbot and Paul Stirton for catching several errors in reading earlier drafts of this manuscript, as well as Vivian Constantinopoulos and Jess Chandler at Reaktion Books, for improving upon it. I am sure mistakes of my own remain but I can only hope that these will come to light years from now, ideally after a well-placed budget cut or dementia releases me from the tedium of reading the inevitable reproachful email.

I am very appreciative of my primary sources, having benefited by watching many working hands and listening to these people who call what they do 'merely work'. Some, like John McQueen, Connie Chapus, Paul Roehrig, Steve Meltzer, Maria Vinka, Karl Malmvall and Ken Sager have provided much needed encouragement. Conversations with Michael Barnett and Ted Hallman, Gerhardt Knodel, Jack Lenor Larsen and the late Karen Karnes and David Weinrib, among others, were influential. I do feel the need to note that both Karen Karnes and Jack Lenor Larsen disagreed with my interpretation; I thank them nevertheless and hope their heroics still shine through. With hope, the long arc of art history will lead to other readings of their work and that of Alice Kagawa Parrott. For my illustrations I am in debt to several of the previously named individuals and firms as well as a few other generous ones: John Wallace, Edward Koren, Andrew Baseman, Wally Haussamen, Dick van Aalsburg, William Peniston, Francesca Scoones, Caitlin Pereira, Jim Stitt, Steinway & Sons, Kohler Company, Mason & Hamlin Company, D. Maldari & Sons and Katherine Griffith.

If this book is a riposte, it is to three pernicious trends. First, craft should no longer be seen as a withdrawal from the everyday world. Second, we need more books to breach the gap to everyday life, and fewer that solely valorize single-author craft, i.e. contemporary art. Finally, the propensity to moralize craft as a method of 'self-improvement' is toxic – either as right-wing macho ideology or as vague left-wing homily among 'craftivists' who promote niche consumerism as radical alternatives to 'rethink corporate culture.' May we survive the euphemistic 'creatives' and our planet the 'creative economy'!

PHOTO ACKNOWLEDGEMENTS

The author and publishers wish to express their thanks to the below sources of illustrative material and/or permission to reproduce it.

Courtesy www.vanaalsburgbv.nl (photograph by Dick Van Aalsburg): p. 32; courtesy Alice Kagawa Parrott Family Trust: pp. 152, 190; photo courtesy Maarten Baas, www.maartenbaas.com: pp. 230, 231; courtesy Lady Jane Barran, Brent Eleigh (photo Ezra Shales): p. 247; courtesy Andrew Baseman Collection: p. 8; courtesy Biblioteca del Progetto, Milan: p. 65; Neil Brownsword (photo): p. 86 (above); Center for Southwest Research, University Libraries, University of New Mexico: p. 41; courtesy Jonathan Clancy: p. 121; courtesy Iftikhar Dadi (photo Ezra Shales): p. 242; Diana and Lawrence Fane Collection: p. 54; Print Jacques Faujour – Musée National d'Art Moderne, Paris (© CNAC/MNAM/Dist. RMN-Grand-Palais/Art Resource, New York © Succession Brancusi – all rights reserved ARS 2017): p. 49; Collection Fenimore Art Museum, Cooperstown, New York: p. 19; Harvard University Art Museums, Harvard Art Museums/Fogg Museum (gift of Sidney and Shirley Singer – © The Estate of Edward Steichen/Artists Rights Society, New York – courtesy Imaging Department © President and Fellows of Harvard College): pp. 45, 114, 150; courtesy Walter Haussamen Collection (print 2014 © Walter Haussamen): p. 37; courtesy Haystack Mountain School of Crafts, Deer Isle, Maine: p. 179; courtesy Herman Miller Inc.: p. 56; courtesy David Higginbotham Collection: p. 134; courtesy Inter IKEA Systems B.V.: p. 99; photo © The Isamu Noguchi Foundation and Garden Museum, New York/ Artists Rights Society (ARS), New York: p. 251; Israel Antiquities Authority Collection: p. 10; courtesy Shoso and Kay Kagawa, Honolulu: p. 191; courtesy Kohler Co. (photos Ezra Shales): pp. 80, 81; courtesy Edward Koren: p. 14; courtesy Ross Lowell (photos Ross Lowell): pp. 59, 178; courtesy D. Maldari & Sons (photo Ezra Shales): p. 83; courtesy Mason & Hamlin (photo Ezra Shales): p. 77; courtesy Steve Meltzer: pp. 244, 245; print Philippe Migeat – Musée National d'Art Moderne, Paris © CNAC/MNAM/ Dist. RMN-Grand-Palais/Art Resource, New York – © Succession Brancusi – all rights reserved ARS 2017): p. 47; courtesy Museum of Arts and Design, New York: p. 64;

courtesy Museum of Innovation and Science, Schenectady, New York: pp. 208, 211; The Newark Museum, New Jersey: p. 11; courtesy Pace Gallery (© Fred Wilson – photo Kerry Ryan McFate): p. 232; courtesy Paley Studios Archive: p. 122; courtesy Peabody Essex Museum, Salem, MA: pp. 108 (artefact #E3505), 139 (artefact #E3618); courtesy the artist (Sopheap Pich) and Tyler Rollins Fine Art, New York: p. 145; Pitt Rivers Museum, University of Oxford (photo Jeremy Coote): p. 105; courtesy Rapexco: pp. 23, 146; Rhode Island School of Design Museum, Providence, RI (photo courtesy Shari Mendelson): p. 235; photos Ezra Shales: pp. 6, 86 (below), 90, 91, 92, 138, 144, 183, 185, 187, 200, 205; courtesy Sikkema Jenkins & Co., New York (© Sheila Hicks): p. 197; courtesy Steinway & Sons (photo Chris Payne): p. 78; courtesy Studio Libertíny: pp. 126, 127 (photo René van der Hulst); Thonet catalog cover (#3311), November 1933 (private collection): p. 98.

INDEX